CONGREGATION

CONGREGATION

STORIES AND STRUCTURES

JAMES F. HOPEWELL

Edited by Barbara G. Wheeler

FORTRESS PRESS   PHILADELPHIA

Excerpts are gratefully acknowledged from: *Mythology* by Edith Hamilton.
Copyright 1942 by Edith Hamilton. Copyright © renewed 1969 by Dorian
Fielding Reid. Adaptation from "Hawthorne Blossom," *The Grimms'
German Folk Tales*, translated by Francis P. Magoun and Alexander H.
Krappe. Copyright © 1960 by Southern Illinois University Press. Reprinted
by permission of the publishers. Material from *The New Larousse En-
cyclopedia of Mythology*, 1959 edition. The Hamlyn Publishing Group.

Third printing 1989

Library of Congress Cataloging-in-Publication Data

Hopewell, James F.
  Congregation: stories and structures.

  Bibliography: p.
  1. Parishes.   2. Theology, Practical.   3. Pastoral
theology.   I. Title.
BV601.2.H67   1987   250   86–45915
ISBN 0–8006–1956–0

3999B89   Printed in the United States of America   1-1956

To my wife, Ruth,
and our children and grandchildren

CONTENTS

ACKNOWLEDGMENTS

Carl Dudley, Edward Farley, David Kelsey, Robert Lynn, and David Pacini graciously read one or more versions of this book, the final form of which reflects both their suggestions and their cautions. I am also indebted to the Lilly Endowment, Inc., for a grant that enabled an earlier year of participant observation in two congregations, to the Association of Theological Schools in the United States and Canada for later help in writing, and to Candler School of Theology and its dean, Jim L. Waits, for their colleagueship and support of the Rollins Center for Church Ministries, the base for my ongoing research. Former constructions of several chapters appeared as the DuBose Lectures of the School of Theology, University of the South, and the Swander Lectures of Lancaster Theological Seminary.

No group has done more in the present decade to promote and enrich congregational analysis than the Project Team for Congregational Studies, whose members include Jackson Carroll, Carl Dudley, Ardith Hayes, Mary Mattis, William McKinney, Loren Mead, and Barbara Wheeler. Their congenial struggle to ground a love of the local church in disciplined study continually refreshed me. The caring argument and exact encouragement of the last named, Barbara Wheeler, affects this book more than any other factor in its development.

JAMES F. HOPEWELL

September, 1984

EDITOR'S FOREWORD

James Hopewell died in October 1984, leaving a complete third draft of his only book. It is a complex work that reflects his varied career and diverse interests. The impetus for the research the book contains came from his assignment to develop a segment of the Candler School of Theology's "contextual" curriculum. Another element of the curriculum, two years of supervised practice in clinical and social-agency settings, was already in place. Hopewell was asked to design a program to deepen students' understanding of ministry in congregations. Since many Candler students serve local churches in pastoral roles while they attend seminary, the kind of field education program common in theological schools, a program that provided elementary exposure to the tasks of ministry, was not appropriate. Instead, Hopewell developed an array of courses of a new kind. Each was held in a congregation, was taught by a Candler faculty member and the church's pastor, and took as its subject matter an actual issue or topic in that congregation's life. The participants were lay church members and Candler senior students.

The aim of these courses was less to solve problems than to gain a critical and appreciative perspective on the dilemmas and strengths of local-church existence. Critical understanding requires analysis, and analysis requires the tools of theory. So Hopewell read systematically through the American and European literature on congregations and ministry of the last several decades, a survey of several hundred works that is recapitulated in this book's second chapter and its extensive notes. His reading revealed that the field to which these works are assigned—variously designated "practical theology," "church studies," or "ministry studies"—is very diverse and imports much from the human sciences. At first, he constructed highly eclectic reading lists for his courses, attempting to cover the field of church studies with examples of its many parts and divisions. But soon he became convinced that the fragmented character of the field was undermining the intent to provide for students a deepened understanding of the nature of the congregation. The enormous variety in the literature notwithstanding, many of the subtleties and nuances of the lives of local churches remained unaccounted for, he felt. Even more serious, the literature neither reflected nor explained adequately how it is that congregations hold together in the face of strains and pressures—a capacity that had impressed him in both the churches that offered Candler's courses and in a congregation he had helped found a few years before. If this ability of congregations to persist was examined sufficiently, he reasoned, an approach might be found that would lend coherence, if not unity, to the great variety of ways congregations are analyzed and apprehended.

With this aim he devoted the sabbatical leave he describes in chapter 1 to the close study of two Protestant churches in a small Georgia town. Hopewell's formal training had been in comparative religion, with a specialty in Islamics, and he drew from this training his principal research technique: participant observation, the method that ethnographers have used to gain firsthand information about religion and other features of non-Western cultures. He spent his sabbatical year, like an anthropologist in a primitive village, omnipresent in the two churches, attending meetings, worship services, and parties, talking to members, sifting documents and publications, observing patterns of community life.

As the year wore on, he made the discoveries this book recounts. The two apparently ordinary congregations had extraordinarily rich, dramatic textures. Though located only a block apart in a small town, each drawing members from the same social and economic stratum of the town's population, the two churches were strikingly different from each other in ways their Baptist and Methodist affiliations did not explain. Each, he concluded, had a distinct culture, as unique and rich as those of the religious communities he had served and studied as a missionary in West Africa early in his career. Like those religious fellowships of Liberia and Sierra Leone, the north Georgia congregations conveyed their culture (later he used the more precise term "subculture") by means of distinct idioms, symbolic dialects constructed both to express and to maintain group identity. To understand the function of idiom (of what anthropologist Clifford Geertz called a "network of construable signs"), he drew on the work of Geertz and Claude Lévi-Strauss. Prompted by these writers and especially by Victor Turner, he explored the special qualities of metaphors. This trail led to the work of Northrop Frye, and Frye's theories of literary structure became the catalyst for what Hopewell regarded as the core of his theory of congregations: his contention that congregational culture is not an accidental accumulation of symbolic elements but a coherent system whose structural logic is *narrative*. As congregations first come into being, Hopewell argued, they construct a narrative that accounts for their nascent identity. They attract to their fellowship those who want to participate in the unique local drama enacted there. They maintain their integrity against incursions by reiterating their distinct local story. And they encounter the world by identifying similarities between its stories and their own.

The rest of Hopewell's work was the elaboration of this major theme. He organized his prior research into narrative categories. The intricate world views and belief systems of congregations constitute the setting of their corporate narrative, while their traditional histories, the sequences of past events selected for retelling, correspond to plot. The ethos of a community—a complex product of its natural conditions, inherited endowments, and considered decisions and choices—become congregational character in a narrative framework. Hopewell used the structures of narrative not only to create his major categories, but also in a secondary way *within* each category. Thus the world views that constitute setting are arranged according to Frye's system of narrative genres. A congregation's traditional history not only represents one element, the plot, of its larger narrative structure, but also functions as a story in itself. And character, Hopewell provocatively proposed, is best grasped if studied in counterpoint with some mythic tale that "matches" a congregation's style, tone, and moral posture, the features of its character.

In the light of this theoretical system, Hopewell developed the research techniques for probing congregational narrative described in chapters 6, 9, and 10. He studied closely several churches in addition to the original two and deployed students to probe several dozen more, whose stories now serve as illustrations throughout the book. He presented his material in lecture series, courses at Candler, scholarly gatherings, and seminars for clergy, laity, and church officials. Last, he began work on a monograph.

Shortly after the sabbatical year, Hopewell had summarized his findings and ideas in a series of essays which he shared but did not publish, since he felt that such a collection would not improve the fragmented state of church studies. He reorganized the essays into the first draft of a book that took as its organizing metaphor the congregation as body. Acknowledging an idea of Mary Douglas about expanding circles of metaphor, he suggested a correspondence among individuals' stories about their own bodies, their corporate narratives, and their tales about the cosmos and its creator. Though this schema remains, in much reduced form, in the present volume, Hopewell found the central image, the body, unsatisfactory as a conveyance for his essentially structuralist arguments about congregational narrative. Stephen Pepper's typology of world metaphors provided a new starting point. Hopewell recognized that his view was not organicist but, in Pepper's term, "formist," an argument from similarity. Finding the structural images of house and household far more adequate, he wrote a new draft and then, in the year before his death, thoroughly rewrote it in response to criticisms and suggestions from the persons named in his statement of acknowledgment.

Despite the number and diversity of strands woven together in *Congregation*, the book is at base not a collage or collection. Like the congregation itself in Hopewell's portrayal of it, the book is unified by its assertions about the power of narrative. It is further bound together by Hopewell's strong theological convictions about how narrative functions as God's work with congregations. In his service as missionary and later as director of the

World Council's Theological Education Fund, he had encountered and dissented from the notion that redemptive Christian norms and ideas transform culture by being imported into or imposed on it. In the course of his work on congregations, he came to believe firmly that the story that catches up and gives pattern to a church's local culture—its beliefs, its mission work, and its everyday administrative transactions—also gives an account of God's intention for that community of believers. Hopewell's use of classical and northern European myths had led some early readers of his work to conclude that congregational story as Hopewell defined it described only the naturalistic, even pagan, stratum of congregational life, a layer that must ultimately be contradicted and transformed by the infusion of gospel principles. Hopewell rejected that view and adamantly maintained, in passages found in nearly every chapter of *Congregation*, that a church's story, even when it recounts pedestrian and trivial activity, is the legend of God's plan, if only its sounds and signs can be heard and read. Further, he insisted, a congregation's particular story, because it draws from a treasury of narrative elements available to all groups of people as they struggle for survival and meaning, is its channel to participation in the worldwide mission of establishing God's shalom. These theological convictions about how God works in the world through particular communities that contain in their narrative life the seeds of their own—and the world's—redemption were the first source of Hopewell's interest in congregations. They molded both the theoretical and the practical development of his work. In the composition of his final draft, they were summarized in the chapter "Christ and Eros" (chapter 11), which he regarded as the book's pivotal section.

The draft that Hopewell left when he died was accompanied by notes for its final revision. I have followed his instructions wherever possible. Specifically, in consultation with Ruth C. Hopewell, his executor, I decided to limit my revisions to rearrangement of the text and editing for clarity and consistency. Where Hopewell's notes dictated expansion, I complied only if I could find appropriate material in earlier versions of the book or in his unpublished essays. As a result, with the exception of a handful of sentences that function only to smooth transitions, nothing has been added to Hopewell's own writing, though it has been, as he wished, substantially reorganized.

The major problem that the book has presented for its own reshaping is that it does not fall into any existing genre. Parallel efforts can be found in other fields. Some sociologists and anthropologists have begun to study community life from the perspective of narrative and dramaturgy. A few structuralist historians have used narrative genres (including Frye's classification) to characterize historical periods. Theologians, philosophers, psychologists, and of course literary theorists are currently exploring the functions of narrative beyond literature itself. Hopewell's book both draws and comments upon—and at points advances—these discussions in social science, literature, and theology, but it belongs in its entirety to none of them. Thus, with the assistance of an extraordinary editor, Davis Perkins of Fortress Press, I have made editorial decisions keeping in mind the serious but mixed audience the book may attract: social scientists interested in religion, theologians concerned about the church and its mission, and clergy and lay leaders who seek to understand their congregations at greater depth.

Hopewell wrote his acknowledgments of assistance and support in haste a few weeks before he died. Among his notes he left a much longer list of persons to whom he was indebted. Heading it is Elizabeth Whipple, who worked with him as editorial assistant as well as typist. Her knowledge of the project and meticulous work preparing the text were invaluable to me. This version could not have been completed without her. Also listed were many members of the Candler faculty and his two closest research associates, Mark Cole and Melton Mobley. Further, he had planned to express his deep gratitude to the congregations "with whom I have labored" and their pastors.

I want to add to this list my own expressions of thanks to those who made what might have been a difficult undertaking a rewarding one instead: Ruth Hopewell, who gave me the privilege of editing the book and consistently aided me in doing so; the Directors of Auburn Seminary, who granted a generous leave for my work on the project in Atlanta; Jim Waits and Elizabeth Smith, who anticipated everything I would need for the work to be done comfortably and efficiently; Lurline and James Fowler, who provided housing and friendship; Channing Jeschke, Candler's librarian, who made available and helped to arrange Hopewell's books and papers; Brooks Holifield, who worked with me on the last and knottiest problems in the text; and David Kelsey, on whose encouragement and sagacity I relied heavily when my assignment seemed most formidable. Finally, I must acknowledge a source of assistance often reported by those who have brought to publication the work of a writer who has died: a strong sense of the continuing collaboration of the author. Throughout, I have felt the lively cooperation of the man whose intelligence, courage, and love of God's world are given form and expression in this book.

June, 1986   BARBARA G. WHEELER
New York City

CONGREGATION

PART ONE

CULTURE, IDIOM, AND NARRATIVE

1

THE THICK GATHERING

Christian congregations took me by surprise. Although I had always been associated with local churches, my curiosity about them came late and unexpectedly while I was engaged with what seemed a quite different set of professional concerns. Twenty years of overseas missionary and ecumenical service had drawn my interest, first, to the traditional and Muslim faiths of Africa and, later, to the religions of Asia. I now teach about these religions in a seminary lodged in a university.

But something happened while I was pursuing religions on the other side of the world. Like Columbus in his search, I encountered an intervening territory that possessed its own riches and fascination. Of course, like Columbus, I was not this area's original occupant. Christian congregations have attracted many investigators in recent years. I venture to add one more volume to the already lengthy list of books and articles about the local church because I think I see from my eccentric angle some aspects of the congregation that may make it for others the surprising new world that it has become for me.

Part of my recent wonder about local churches grows from my need as a professor of world religions to demonstrate how my courses meet concerns in the ministry that my students will enter. The close attention to such parish features as ritual process and the use of Scripture encouraged in my courses does indeed help forge links to other religions, but studying the congregation because it provides a rationale for courses in other faiths remains only a part of the reason for my interest. What proves more tantalizing are the ways in which the study of other religions gives me fresh access to the nature of congregations, enabling me to glimpse better how local churches particularize their religious behavior and concretely express the faith. A congregation, undeniably Christian, nevertheless uses forms and stories common to a larger world treasury to create its own local religion of outlooks, action patterns, and values. I have begun to see how astonishingly thick and meaning-laden is the actual life of a single local church. Ministry in even a small church occurs

3

in a much more abundant world of signals and images than I and, I suspect, many others had assumed.

My interest in exploring the thick culture of local churches was first prompted by an unsettling experience. Beginning in 1975, a new congregation grew up around me. A group of Episcopal laity and I as their priest set out to form a loose fellowship that would meet for Communion each Sunday to supplement our participation in the community's existing churches, none of which was Episcopal. Because of my university commitments I could give very little time to the group; in fact, I took great interest in keeping its activity as simple as legitimately possible. My behavior could be used by church growth advocates as a case study of unpromising leadership. I was unaggressive and nonauthoritative; I was more interested in intimacy than expansion; I avoided ecclesiastical trappings and tried to promote service to the neighborhood instead of the internal activities of an organized church.

To our first Eucharist, held in a bank, I brought the bare minimum: bread and wine, prayer books, and a card table. On the second Sunday, however, someone brought a cloth to cover the table. The following Sunday another person produced a cross and candlesticks, and at our fourth gathering still another announced that the women of our church would meet the following Thursday to plan the bazaar. Despite my style, our fellowship became a congregation. Within a few years it constructed its own building, grew to full parish status, called its own rector, and burned its mortgage.

What caused its growth? God gave the increase, but God used other means than its first ordained leader for its planting and watering. As the four years of my tenancy passed, I learned to appreciate the capacity of an ordinary group of Christians to bring to maturity a unique and vibrant congregation. That this culture developed, convoluted, and achieved a church around my passive if permissive leadership more and more intrigued me. Most of what constructed our congregation did not occur by deliberate planning or goal setting; rather, a particular language developed among the members, an idiom that came to bind their actions and perspectives. Though its terms were drawn from the vast world repertoire of religious and social imagination, they were particularized in a local language that expressed our own views, values, and actions. Together we wove a network of audible and physical signs that, informed by humanity's symbolic struggles for community, now shaped our own. What was the grammar, I began to ask, of the new language that the members of this congregation seemed to create? What images and twists of phrase constituted their common communication? How did their common structures build them into a household of God?

Questions such as these began to nag me. It was fairly easy to identify elements in our local idiom derived from Christian and denominational sources, but much of what we expressed and meant to each other had other origins. I was struck by the resemblances between our growing church and bonding features I had earlier seen in African villages: the critical importance of narrative, a coalescence of world view, the link of myth and ethos. Could it be that here in suburban America there grew around me a church that partook of powerful religious forms that I had previously associated only with another continent?

At the next opportunity, a year's sabbatical, I set out to pursue these questions. What I did on that sabbatical was to observe two ordinary congregations, both long established in the same town in which my Episcopal congregation had sprung up. By sitting sympathetically through a year's worth of meetings, conflicts, services, and conversations, I sought to determine what their participants were saying to each other, what meanings they were sharing, what drama they as actors were together unfolding. By year's end I was convinced that parish life, in these two local churches as much as in my own, was a rich and multilayered transaction that seldom got the description it deserved. The life of each was like a fascinating tapestry woven with distinctive values and outlooks and behaviors, each telling its own pattern.

I do not think these churches each had by chance an unusually rich character that oozed meaning. An abundant system of language and significance seems to come with any congregation, whether growing or declining, be it as flashy as the Crystal Cathedral or as lukewarm as Laodicea. At the end of the year I concluded that a group of people cannot regularly gather for what they feel to be religious purposes without developing a complex network of signals and symbols and conventions—in short, a subculture—that gains its own logic and then functions in a way peculiar to that group. That conclusion changed the course of my research and my career. My explorations along this new path, leading, I hope, to insight into the structures of expression in local churches, form the body of this book.

IDIOM

What struck me first and most forcefully in these three churches—the one I led and the two others I studied—was the surprisingly rich idiom unique to each. As slight and predictable as the language of a congregation might seem on casual inspection, it actually reflects a complex process of human imagination. Each is a negotiation of metaphors, a field of tales and histories and meanings that identify its life, its world, and God. Word, gesture, and artifact form a local language—a system of construable signs that Clifford Geertz, following Weber, calls a "web of significance"[2]—that distinguishes a congregation from others around it or like it. Even a plain church on a pale day catches one in a deep current of narrative interpretation and representation by which people give sense and order to their lives. Most of this creative stream is unconscious and involuntary, drawing in part upon images lodged long ago in the human struggle for meaning. Thus a congregation is held together by much more than creeds,[3] governing structures, and programs. At a deeper level, it is implicated in the symbols and signals of the world, gathering and grounding them in the congregation's own idiom.

Most of us can recall several quite distinct manifestations of parish idiom. A pastor moving from one charge to another encounters strikingly different expressions of value and style in the new church. To communicate effectively within the new congregation the pastor must master its particular language. Moreover, potential church members, like househunters, do not find a wide range of acceptable habitations in a new town. They may search diligently before discovering a congregation that catches the intonations of their own language. Some give up the search and stay home. It is not that the churches they rejected were not reasonably pleasant and worshipful, and it is not, as hyperactive help books on the market assert, that better or different programs would necessarily lure them in. In hunting for a church, Christians are not only buying a product that must be attractively presented, they are also testing their own symbolic expression against that of the prospective church. Silently they ask of the congregation: What does this place say about us? What does it signify about our values and the way we see the world?

For both pastor and laity, entry into a new church is only the beginning of the encounter with its idiom. Parish communication constitutes virtually every parish event. Conflicts of any duration usually arise from different interpretations of parish idiom. Parents and education committees perennially worry about how the young are to learn the church's language. Each week teachers struggle to relate standard curriculum materials to the information that the congregation's members already convey to each other. Members of boards and committees map out campaigns and policies along lines of discourse that function to gather the congregation. The youth group strives to entertain the church's sense of the absurd in its skit at the next parish supper. A recovered invalid chooses to express thanks to a helpful congregation in a manner authentic to its nature. The pastor spends much of the week weighing words—phrases in prayers, terms in appeals, points in sermons—so that they sink into the communicated stuff of parish idiom.

Later chapters will explore ways of analyzing the expressive nature of the congregation: how it views itself and the world, how it behaves symbolically, and how it communicates its character. To start, however, I want to call attention to examples of signals and symbols in parish idiom, the first feature of congregational expression to attract my own attention. So accustomed are all of us to conceive the church as an assortment of either consciously planned programs or irrational religious feelings that illustrations of symbolic interaction are necessary to warm us to the notion that congregations have cultures as well as activities, policies, and emotions.

Consider the church in which it has been the practice of the members to leave abruptly after the worship service. Appeals to conscience ("We are depending on *you* to help create a time of fellowship after church") or a planned program to attract after-church participation are unlikely to change the habits of most members. But suppose changes are made in the symbolic code by which worshipers may remain comfortably in each other's presence after service, perhaps by giving each a doughnut. Neither provided nor consumed for the sake of nutrition, the after-worship doughnut (and the manner of its provision and eating) is, rather, intended as new bit of idiom that influences the tone, timing, and identity of life together. A doughnut might seem a strange example of congregational language, but it is a signal that conveys a message significant to the corporate life of the congregation. A congregation knows its specific meaning, which is an invitation to linger good-naturedly. Substances that express such messages, many only locally understood, are part of a congregation's idiom.

Most available substances do not have idiomatic implications. To offer glasses of water in the church foyer after worship would cause bewilderment, as would the distribution of gum or grits. "What's this *for?*" worshipers would ask, uncertain of the intended meaning. Some substances, nevertheless, as well as some sounds, gestures, and marks—and even some smells such as sanctuary musk and kitchen spices—do serve as signals within a congregation, which by the convention of its idiom understands each to stand *for* something else. Both universal and home-grown signals, their combinations, and the rules regarding their significance form the idiom of the local church. As many testify, idiom differs from congregation to congregation, subtly but insistently presenting in each its own character.[4] Each idiom is a wondrously complex language, largely built of written and spoken words and phrases, but also including matter as tangible as doughnuts and mute as handshakes and pouts. Together the signals make up the idiomatic code by which a congregation communicates itself, enabling it to identify and integrate itself, to express its faith and love, to govern and sometimes to change its corporate behavior.

Within congregational idiom are special signs called symbols. We shall use "symbol" to refer to a signal that commands markedly higher recognition and respect from members as an element essential to parish life. As an East Coast pastor recently discovered, symbols are not tampered with:

> It was the damndest thing. I preach unorthodox, even heretical sermons fairly often, and, three years ago, the board took the results of the sale of some property, over a million dollars, and set the proceeds aside . . . for the meeting of human need in this city. There's never a peep about the preaching, nor a single complaint about that dramatic action on the part of the board. But when we said that we wanted to move the pulpit a couple of meters to the left and the lectern just a couple to the right, there was a . . . storm, and that is not too strong a term.

An arrangement of sanctuary furniture for this congregation proved to be more inviolable than either its budget or its sermons.

Symbols differ from signals like doughnuts in another way: the meaning of the symbol is markedly less specific. Even young children know what after-worship doughnuts mean, but probably no member in the East Coast church, no matter how irate, could explain what the sanctuary arrangement precisely meant. That "multivocality," in Victor Turner's phrase, is in the nature of the symbol.[5] Members fight for its significance but cannot agree upon a single particular referent. Thus the meaning of a symbol is not easy to grasp because it abounds in meanings that touch many parts of a parish identity.[6] The transformative power of symbols resides in the abundance of meanings stored in them,[7] so members are quick to champion, but slow to explain, the symbols of their identity.

What an observer of parish symbols soon discovers is that a large portion of them are not specifically Christian in nature. Both signals and symbols in congregational idiom can arise from any source in the experience of the congregation's members. Money is such a powerful, not specifically Christian, symbol. Though the disposal of a million dollars did not seem very significant to the East Coast church, money is frequently an emotion-laden metaphor that both expresses and provokes the identity of a particular congregation. Different local churches use the symbol in different ways. One parish develops an elaborate system for hiding its display, issuing awkward campaign letters that barely mention the subject, publishing no budget, and treating the Sunday offering as an embarrassing moment to be quickly concluded. But in another church, just down the road, the subject of money comes up in most conversations. There it functions as a potent expression of superabundance and fertility. Yet another church close by treats money as a principal adversary, waging a symbolic and sometimes ingenious guerrilla war against its power to dominate. And a fourth congregation in the vicinity uses the topic of its financial difficulties primarily to voice its disappointment with a world that, through changing population patterns in the neighborhood, seems to have drained that church of its membership and power.

Jesus' insouciance toward money, taking it from the mouth of a fish, typifies the idiom of none of these congregations. Their seriousness about money comes from other sources. Such parentage does not mean that the ways they treat money are therefore sub-Christian, but rather that a household of God draws its idiom from its complex heritage of Christian and non-Christian sources.

Another world symbol in congregational idiom is children, also an emotion-laden metaphor. Different churches treat their children in different symbolic ways. One secretes them in soundproof rooms and becomes uncomfortable if too many appear in the sanctuary. A neighboring congregation, expressing its fecundity, arranges the public display of its children at worship. Another church close by devises creative campaign strategies to attract more young people and families with children, while yet another acknowledges the absence of children as it grieves its own aging.

As described here, there are similarities between the symbolic operations related to money and children. It is not the case, however, that a given congregation's idiom would express a similar action or attitude in each matter. A congregation may flaunt its money and hide its children. The distinctive idiom of a church rests on such permutations of many symbols and signs. Its language is constructed from key verbal phrases, furnishings, rituals of conflict and conciliation, displays of technical competence, ways of showing care and worth, and much more. Given the variety of options available within any of the categories, it is easy to see that the idiom of any single church is necessarily distinct.

The local church suffers when it does not take its idiom seriously. If the congregation views itself as merely the repository of meanings better expressed elsewhere, it fails to appreciate its genius, its microcosmic capacity to reflect in uniquely lived form the sociality of humankind. When a congregation considers its own language neither interesting nor important it devalues its identity and thus its names for and before God.

EXPLORING CONGREGATIONS

There are three further reasons why I and other students of congregational life invite a wider probe of the idiomatic local expression of church life. The first is that the image that many members now possess of their parish tends to embarrass them, and I believe that a deeper understanding would enable their greater appreciation of their congregation's value and potential faithfulness. Second, a more acute sensitivity to a congregation's idiom should increase the facility with which the gospel is proclaimed and heard in its midst. And, third, a perception of how the parish uses the cultural forms of other human communities should deepen its consciousness of its solidarity with peoples throughout the world in their mutual search for shalom. Each of these reasons requires more extended discussion.

1. *Seeing beyond the embarrassment.* Observers of congregational life today are more often chagrined than impressed: too often congregations deviate substantially from ideal concepts of Christian community. The charge of hypocrisy is made more frequently against church members than any other group of Americans. The contemporary local church, despite occasional enthusiastic advertisements and placid self-descriptions in annual reports, is often discouraged and sometimes cynical about ties that bind its members. An educated congregation these days knows more sociological and psychological explanations for its collective behavior than it dares, in its embarrassment, to apply. Moreover, the instances in which parish culture and structure are most evident usually hold bad news. As long as a congregation seems to surmount its problems of social interaction, it is easy to forget its congregational aspects and to view its members as free agents who spontaneously collaborate to practice high Christian precepts. When trouble strikes, however, the residual, structured, idiomatic household image of the parish becomes starkly visible.

Take a case in which church teenagers are caught using marijuana at a youth group party. The alarm system of the congregational household immediately alerts its members. Angry parents and others spread the signal. Their

anxiety about the world of drugs turns to outrage when pot invades their corporate precincts. They may summon credal and biblical support as ammu-
nition to defend their position, but their basic defense guards a more primal
symbolic integrity. They raise questions about cultural identity: Who do they
think we are? They recognize intrinsic values: Where do we stand? Where do
we draw the line? Members also devise symbolic strategies: they formulate
house rules to outlaw the behavior and adopt catchwords to belittle its perpe-
trators. The pastor plans a severe talk to the teenagers. Throughout the
trouble the structure of the congregational household is painfully manifest
to its members. They test and voice its boundaries. They employ its systems
of value and communication. They display its purpose, and they use its resources to accomplish that goal. The pastor, prepared, does indeed talk to the
adolescents, and several never return to the house.

What the congregation senses in the marijuana incident to be its own structure is doubly disappointing. Its culture first becomes clear to its members in
a trying crisis and is, as usual, associated with social predicament. When revealed, furthermore, the form and character of their household appears all
too common. Household actions are homely, made from human stuff. In
their bout with marijuana, members use vulgar weapons—gossip, pressure,
threat—to fight in defense of their house. They are also puzzled by the fact
that their culture at least tacitly gives access to a drug and then expels its
users. Neither feature seems Christian, and life in the congregation appears
all too human, cramped, and predictable.

A common response to social crises like the marijuana incident is to look
more to what the local church should be than to whatever in fact it is. Congregations that respond in this way often succeed in convincing themselves
that the church is invisible or, at least, different from its local manifestation.
Aided by judicatory and seminary personnel to whom the congregation seems
more beneficiary than source of Christian praxis, local churches usually assume that a more definitive form of church life exists somewhere else. I gain
the impression from some denominational meetings and seminary lectures
that the real church can be located just outside the network of concrete parishes and might well function better without them. Caught themselves in
their embarrassing finitude, local churches are also relieved to hear that superior church life occurs somewhere else.

But the thick gathering that constitutes congregational life is more substantial than is usually acknowledged. As I discovered in my early studies,
the local church is a microcosm of human culture, an immediate instance of
the world's symbolic imagination. Its specific disappointments and predictable sins are real, but they are also the lot of humanity caught everywhere in a
story of accomplishment and failure, of devotion and disobedience. Itself a
potent example of the ambiguity of human association, the congregation
nevertheless dares to accept its designation as the body of Christ and the

household of God, proclaiming in its acceptance the incarnate nature of its God who took on servant form. The thick gathering of the congregation is much more than a hypocritical assembly; it is for Christians the immediate outworking of human community redeemed by Christ.

2. Hearing and proclaiming the gospel. Disappointed by the homely behavior of the local church and embarrassed by its parochialism, church leaders have launched major schemes, especially in the last quarter century, to convert the congregation into a fundamentally different sort of community. We have tried to turn the church around or inside out; we have introduced new programs and planning devices; we have sought the missionary structure of the congregation and plotted its numerical growth. The results have usually been disappointing. The reported size of the average non-Roman Catholic congregation in the United States in 1970 was 273 members; in 1980, 274.[8] Despite massive deliberation and effort throughout the nation, the basic shape, size, and character of the local church remain essentially unchanged. Its worship may be more varied today than it was in earlier decades, and its leadership may now be more representative of its members as a whole, but the fundamental patterns of congregational culture that most of us encountered as children will probably cloak our aging and burial.

An analysis of both local congregational idiom and the way the gospel message confronts and yet is conveyed by that language would be a better starting point for efforts to assist the local church. Rather than assume that the primary task of ministry is to alter the congregation, church leaders should make a prior commitment to understand the given nature of the object they propose to improve. Many strategies for operating upon local churches are uninformed about the cultural constitution of the parish; many schemes are themselves exponents of the culture they fancy they overcome. For several centuries the gatherings of the dominant class in American society, white Anglo-Saxon churches have tended to assume that they themselves have no cultural particularity and therefore no reason to investigate their own ethos, tradition, and world view. These features were attributed to "ethnic" groups; the dominant white Protestant churches considered themselves beyond ethnicity, responsive primarily to universal precepts and revelation. Only recently has their cultural specificity been recognized.

To ponder seriously the finite culture of one's own church, given the promise of God's redemptive presence within it, opens up a vast hermeneutical undertaking. The congregation recedes as primarily a structure to be altered and emerges as a structure of social communication within which God's work in some ways already occurs. The hermeneutical task is not merely the mining of biblical revelation in ways meaningful to individuals. It is more basically the tuning of the complex discourse of a congregation so that the gospel sounds within the message of its many voices.

3. *Solidarity with the world.* The congregation is a specific and available instance of human society expressed in symbolic activities that grasp society's plight and hope. That is the basis for calling it God's household. The local church is specific, with commonplace boundaries that prevent flights into generalities about the church, humanity, and the nature of the redeemed life. The congregation is also available, present to all for entry and inquiry; one need not seek some more remote or less obvious ecclesial home. The local church is, further, because it speaks an idiom of human language, an instance of human society that distinguishes itself from many other kinds of societies by the high proportion of language it spends on struggle and grace. The plight and the hope of the world are not entirely concealed in other forms of social grouping, but the idiom of the congregational household often expresses for Christians most persistently and poignantly God's call and the human cry.

Servants belong to households. When Christ emptied himself, he took the form not only of a servant but also of the household that bound his servanthood. That house was at once the *oikoumenē*, the whole inhabited world, and all local households, all homely, and all served by the house servant Christ in their limited but imaginative form. Thus careful attention to a congregation's domestic idiom yields a healthier self-image and a clearer sense of the gospel's intonations in that congregation's midst, but most important, a means of solidarity with the struggle of all human groups for survival and meaning, no matter how distant and strange the settings in which they are housed.

CHARACTERISTICS OF THE
CONGREGATION

Before we elaborate the modes of congregational idiom and the narrative forms they assume, a task that will occupy all the subsequent chapters of this book, we must dispatch two preliminary matters: a definition of the congregation as one among several forms of religious association and some comments on the relation of the congregational form to specifically Christian witness and mission, a discussion that forms the last section of this chapter.

Common as they are in several religious traditions, congregations have never dominated the totality of the world's local religious organizations. Human groups more frequently express their faith through corporate forms other than the congregation. Interwoven with familial, civic, devotional, and secular configurations that are structurally different from the local church, other religious groupings offer alternative patterns of collective reverence and incidentally suggest other ways by which Christianity might conceivably have spread among peoples. The congregation is not as inevitable as church members might assume. To study the congregation in any detail requires more precision about the way it differs from other pious gatherings.

My working definition of the congregation is this: *A congregation is a group that possesses a special name and recognized members who assemble regularly to celebrate a more universally practiced worship but who communicate with each other sufficiently to develop intrinsic patterns of conduct, outlook, and story.*[9] We can sharpen our appreciation of congregational structure by comparing its thick culture with that of other religious associations.

One pervasive form of pious gathering occurs within the family. Whether the family is nuclear or extended, a twosome or a tribe, its propensities for reverence and ritual often express a religious process that relates home-grown myths, honors domestic symbols, and follows devotional sequences that intensify faith in that family and allegiance to its own images of ultimacy. While such piety might seem more evident among people who live in clans and who honor ancestors, it also characterizes family reverence in societies such as our own.[10] Consider the motivation of the crowds that attend Christmas and Easter services in any local church. The absentees who appear on those occasions probably are present to acknowledge less the calendar of the church than their family's own cycle of birth, childhood, life, and death. Out of loyalty to their folk they participate in events that briefly synchronize the pageantry of the Christian year with the consuming drama of kinship. To scold Christmas and Easter crowds as lapsed Christians may miss the point: that they are loyal family members performing their household rites of affinity.

A congregation differs from a family at prayer. The local church bears a distinctive name to indicate, even in cases where one family rules the parish, that the congregation is not synonymous with a particular bond of flesh. It is called St. Paul's or Newtown Church, not often Smith Church even if the Smiths dominate the congregation. Moreover, the congregation identifies its own membership, initiating its catechumens rather than taking for granted their incorporation by reason of blood. The flesh and blood the congregation celebrates are not therefore those of a family but those of a universal Lord whose worship transcends the local church to embrace all assemblies that call themselves Christian.

Political units such as towns and nations exercise their own forms of collective piety. Ceremonies such as Memorial Day celebrations[11] and certain sporting events[12] express a corporate devotion to civic hopes and ideals. Again aggregates of people collaborate to recall mythic memories, to symbolize present accomplishment, and to project a final triumph often wrought from great peril. Robert Bellah has demonstrated how even a supposedly secular nation manifests a civil religion that provides for most American communities a powerful amalgam of Christian and patriotic images and values.[13]

Though congregations may be closely identified with specific political units, as were parishes in medieval Europe, local churches nevertheless resist total identification with their secular magistracy. Congregational sacraments, though they may support civic intentions, are rarely subsumed within civic observances. Even those who automatically are members of state churches undergo baptism and thereafter participate to varied degrees in the distinctive life of local churches. Such local groups are often deeply implicated in the piety of the state, but nonetheless each congregation retains a culture distinguishable from the pattern of the civil religion.

In Asia one encounters two other forms of religious assembly that are, again, structurally different from the congregation. One is the type of corporate observance that occurs within the precincts of temples, shrines, and other holy places. In these settings a small corps of priests or other functionaries, or perhaps a single religious leader, provides ceremonial proficiency and continuity for a larger lay populace whose participation, while not casual, tends to be more occasional and informal than the ordered activity of church attendance. Pilgrims and local devotees seldom attend regular services or expect to take their places in a fixed lay community. Most worshipers at a shrine on a single day do not communicate sufficiently with each other to develop the unique pattern of conduct, outlook, and story that distinguishes the local congregation.

A similar amorphism of the attendant community accompanies another form of religious gathering prevalent in East and Southeast Asia. Here the lay followers of the Buddhist monastic order, the Samgha, may gather in groups to perform meritorious rituals of devotion at the monastery, but their participation is individual and limited, unlike that of the congregation of monks whose corporate life they support.

As these illustrations suggest, congregations are only one of several sorts of collectivities by which human beings corporately express their religion. In Christianity, however, the congregation is the primary community by which the faith is expressed and perpetuated. Though organized into larger ecclesial units such as dioceses, denominations, and, ultimately, the worldwide church, the congregation is nevertheless the persistent and immediate form by which the church is manifested in almost every community. When people join the church or are ordained for ministry in the church, they almost invariably enter the culture of a specific congregation whose conduct, outlook, and story will occupy most of what their church membership entails.

HOW CONGREGATIONS MAY
BE CHRISTIAN

So closely do local churches accompany the growth and perpetuation of Christianity that their structure may seem an apostolic invention, but the followers of Jesus founded only particular churches, not the pattern of the congregation itself. The apostles, in fact, grew up in congregations. For several centuries before it came to characterize Christian assembly, a congregational form of organization shaped the local gatherings of both Judaism and some Mediterranean mystery religions. This older pattern of pious community was adopted by early Christians to support and express their newfound faith. From its beginning the Christian church used social forms already common to other human groups.

The congregating of a contemporary Protestant parish reflects its complex parentage. Although it honors Christian precepts, it also inherits many other social codes that help it cohere and survive. Some of its structures and practices have obvious origins in Christian traditions; others, equally widespread and apparently necessary to Christian congregational identity, have murkier sources or explicitly secular ones. No congregation is a "pure gospel" church, composed solely of inarguably Christian practices; no living church escapes the contribution that a wider culture makes to its nature and continuing history.

This complex heritage may be evaluated from several different perspectives. One might consider much of what appears to be unidentifiably Christian as mere baggage, the social impediments that must travel along with the activity of recognizable devotion so that the church can persist through the many moments and circumstances each week during which members are not engaged in specific witness to their Christian faith. From this perspective one might be willing to tolerate large investments of parish energy in events whose sanctity is obscure, because they are functions needed to escort more obviously Christian practices. Fairs, elections, and building plans, for example, can be seen as the necessary but finally indifferent stuff the congregation creates to convey through time and space a more distinctively Christian ministry.

A quite different viewpoint, which I have already advocated, considers the total mix of parish life as the primary opportunity for members to see close at hand the struggle of human society through which the gospel is proclaimed. Instead of dividing the complex activity of a congregation into categories of sacred behavior and secular baggage, this approach sees God's meaning as fully available only to members who perceive the entirety of social links that make their group whole. The worldwide toil to knit a human community out of disparate motives and symbols occurs in specific instance in the local church; the congregation, as was earlier suggested, is an immediate microcosm of all society's attempts to associate.

In this view, the depiction of the congregation is more appropriately Paul's image of the household than his metaphor of an earthen vessel holding separate treasure. The household is both container and treasure. The household works to coalesce its separate parts, like a congregation striving to incorporate various social forces and histories, like a world struggling to reconcile its different classes and peoples. A congregation's appreciation of its own labor of embodiment, its recognition of its own attempt to fuse its many actions, can also, as I have said, deepen its sense of commonality with efforts of human societies throughout the world to gain their own shalom.

How a congregation views its institutional actions, moreover, is inextricably linked to its understanding of mission. One pastor, concerned about parish mission, notes that on the same day, her congregation celebrates Communion, fights over its music program, and fixes its plumbing. Were she to understand her church by the first perspective that extracts recognized piety from other behavior, she might identify Communion as specifically Christian and the other activities as the unavoidable, self-oriented burdens of corporate life. To prepare for mission, in this view of things, would require the members of a congregation to discount their self-serving stuff, attempting to slough it off in order to offer their more recognizably Christian hopes and actions, such as the grace and love witnessed in their Communion, to other people. Mission in such terms assumes the separability within the congregation of purer Christian expression from the general travail of corporate intercourse. In this view, the congregation communicates by word and deed what is uniquely Christian, in the hope that other sectors of society will receive the offering into their own community struggle.

Or the pastor, following a course similar to the one I propose, might ponder whether the Communion, the music dispute, and the plumbing repair were themselves interlocked in some more complex congregational configuration whose whole reflects the plight and promise of other communities throughout the world. The three events do, after all, involve breaks: one of bread, another of harmony, and the third of water. In each case the fraction can disclose the basic human imaginative working that through millenia has given form to primal sound and matter to render it Word and Sacrament, melody, and cleansing. Furthermore, each instance in some way depicts a community in trouble. Although the congregation knits itself together by inspired strands such as liturgies, musical programs, and water systems, each by the activity of the same congregation also corrupts its nature and threatens the congregation's own life together. Death and betrayal, foretold in eucharistic action but belying that action's intent, nonetheless continue to occur within the church. Strife tears processes apart; use makes resources such as plumbing fail. The events of Eucharist, broken pipes, and congregational conflict may seem to be atomized happenings of widely separated meaning. They are, however, the components of a larger human story whose themes embrace recurrent antinomies of saving and losing, hope and routine. The story relates a struggle throughout history for community leavened both by decay and evil and by the gospel of God.

Mission for a congregation conceived in images that embrace the totality of parish experience has a different starting point than that which extracts from the whole a designated piety. Such mission begins with a greater appreciation of a local church's own finitude, its own ethos drawn from the world's symbols but particularized in a cultural pattern specific to its own corporate life. Were it to recognize its own structured custom, a congregation might find in other societies, bodies in their own right, a strange consonance, distinct but bonded to that local church in a similarly symbolic toil for community. While congregations and other types of society possess obviously different intentions, they nevertheless work through analogous forms of culture in which a local church might recognize its deeper solidarity with other human groups.

Such a perspective for congregational mission implies that Christ is already present in every community struggle, not just churchly ones, and that the gospel the congregation witnesses to other groups is more likely encountered in those groups' own setting than imported from our parish home. Given such a perspective, missional words and actions would spring less from a sense of extracting out of our social dross an identifiably golden Christian behavior for application elsewhere than from the promise that God is already in Christ reconciling the world of each group to Godself, including the territories, nearby or distant, that our local church is privileged to approach in mission.

My personal experience illustrates the difference between a parish missiology based on extraction and one based on discovery. After my seminary training, my family and I went to West Africa as missionaries. As with other new missionaries, my goal in 1954 was to bring Christ to Africa, a continent not dark but dusky enough in my view to need the light that shone more brightly in my American home. It was a case of believing that one area had what another lacked and of being at a time in history when I felt I could personally act as a bridge that permitted the transfer of that good from one area to the other. Traffic on the bridge, moreover, was to move both ways: concepts and methods of the gospel were indeed to flow from their American abundance to Africa, but in the other direction was to run the electricity of Africa to listless, self-serving churches in my native land. One realm which excelled in knowing what and knowing how could be linked symbiotically, it seemed, with another which instead had pointed energy, if only bridges were to span the gap between them.

I learned several lessons during our years in Africa. The first was that I could not to any significant degree shed my foreign character; thus my words about Christ and my, I hope, Christian behavior were saturated with the culture I had wanted to leave at home. Try as I might, I could extract no separate Christian word and deed. Second, I learned that I did not function as the primary expression of the gospel in an African community. The community itself did. What I came to discover in Africa was that Christ was already there and that, far from being the bridge for his entry, I, as my own dusk thinned somewhat, might have been a minor witness to his presence, already embedded in people's life together. In the later 1950s, as I matured within the loving bonds of that society, Africa became for me not one side of a bridge but a whole sphere of redemptive life, sustaining within itself those features which earlier I had felt must come from outside.

The remainder of this book follows some implications of realizing that congregations everywhere are thick gatherings of complicated actions, each parish distinctive in its expression, each possessing its own genius yet incarnating in that peculiarity the worldly message and mission of Christ. We shall explore the congregation as we might a village, trying to learn the particular cultural patterns by which it attempts to make itself whole, but also finding within it forms by which other groups in the world coalesce, disintegrate, and yet manifest the gospel.

NOTES

1. A survey of recent studies of the local congregations is the basis for chapter 2 of this book. In somewhat different form, the survey appears in James F. Hopewell, "Ghostly and Monstrous Churches," *The Christian Century* 99 (1982): 663–65.

2. Clifford Geertz, *The Interpretation of Cultures*, chap. 1.

3. Wade Clark Roof, *Community and Commitment*, 178–79, takes issue with research that construes belief primarily from the credal statements of a church: "Theological doctrines are always filtered through people's social and cultural experiences. What emerges in a given situation as 'operant religion' will differ considerably from the 'formal religion' of the historic creeds, and more concern with the former is essential to understanding how belief systems function in people's daily lives."

4. "Individual congregations within one judicatory have very different ideological systems. . . . The difference between the extremes of the systematic value structure of congregations has grown tremendously" (James D. Anderson, *To Come Alive!* 32). "Congregations are unique. No two congregations are alike" (Loren Mead, *New Hope for Congregations*, 96). Sociological confirmation of the heterogeneity of congregations within a single denomination is found in the various articles of James D. Davidson listed in chapter 2, n. 22, of this volume; in Donald L. Metz, *New Congregations: Security and Mission in Conflict* (Philadelphia: Westminster Press, 1967), 25; and in William H. Anderson, "The Local Congregation as a Subculture," *Social Compass* 18 (1971): 287–91.

5. Victor W. Turner, *Dramas, Fields and Metaphors*, 29.

6. Referring to what he terms their "multivocality," Victor Turner proposes that symbols condense within a single formulation a number of meanings and values significant to a people (*The Forest of Symbols: Aspects of Ndembu Ritual* [Ithaca, N.Y.: Cornell Univ. Press, 1967], 19–41). Cf. Turner's introduction to Edward R. Spence, ed., *Forms of Symbolic Action* (Seattle: Univ. of Washington Press, 1970). Turner finds in each symbol a polarization of physiological referents and those which disclose a "depth world of prophetic, half-glimpsed images. . . . Symbols resonate with meanings."

7. Symbols perform, for Geertz, a synthesizing action that relates their stored meanings and depicts a social behavior they also evoke (*Interpretation of Cultures*, 87–141).

8. Average congregational size is computed from statistics in the 1970 and 1980 editions of Constant H. Jacquet, Jr., ed., *Yearbook of American and Canadian Churches* (Nashville: Abingdon Press).

9. Congregations have received such casual analysis that few technical definitions of their nature exist. Mine builds upon Morris Freilich's concept of community in his *Marginal Natives*, 520. As is already evident, I also use the terms "local church," "parish," and occasionally "church" to denote the congregation.

10. Gwen Kennedy Neville describes forms of "religious familism" and its tension with congregational character in John H. Westerhoff and Gwen Kennedy Neville, *Generation to Generation*, and again in their *Learning Through Liturgy* (New York: Seabury Press, 1978).

11. William L. Warner, *The Family of God: A Symbolic Study of Christian Life in America* (New Haven: Yale Univ. Press, 1961).

12. Gregor T. Goethals, *The TV Ritual: Worship at the Video Altar* (Boston: Beacon Press, 1981).

13. Robert H. Bellah, *The Broken Covenant: American Civil Religion in Time of Trial* (New York: Seabury Press, 1975).

2

HOUSEHUNTING

Since 1960 over two hundred books and countless reports have examined either single congregations or their species, and any new work such as mine gratefully follows the tracks that many sorts of explorers—consultants, management specialists, sociologists, psychologists, ethnographers, historians, and others—have already laid down.[1] Prior to 1960 the investigation of the local church was more occasional, and except for a few books written to enliven parish programs[2] and the pioneering sociology of H. Paul Douglass,[3] the analysis occurred primarily in Europe.[4]

All studies, including mine, follow lines that are curiously similar to the ways a family examines a house or an apartment in which it might dwell. There are four approaches from which one examines a potential dwelling: contextual, mechanical, organic, and symbolic.[5] To consider seriously the capacities of either houses or local churches, in other words, is to view them as textures, mechanisms, organisms, and means of signification. While all four perspectives are in play in any single instance of inquiry, one of the four generally dominates.

Househunters look at the *contextual* nature of a possible dwelling. No house or apartment is entirely isolated; it is set in an environment that not only physically surrounds the building but also conditions all household activity. Househunters look at the manner in which its larger context creates the warp and woof of the dwelling's living texture. They therefore inquire about local costs; they check out the neighbors; they examine the neighborhood—its schools, services, climate, demographic trends—to satisfy themselves that the context is suitable and the place secure. Viewed in this way, a dwelling is a texture whose weaving reveals the strands that originate in the larger context of the neighborhood. No matter how attractive the house or apartment itself, its textured dimensions may be sufficiently disadvantageous to persuade the househunter to look elsewhere. Or the neighborhood context may be so desirable that shortcomings apparent from other perspectives are overlooked.

Dwellings are also viewed as *mechanisms*, that is, implements that accomplish certain ends, such as shelter, protection, and the delivery of heat, light, and water. Sometimes an engineer is employed by the househunter to check out the mechanical dimensions of the dwelling: its structural stability, the efficiency of its systems, its capacity to withstand whatever undesirable forces the contextual perspective has discovered in the environment. Such engineers are not necessarily concerned about the neighborhood or about the symbolic and familial potential of the place; they seek instead to determine how well the house mechanically operates, how well it does its job.

The *organic* perspective of the househunter looks at how the dwelling enhances the life and development of its occupying family. Unlike the mechanistic approach that examines the physical work that the house accomplishes in itself, the organic view unites it to the biography of a particular family and focuses on the dwelling's capacity to create for that household a "happy home." In probing a dwelling's organic capacity, househunters envision the way their family would use the property, where and how gracefully the group would eat, sleep, and encounter each other yet each pursue his or her own interests. More the realm of the architect than the engineer, organic considerations include issues of familial style, cohesion, and social grace.

The fourth perspective, the *symbolic*, is also essential. A dwelling not only simulates its environment, performs tasks, and supports the life of its inhabitants, it also conveys meanings. Househunters examine the capacity of a potential house or apartment to reflect their character. Identity is often critically linked to the building in which one lives. What does this place, househunters ask themselves, suggest about who we are? What are we saying to ourselves and to visitors by the form and symbolic pattern of this house? As real estate brokers attest, it is frequently the image projected by a house that first attracts or repels prospective occupants and that finally clinches a lease or a sale. "This house is us!" cry some househunters when they find their choice, referring to its symbolic identity.

Congregational researchers also use contextual, mechanical, organic, and symbolic approaches to assess the local church, because congregations are also dwellings, but for a different kind of household. Sorting out research approaches according to the four categories throws light on the intentions of each study. It can also reveal the author's attempt, present in most studies if only by implication, to correct what the writer feels is an overemphasis in the corpus of previous studies on another perspective.

It will be evident that particular categories have dominated certain periods and types of church life in the last twenty-five years. It is important to remember, however, that any congregational inquiry, like the househunt, of necessity employs all four perspectives and may acknowledge their utility. One of the four approaches nevertheless seems to characterize each single inquiry and to encompass its major findings.

CONTEXTUAL STUDIES

The acceleration of congregational studies in the last quarter century sprang in part from fresh and troubling inquiry by sociologists who probed the parish as a social organization. Instead of replicating already familiar and usually benign survey analyses that counted and sorted churchgoers, researchers such as Joseph Fichter, Peter Berger, and Gibson Winter[6] disclosed disturbing data about motivation for church membership and its relation to social behavior. Their critique coincided with the swell of the ecumenical movement, a formidable attack mounted by mainline Protestantism against parochialism in the church. Theological hesitations in the 1960s about the church in its congregational form were thus reinforced by both sociological conclusions and ecumenical convictions. In this climate a study apparatus of unprecedented scope for the examination of congregations was established by the World Council of Churches and its national counterparts. Working in groups in western Europe, North America, and to a lesser extent elsewhere, the study team produced and encouraged many papers and books on the problem of the local church.[7] Naming as its focus the Missionary Structure of the Congregation, the study proposed that radically different forms of Christian assembly and witness be fostered within the secular context. No longer a protected shelter, the congregation was by ecumenical design to become present in the environment of the workaday world, in its cities, its dilemmas, and delights. Earlier writings of clergy in France and the United Kingdom, who sought to treat their parishes as mission fields, set the stage for this more expansive understanding of congregation as Christian corporate life best fulfilled in its larger secular context.

A remarkable feature of the Study of the Missionary Structure of the Congregation was its inattention to the internal aspects of existing churches: their mechanisms and organic and symbolic functions. The North American working group of the Study, declaring themselves frustrated with the Study's defined scope, tried to avoid such topics altogether by making a clear but severe decision for a contextual approach:

> Instead of starting from the *church* and the problem of "what is the true church?", why not start our investigation in the *world*, especially where attempts are being made to respond to the agenda of the world?[8]

Although their mandate directed them also to study "existing patterns of church life,"[9] all the working groups were generally reluctant to consider the existing structure of the congregation with the same interest and skill they brought to probing its relation to its environment. Some church groups, such as the Lutheran World Federation, objected to the Study's skewed focus,[10] and the editor of one of the project books acknowledged that:

> the emphasis on "new forms" of missionary action has incurred the criticism that this study is not living up to its title insofar as it does not show great interest in

the work of existing congregations where, it is said, the church after all carries on its major work. . . . It became soon evident that we were talking not so much about a missionary structure for a congregation, but we were concerned for structures for missionary congregations.[11]

Such deliberate and thorough avoidance of the internal operations, processes, and symbolic structures of congregations reflected in part a simmering exasperation with parish hypocrisy. "How can we build a church that will not stand in its own way," begins one study report, "whose organizational structure is not forever contradicting what it says on the mystery of the church, whose budget does not make a mockery of what the church teaches?"[12] Members content with things as they are were warned that they practiced a "morphological fundamentalism"[13] that prevented the church from revising its structure to assume a more faithful form determined by the needs of the world. Like their individual Christian members, local churches should live not for themselves but for service to their neighbors in crisis. As one book title put it, the congregation was to become "the church inside out."[14] No longer should a church tend its inward processes; rather, it should turn outward to the larger environment that resources the strands from which its textured life is woven.

A congregation serving in a worldly context would not, of course, be primarily interested in an understanding of mission as the conversion of peoples to either doctrinal or morphological fundamentalism. Instead, the missionary action envisioned by the congregational studies of the 1960s was the participation of churches in the *missio Dei*, the all-encompassing act of God toward God's full creation. One was to attend society[15] in its struggle in the presence of God. One could not assume that the outcome of this missionary action would be new church members.

This thoroughgoing emphasis upon context raised questions about what would be the form of a congregation turned out to its environment. An analysis of how a church converted to the world nevertheless could remain distinguishable from it occupied George Webber's *God's Colony in Man's World*.[16] He conveyed images, which other works later amplified,[17] of pilgrimage and poverty distinctly Christian yet subordinate to society at large. Toward the end of the decade a number of other studies, almost all directed to the ecumenically oriented sector of Protestant church life, also portrayed the church as transient institution. They argued that a renewed[18] or reshaped[19] congregation should respond to an era described as one of rapid social change.[20] The later studies drew their theory largely from earlier works, but they were designed by denominations to present to broader publics the contextual message. Several contained case studies of congregations considered unusually responsive to the challenge of their environment.

The proportion of congregations in the 1960s and 1970s that actually responded as prescribed to their contexts was in fact very small.[21] As neighborhood populations changed racially, some churches whose physical and financial resources lingered after their former membership fled introduced service programs to assist the poor, but the adjustment seems in most cases to have stemmed from necessity or default rather than from deliberate reorientation and restructuring by members who themselves stayed on to be transformed.

The general appeal of contextual studies of the congregation waned rapidly in the early 1970s, leaving the contextual perspective once again almost exclusively to the sociologists.[22] Reflecting the introspective tendencies of the period, Protestant Americans began in the 1970s to assert widely that "the local church is a lot livelier than most people think."[23] Church leaders turned from the environment to examine the interior processes of the congregation. Contextual procedures that in the 1960s had promoted the opposite view fell into disuse.[24] In part the shift reflected the increasing difficulty of the mainline churches in sustaining contextually oriented agencies and studies whose intention was to revise the church's basic form of association. In addition, those who had labored for a contextual redirection themselves grew discouraged. The denominations that had earlier supported the missionary structure study and other liberal arguments became increasingly aware that they were losing both membership and financial support while denominations less ecumenically inclined that had avoided the contextual issue grew in size and power.[25] For all these reasons, a more traditional interest in the vitality of the congregation quickened, as the 1970s progressed, among church bodies that in the previous decade had promoted its restructuring.[26] That interest developed along two lines, one that explicated the congregation in mechanistic terms and the other that took an organicist approach. The more popular of the two developments was the analysis of the mechanical qualities of the local church.

MECHANISTIC STUDIES

A mechanistic examination of a potential dwelling uncovers how effectively the house fulfills its functions. Whatever the environment may tell a househunter about the house's milieu, the surroundings by themselves give inadequate information about the specific condition of the dwelling itself. Only a look at the house's actual mechanisms satisfies our concerns about its capacity to accomplish its purposes as a shelter. How well do things work? Is the house sound or decrepit?

Such concerns about the efficiency of a dwelling also characterize a type of inquiry about congregations that came to national prominence as contextual approaches receded. New emphasis was placed on the internal operation of the local church, as less stress was placed on its environment. Though aware of the social and cultural context of the church and the necessity of an evangelical engagement with it, advocates of the mechanist approach required that prior attention be given to the adequacy of the instrumentality that undertakes the engagement.

Mechanist approaches focus on program effectiveness. Of the several recent schemes that assess and promote accomplishment in the local church, the church growth movement has best captured mechanist hopes for competent congregations. "Growth" in the church growth movement refers to the effective numerical enlargement of the congregation. (Growth as the development of mature sensibilities is an organic image, discussed in a later section.) Churches that are growing in size both signify and accomplish the work of the Lord. "We can learn more about the way God works"[27] when a congregation is studied by church growth principles. "Bigness" is, moreover, a "powerful evangelistic tool"[28] and provides the resources necessary for effective programs of worship and ministry.[29] The local church is here viewed as a mechanism with the capacity for greater or lesser efficiency in doing the work of God.

Principles for church growth were first devised by Donald MacGavran, who examined churches in the Third World[30] and later founded the Institute for Church Growth in Eugene, Oregon. An Institute for American Church Growth was founded by a MacGavran disciple in the early 1970s. The first book that built on MacGavran principles but was directed toward the United States was probably that published by the Episcopalian Boone Porter in 1968.[31] In 1971 W. Wendell Belew published *Churches and How They Grow*;[32] it was followed in 1972 by Dean Kelley's ecumenical and provocative *Why Conservative Churches Are Growing*.[33] Thereafter the growth movement accelerated and many works appeared.[34] Studies critical of the movement[35] and sociological accounts of church growth and decline[36] followed. Several studies that countered the emphasis on growth by affirming the integrity and beauty of small churches[37] also emerged, but the number of such works is dwarfed by the prodigious literary production of the church growth movement.

Mechanist approaches operate according to rational principles. A chief spokesperson of the church growth movement, C. Peter Wagner, describes on several occasions the "seven vital signs" of a healthy church. They indicate the value the movement places upon the purposive effort of the congregation, noting the functions and faculties required to accomplish the Christian task.

1. A pastor who is a possibility thinker and whose dynamic leadership has been used to catalyze the entire church into action for growth.
2. A well-mobilized laity which has discovered, has developed and is using all the spiritual gifts for growth.
3. A church big enough to provide the range of services that meet the needs and expectations of its members.
4. A proper balance of the dynamic relationship between celebration, congregation and cell.

5. A membership drawn primarily from one homogeneous unit.
6. Evangelistic methods that have proved to make disciples.
7. Priorities arranged in biblical order.[38]

Mechanistic images power most of Wagner's points: dynamics, catalysis, mobilization, size, range, balance, unit, priority, and order.

The mechanist approach differs in both missiology and method from the contextual view, and in each case choice of method is related to missional stance. Contextualism discerned the saving activity of God primarily in the world at large and looked to sociology and ethics to provide information about the world and its requirements. The church growth movement, by contrast, saw God's salvation occurring in individual souls and thus sought reliable formulas for gathering large numbers of persons into congregations. For dependable, sophisticated techniques it turned to organization science. Wagner compares the movement's discoveries to a major scientific breakthrough:

> Church growth as a science helps us maximize the use of energy and other resources for God's greater glory. It enables us to detect errors and correct them before they do too much damage. It would be a mistake to claim too much, but some enthusiasts felt that with church growth insights we may even step as far ahead in God's task of world evangelism as medicine did when aseptic surgery was introduced.[39]

What Wagner describes in his approach as "consecrated pragmatism"[40] would, a decade earlier, have been dubbed "morphological fundamentalism." By the same token, the contextual requirement that the church empty itself makes little missional or methodological sense from the mechanist vantage point. Why abandon an enterprise sure to succeed? "The principles of success are all here!" vows the outer cover of one mechanistic study.[41] Contextual inquiry presented an ethical critique of parish life; mechanistic studies provided the engineering to empower parish life.

By the end of the 1970s, church growth had become for most denominations the most frequent topic of conferences and consultations. Advocates of the church growth movement now claim the substantial attention of churches throughout the country. Wagner notes that "although some overhang from the 1960's still persists like a pesky cough after a head cold . . . , by and large, church growth has edged up toward the top of the agenda in the churches across the board."[42]

Church growth science is only one scheme within a much larger battery of methods that examine the congregation as a machine. The technique most relentlessly employed, of course, is the annual report prepared by almost every congregation. Although a few of these may refer primarily to other images, the average report portrays the congregation as a machine whose work is detected by quantitative measurements and program vectors. Data—often crushingly dull—about money, membership, and meetings make up most of the report of collective activity in the previous year. Statistics comparing this year with last are included to reveal the relatively greater efficiency of the parish mechanism; program descriptions attest the frequency and intensity of parish activity. A satisfactory account, by mechanist standards, reports the hum of increased funds and attendance expanded in programs that themselves turn like dynamos.

Many professional church consultants follow mechanist approaches that work to increase the effectiveness of congregational programs. Lyle Schaller, the best-known church consultant in America today, uses a model of intervention and planning that is essentially mechanistic in its pattern.[43] Like most others who help the church professionally,[44] Schaller advocates the presence of a consultant to mobilize leaders to examine their potential and plan for a more productive future.[45] He eschews both the contextual approach[46] and situations where severe interpersonal problems require an organic solution.[47] Instead, he enters a congregation as a planner, to diagnose its internal dynamics. After examining the impact of such factors as physical setting,[48] size, tenures of staff, ages, roles, and religious intentions of the church and its members, Schaller tailors a planning process that recognizes the strength of the organization and encourages members to gain an understanding of their situation and alternative futures. He follows what he calls an "affirm and build" model that acknowledges the working elements in the congregation and mobilizes their power for the purpose of the church.[49]

Like householders who insist that a dwelling first possess efficient components and systems, the mechanistically disposed analysts of the congregation argue that, unless basic structures are sound and dynamic, any sort of parish goal is in jeopardy. Mechanists are not opposed to the intentions of service, fellowship, and interpretation advanced in other approaches. They anticipate and welcome such achievements, but to them the primary need of churches today is the rationalization of congregational process and the animation of social will to achieve results.

ORGANIC STUDIES

A congregation may also be treated as an organism, a living entity given not to mechanical production but to sensitivity and maturation. In our househunting analogy, the organic inquiry of the seeker tests the capacity of the dwelling to develop household vitality and style. Whether the house works efficiently is less important to an organicist than whether it enlivens and harmonizes its dwellers. Is the place conducive to good relationships? Does it aid the development of a happy home?

Similar priority is placed on matters of style and fellowship in organic studies of the congregation. Unlike church growth science that works for an efficient homogeneous unit to mobilize the congregation,[50] organic approaches recognize the heterogeneity of members and their deep need to be reconciled in a common, if complicated, life. For advocates of the organic view, such as Robert Worley, a local church is "a gathering of strangers"[51] whose members are alienated from each other in ways that mechanist approaches tend to overlook. Worley describes the present disarray of church members:

> Our current lack of common definitions has led to frustration, bitterness, and even withdrawal from the church by both clergy and laity. The absence of commonly accepted definitions means that people do not feel they have a place, do not know who they are in the congregation. It means that they are not established as persons in the church. In the turbulence of contemporary congregational life diverse definitions of behavior, attitudes and interests exist. Church members have great difficulty dealing with this diversity. In the midst of competing and conflicting ideas and expectations, they suffer an identity crisis.[52]

Gone from such accounts are not only ideals of homogeneous units but also any mechanistic disposition to employ a diagnostic process that might propel the church to greater efficiency. Organic studies of the congregation instead begin with the disparity of parts; they acknowledge breakdown; they embrace the perplexities of modern association. But they also offer hope that sensitive attention to organization development will create a new, more complex church body.

Organic assessments of the congregation assume its similarity to a living organism that can mature to stages of equilibrium and insight not evident in its present state. Such studies generally have three characteristics: they recognize in the parish a potential fellowship that can transcend the differences and conflicts among its parts; they employ organization development methods; and they encourage all members to participate equally in a congregation's ministry.[53] Each feature deserves separate attention.

First, organicists view the whole of a congregation as greater than the sum of its parts, and they use the term "community" to express the special value and power of the whole. A social body develops through the purposeful interaction of often quite disparate members. "Community is a way to be together," declare Evelyn and James Whitehead, emphasizing the integrity that develops from the participation of parts. Community, however, does not, for the Whiteheads, imply uniformity:

> Community does not point to one particular structure of group life. Rather, the term refers to a range of social forms, a variety of patterns of interaction and communication within groups. One group will incorporate several elements and expectations of primary relations. Another will show more concern for formal patterns of organization. But each may be understood as an intermediate style of group life, as a community.[54]

In Wagner's mechanism, the seventh sign of church growth insists upon priorities arranged in biblical order. The system advocates seem, in comparison, more at home in chaos, with its paradoxical promise of integrity.[55] How the change from disorder to wholeness occurs is the second characteristic of organic systems approaches: organization development. "The parts of the whole work together," Mansell Pattison relates.

> In any system the subsystems interact with each other and adjust to one another
> so that the whole is self-modifying. The system exists in an equilibrium between
> the parts, but an equilibrium that is forever changing. The system is not static
> but grows and moves. . . . The possibilities are kaleidoscopic and the process
> open-ended.[56]

Although organicists recognize the crisis inherent in discordant parts, they are essentially optimistic about the course of organizational process. A favored term of organic proponents is vitality,[57] used to describe robust interaction among members who, possessing different gifts and opinions, are synthesized to new corporate fulfillment.[58] Vital congregations are not distinguished by ordered accomplishment; they are lively, instead, by dint of the intensity of their community interaction.

A third characteristic of organic approaches is their emphasis upon full participation. "The systemic purpose is shared by all subsystems," says Pattison.[59] All parts count. They take on the common shape and intention of the whole and are responsible to each other for its future integrity. Worley summarizes the characteristics of an organic participation of all members within their congregation:

> Power to contribute, to share, to be involved meaningfully; justice in structures,
> communication, and decision-making processes; love in relationships and self-
> understanding as a genuinely contributing member are the elements of reconcili-
> ation and the true sign that the institutional church as the body of Christ has as
> its head Jesus of Nazareth.[60]

Leaders, in the organic view, have none of the singular authority given by mechanists to leaders of growing churches, who are "motivated by the assurance that they have understood the revealed will of God for world evangelization and that they are attuned to what God expects to accomplish through them."[61] In the organic approach, all parts are responsible for the whole as full partners in decision making, as attested by a number of books that began to appear in the 1970s to promote the democratization of congregational leadership. Many of the books invite the holistic involvement of the congregation in a specific responsibility previously considered part of the clerical role, such as the priestly,[62] prophetic,[63] kingly,[64] and pastoral[65] offices. In each case, the point is that the congregational body best performs its ministry by the collaboration of all of its parts. As an organism the local church grows, not necessarily to greater size and efficiency, but to a full ripening of its communal nature.

SYMBOLIC STUDIES

Still another perspective illuminates the local church, one less frequently advanced, the one this book primarily advocates. The approach considers the congregation less a texture or machine or organism than a discourse, an exchange of symbols that express the views, values, and motivations of the parish.[66] While the other approaches explore, respectively, the context, effectiveness, and communal development of the congregation, the symbolic outlook instead focuses upon its identity. Identity mirrors the "we" of a church that persists through whatever changes environment or revised program or interpersonal growth may effect in its midst. Throughout such changes any congregation remains itself, irrepressibly recognizable to its members and other observers. The marks and patterns of that recognition are the symbols this fourth approach seeks to discover.

In househunting terms, the symbolic search is the one undertaken to find a residence that reflects the identity of the family, a place that expresses the self-understanding of its occupants and their transaction with the world. When househunters contemplate the symbolic language of a potential dwelling, they look at a quality different from its neighborhood, efficiency, or familial appropriateness. They ask: What, in any circumstance, does this place say about us? What does it express about our values and the way we engage the world?

Pastors frequently acknowledge congregational identity by speaking of the symbolic network of a congregation as its "personality." They note that parishes that have similar contextual, mechanical, and organic features display remarkably different personalities. The analysis in congregational literature of symbolic networks, or identity, has proceeded desultorily, not in a widespread or consistent movement like those which have propounded the other approaches. A few histories of local churches have examined the identifying cultural traits of their subjects, exploring the symbolic patterns that give a particular congregation its unique character, instead of the far more common topics of local church history, such as campaigns, catastrophes, and clergy. In 1967, possibly in reaction to the dominantly contextual interpretations of the time, three books appeared that probed congregational culture in other, nonhistorical ways. One was the work of a sociologist, Earl Brewer, who, with the aid of a theologian and a ministries specialist, sought by an extensive content analysis of sermons and other addresses given in a rural and an urban church to differentiate the patterns of belief and value constituting those two parishes.[67] The second was the inquiry of a religious educator, C. Ellis Nelson, who departed from a curricular definition of education to envision the congregation as a "primary society" whose integral culture conditions its young and old members.[68] James Dittes, the third author, described more fully the nature of the culture encountered in the local church. He called it intractable stuff:

This "stuff" about which the minister develops and exercises intentions—the moods and motives, the whimsies and wiles of people, their responsibilities and irresponsibilities, the structures and clashes of groups, their forms and formalism, commitments and inceptions, ideas and ideals—this "stuff" is active, reactive, insistent, and sooner or later must have the final word.[69]

Later a pastor, John Harris, likened the stuff to an iceberg:

> [The] network of beliefs and behaviors . . . in every church . . . varies enor-
> mously, but it is maintained by the church's influential members and by the sur-
> rounding environment's expectations of a "good church." The consensus is like
> the tip of an iceberg, . . . a small bit visible to the eye while the vast bulk of it lies
> beneath the surface of consciousness, unspoken and powerful. Whatever form it
> takes the consensus can be felt as an alive, "electric" network of symbols and
> sanctions—it is *there*, a brute, essential organizational fact.[70]

In the 1970s the study of symbolic interaction in the congregation became
increasingly the domain of ethnographers. As might be expected in a society
in which white Anglo-Saxon Protestants are slow to recognize their own
ethnicity, the first, and still the best, ethnographies of congregations are
Samuel Heilman's study of an orthodox synagogue and Melvin Williams's description of a black Pentecostal church.[71] Heilman and Williams conclu-
sively demonstrate the power of even small, marginal congregations to gener-
ate among themselves a rich symbolic communication that gives each its
meaning and cohesion. Only a single theologian, Urban T. Holmes, has
given protracted attention to the culture of the local church and the symbolic
implications of ministry conducted within its network of signs. Holmes's several books on the ministry sought to counter the mechanist and organic orientations that guide works that view ministry primarily as social profession.[72]
Since Holmes, a few other theologians have explored, differently and far less
extensively, the function of symbols in the life of the congregation.[73]

The remainder of this book will offer various ways to detect the symbolic
and idiomatic discourse of a congregation and to probe its significance to the
church members who convey it. To introduce that effort, however, several
characteristics of the symbolic approach to congregational study are here set
forth that distinguish it from the other principal modes of analysis. The
marks are its attention to a pattern of motifs, its use of a linguistic model, and
its narrative dimension.

Critical to the cultural analysis of a congregation is the discovery of significant motifs, or themes, that through their conscious and unconscious repeti-
tion by church members sanction the world view, ethos, and praxis of the
parish. Heilman explains how he established what motifs conditioned the life
of Kehillat Kodesh synagogue:

> When the events I observed in the setting ceased to reveal novelties to me, I took
> my six volumes of notes and began to look at what I had gathered. While certain
> themes had spelled themselves out in the course of the observations, others be-
> came apparent only after all the notes were analyzed.
>   Only a small part of the information I collected could be incorporated in this
> study. The themes that are treated must therefore not be presumed to describe
> everything there is to know about Kehillat Kodesh. Rather, they represent those
> aspects of the setting and action that are most representative of American modern
> Orthodox Jewish synagogues, as I comprehend them, or vital for a comprehen-
> sion of the particular social interaction at Kehillat Kodesh.[74]

Unlike the contextualist who endeavors to explain the congregation in the light of social ideas and forces at work throughout the larger community, the symbolist observes the structure of ideas and actions within the church itself that particularize its outlook and behavior. Note also in Heilman's remarks the absence of the mechanist concern to modify congregational behavior in order to increase its efficiency. Organicists and symbolists do have in common a focus upon internal community, but for symbolists the task is a search among existing cultural data to discover the matrix of the community already existing, while organicists advocate a social process that develops a future community not now realized.

A second feature of the symbolic approach is its use of a linguistic model to depict congregational culture. Symbolic analysis demands on-site observation, usually for an extended period of time, to detect the signals that convey a church's culture. The analyst watches, participates, listens, interviews, and reads all that occurs within the life of the congregation. The data the researcher collects must then be shaped in a model that gives it sense and coherence. The model employed is that of a language, the communication pattern Clifford Geertz calls "construable signs." As noted in the preceding chapter, the idiom of an individual congregation includes not only verbal and written signs but also gestures, smells, touches, and physical configurations. Viewing such data as part of a rich language that members express to each other as information provides the paradigm for ordering and weighing what is observed.[75]

The third characteristic of the symbolic approach emerges from the other two. When an ethnography finds formal motifs or themes in symbolic discourse, it is disposed to treat the culture it examines in literary terms. Geertz in fact likens the work of an ethnographer to that of a literary critic, and Heilman deliberately sets his study in a dramaturgical framework, suggesting that the relation of empirical study to narrative art may be closer than usually believed. "To those defenders of quantitative social science who will denounce my tendency toward a narrative style," he writes, "I can only reply that, unlike the novelist, who seeks to make the facts conform to his art, I have throughout made my art conform to the facts."[76] Historians who offer a symbolic approach to the study of the congregation also employ a narrative style to depict their findings. My own understanding of the parish is decidedly narrative in its orientation,[77] so much so that the following chapter addresses that topic almost exclusively, and narrative categories will frame the remainder of the book.

So unexpectedly complex is the congregation that it requires comprehension from four quite different perspectives. It cannot be correctly understood without an exploration of the textural qualities that tie it to its larger context. Nor does its function become clear without analysis of the mechanist qualities that trace its dynamics and performance. Nor does this household of God come to life without organicist attention to its growth in community. And the observation of a congregation's symbolic interaction discloses its identity and web of meanings. I will emphasize this final approach, not because of a lack of appreciation for the other three, but because to date it has been dangerously underrepresented in works that analyze the local church.

NOTES

1. Carl S. Dudley, ed., *Building Effective Ministry*, contains an extensive examination of various approaches to congregational analysis and a selective bibliography of local church studies produced since the late 1950s.

2. Willard Augustus Pleuthner, *More Power for Your Church: Proven Plans and Projects* (New York: Farrar, Straus & Young, 1950); and see Murray Leiffer, *The Effective City Church* (New York: Abingdon Press, 1955), which preceded plans of the National Council of Churches to study "the effective city church." Unlike the later contextualist interpretations of the urban church, an instrumentalist emphasis characterized studies and plans of the 1950s. Power was to be evoked, multiplied, and redistributed. Roman Catholic literature in the period follows the same motif but with considerably greater attention to the manner in which power is to be recognized and shared between diocese and parish. See Hugo Rahner, *The Parish: From Theory to Practice* (Westminster, Md.: Newman Press, 1958); Leo R. Ward, *The Living Parish* (Notre Dame: Fides Pub., 1959); Casiano Floristán, *The Parish—Eucharistic Community* (Notre Dame: Fides Pub., 1964); Alex Blöchlinger, *The Modern Parish Community* (New York: P. J. Kenedy & Sons, 1965).

3. H. Paul Douglass, *1000 City Churches* (New York: George H. Doran, 1926); *The Church in the Changing City* (New York: George H. Doran Co., 1927); *How to Study the City Church* (Garden City, N.Y.: Doran & Co., 1928). An assessment of Douglass's contribution both to sociological method and to the study of the local church is contained in Jeffrey K. Hadden, "H. Paul Douglass: His Perspective and His Work," *Review of Religious Research* 22 (1980): 66–88.

4. George Michonneau, *Revolution in a City Parish* (Westminster: Newman Press, 1950); Tom Allan, *The Face on My Parish* (New York: Harper & Row, 1957); Ernest Southcott, *The Parish Comes Alive* (New York: Morehouse-Barlow Co., 1956). Several of the Roman Catholic works cited in n. 2 appeared first in European editions.

5. Approaches to househunting and to congregational study resemble Stephen Pepper's well-known typology in *World Hypotheses: A Study in Evidence* (Berkeley and Los Angeles: Univ. of California Press, 1942). Mary Douglas, *Natural Symbols*, points out the consonance of perceptions that a people hold about their bodies, their society, and the cosmos. Similar isomorphisms about habitations—house, congregation, and world—seem to operate in the present instance. Pepper's four world hypotheses correspond to house and congregational hypotheses in the following order: *Contextualism* employs the historical event as its root metaphor and emphasizes the pragmatic truth found in encounter. What is significant about the world is not its form or process but incidents in specific environments. *Mechanism* works from a machine as root metaphor and emphasizes the discovery of factors as agencies and the delineation of action. For mechanists, the world is a field of force whose properties are basically numerical and instrumental. *Organicism* develops from the root metaphor of an organism and emphasizes the systemic nature of occurrences. The world is basically a developmental process that works toward an ultimate unity or absolute. *Formism* builds upon a root metaphor of similarity and emphasizes the correspondence of forms between otherwise unrelated things and events. The world is imagined as certain persistent structures in which life participates.

6. Joseph H. Fichter, *Dynamics of a City Church* (Chicago: Univ. of Chicago Press,

1951); Peter Berger, *The Noise of Solemn Assemblies: Christian Commitment and the Religious Establishment in America* (Garden City, N.Y.: Doubleday & Co., 1961); Gibson Winter, *The Suburban Captivity of the Churches*. Fichter's investigation of a New Orleans parish proved so disturbing to Roman Catholic officials and those of his university that he was prevented from publishing further volumes in what was to be a series entitled *Southern Parish*.

7. World Council of Churches Department on Studies in Evangelism, *Planning for Mission: Working Papers on the New Quest for Missionary Communities*, ed. Thomas Wieser (New York: United States Conference for the World Council of Churches, 1966); World Council of Churches, *Concept*, newsletter published by the Department on Studies in Evangelism, WCC; World Council of Churches, *The New Delhi Report: The Third Assembly of the World Council of Churches, 1961* (London: SCM Press, 1962), 189–91; World Council of Churches, *New Delhi to Uppsala: Report of the Central Committee to the Fourth Assembly of the World Council of Churches* (Geneva: WCC, 1968), 66–70; World Council of Churches, *The Uppsala Report: Official Report of the Fourth Assembly of the World Council of Churches*, Uppsala, July 4–20, 1968 (Geneva: WCC, 1968), 33f., 200f.

8. World Council of Churches, *The Church for Others and the Church for the World* (Geneva: WCC, 1967), 61.

9. World Council of Churches, *New Delhi Report*, 189.

10. Herbert T. Neve, *Sources for Change: Searching for Flexible Church Structures* (Geneva: WCC, 1968).

11. World Council of Churches, *Planning for Mission*, 26.

12. World Council of Churches, *New Delhi to Uppsala*, 66.

13. World Council of Churches, *Planning for Mission*, 134.

14. Johannes Christian Hoekendijk, *The Church Inside Out* (Philadelphia: Westminster Press, 1966). Cf. Colin Williams, *Where in the World?* (New York: National Council of the Churches of Christ in the U.S.A., 1963), and *What in the World?* (New York: National Council of the Churches of Christ in the U.S.A., 1964). Williams's books, widely circulated, were guides that provided for laity a clearly argued theological basis for missionary structure.

15. In some study papers it was proposed that although the church might be of prophetic service in a variety of arenas of public life, the primary locus of church mission should be the urban community. Unlike the congregational studies of earlier decades that treated an urban context as, at most, an environment outside and distinct from the major business of the church, the literature of the 1960s projected urban society as the pervasive ethos of the congregation itself. Only insofar as the congregation as texture strengthened the fabric of urban community would it gain its true nature. See Walter Kloetzli, *The City Church, Death or Renewal: A Study of 8 Urban Lutheran Churches* (Philadelphia: Muhlenberg Press, 1961); Robert Lee, ed., *Cities and Churches: Readings on the Urban Church* (Philadelphia: Westminster Press, 1962); Richard E. Moore and Duane L. Day, *Urban Church Breakthrough* (New York: Harper & Row, 1966); George W. Webber, *The Congregation in Mission* (New York: Abingdon Press, 1964); Gibson Winter, *The New Creation as Metropolis* (New York: Macmillan Co., 1963). See also Ezra Earl Jones and Robert L. Wilson, *What's Ahead for Old First Church?* (New York: Harper & Row, 1974), and Gaylord Noyce, *Survival and Mission for the City Church* (Philadelphia: Westminster Press, 1975). Published in the next decade, the works of Jones and Noyce are more centripetal in their focus, treating the city as surrounding environment rather than the total context for church life. Several books of the contextual sort also considered the suburban environment: Andrew W. Greeley, *The Church and the Suburbs* (New York: Sheed & Ward, 1959); Frederick A. Shippey, *Protestantism in Suburban Life* (Nashville: Abingdon Press, 1964); Gaylord Noyce, *The Responsible Suburban Church*

(Philadelphia: Westminster Press, 1970); W. Widick Schroeder, Victor Obenhaus, Larry Jones, and Thomas Sweetser, *Suburban Religion: Churches and Synagogues in the American Experience* (Chicago: Center for the Scientific Study of Religion, 1974).

16. George W. Webber, *God's Colony in Man's World* (Nashville: Abingdon Press, 1960). See also Steven Rose, *The Grass Roots Church: A Manifesto for Protestant Renewal* (Nashville: Abingdon Press, 1966), which poses a more visionary structure of Christians organized not in congregations but in clusters for service and teaching.

17. Gerald Jud, *Pilgrim's Process: How the Local Church Can Respond to the New Age* (Philadelphia: United Church Press, 1967). Defying the different ecclesial tastes of the 1970s, George W. Webber also published *Today's Church: A Community of Exiles and Pilgrims* (Nashville: Abingdon Press, 1979), which advocates a style of transience more radical than the one proposed in his earlier works.

18. Robert W. Long, ed., *Renewing the Congregation* (Minneapolis: Augsburg Publishing House, 1966); M. Edward Clark, William L. Malcomson, and Warren Lane Molton, *The Church Creative* (Nashville: Abingdon Press, 1967); Waldron Howard, *Nine Roads to Renewal* (Waco, Tex.: Word Books, 1967); Wallace E. Fisher, *Preface to Parish Renewal: Study Guide for Laymen* (Nashville: Abingdon Press, 1968); Gerald H. Slusser, *The Local Church in Transition* (Philadelphia: Westminster Press, 1966); Joan Thatcher, *The Church Responds* (Valley Forge, Pa.: Judson Press, 1970); William R. Nelson and William F. Lincoln, *Journey Toward Renewal: New Routes for Old Churches* (Valley Forge, Pa.: Judson Press, 1971); Anthony Wesson, *Experiments in Renewal* (London: Epworth Press, 1971).

19. Robert A. Raines, *New Life in the Church* (New York: Harper & Row, 1961); *Reshaping the Christian Life* (New York: Harper & Row, 1964); *The Secular Congregation* (New York: Harper & Row, 1968); Rudiger Reitz, *The Church in Experiment: Studies in New Congregational Structures and Functional Mission* (Nashville: Abingdon Press, 1969); Eugene Stockwell, *Claimed by God for Mission: The Congregation Seeks New Forms* (New York: World Outlook Press, 1965).

20. Marvin Bordelon, ed., *The Parish in a Time of Change* (Notre Dame: Fides Pub., 1967); Grace Ann Goodman, *Rocking the Ark: Nine Case Studies of Traditional Churches in the Process of Change* (New York: United Presbyterian Church U.S.A., 1968). More recently, B. Carlisle Driggers, ed., *Models of Metropolitan Ministry: How Twenty Churches Are Ministering Successfully in Areas of Rapid Social Change* (Nashville: Broadman Press, 1979).

21. Robert S. Lecky and H. Elliott Wright, *Can These Bones Live? The Failure of Church Renewal* (New York: Sheed & Ward, 1969).

22. Theologians such as Joseph C. Hough have since insisted that the congregation needs to be analyzed "in the light of the universal theological dialogue in the church about the mission and ministry of the church as the body of Christ in the world" (in Dudley, *Building Effective Ministry*, 112), but most theological studies of the church since 1970 do not analyze the local church. Sociological studies of congregational context since 1970 include Arthur L. Anderson, *Divided We Stand: Institutional Religion as a Reflection of Pluralism and Integration in America* (Dubuque: Kendall/Hunt Pub. Co., 1978); Thomas C. Campbell and Yoshio Fukuyama, *The Fragmented Layman: An Empirical Study of Lay Attitudes* (Philadelphia: Pilgrim Press, 1970); James D. Davidson, "Religious Belief as an Independent Variable," *Journal for the Scientific Study of Religion* 11 (1972): 65–75; James D. Davidson, "Religious Belief as a Dependent Variable," *Sociological Analysis* 33 (1972): 81–94; James D. Davidson, "Patterns of Belief at the Denominational and Congregational Levels," *Review of Religious Research* 13 (1972): 197–205; David R. Gibbs, Samuel A. Miller, and James R. Wood, "Doctrinal Orthodoxy, Salience and the Consequential Dimension," *Journal for the*

Scientific Study of Religion 12 (1973): 33–52; William McKinney, and others, *Census Data for Community Mission* (New York: Board for Homeland Ministries, United Church of Christ, 1983), part of a denomination-wide study of census data relevant to each congregation in the United Church of Christ; David O. Moberg, "Theological Position and Institutional Characteristics of Protestant Congregations: An Explanatory Study," *Journal for the Scientific Study of Religion* 9 (1970): 53–58; Wade Clark Roof, *Community and Commitment*; Thomas Sweetser, *The Catholic Parish: Shifting Membership in a Changing Church* (Chicago: Center for the Scientific Study of Religion, 1974).

23. Edgar R. Trexler, *Creative Congregations: Tested Strategies for Today's Congregations* (Nashville: Abingdon Press, 1972), 9. Cf. James B. Sauer, *Congregational Vitality: Foundation for Integrity in Evangelism* (New York: National Council of the Churches of Christ in the U.S.A., n.d.), 1: "The local congregation is a lot livelier than most people think."

24. Writing in 1982, after a decade in which the church as a whole had pursued the inner mechanisms of congregations, several sociologists reported as follows: "We share the conviction that in recent years congregational analysis has over-emphasized the internal dynamics of congregational life and has failed to sufficiently account for the influence of the social and ecological context of the church's inner life. We argue, in other words, that congregational analysis should work from the 'outside in.' While we do not subscribe to a deterministic view, we believe that the environment both sets limits on and provides opportunities for a congregation." Jackson Carroll, William McKinney, and Wade Clark Roof, "From the Outside In: A Sociological Approach," in Dudley, *Building Effective Ministry*, 84–85. See also David S. King, *No Church Is an Island* (New York: Pilgrim Press, 1980).

25. Dean A. Kelley, *Why Conservative Churches Are Growing* (New York: Harper & Row, 1972).

26. C. Peter Wagner, *Your Church Can Grow* (Glendale, Calif.: Regal Books, 1976), 43.

27. Ibid., 1, 28.

28. Ibid., 89.

29. Ibid., 87.

30. Donald A. MacGavran, *Bridges of God* (New York: Friendship Press, 1955); *How Churches Grow* (New York: Friendship Press, 1959).

31. H. Boone Porter, *Growth and Life in the Local Church* (New York: Seabury Press, 1968).

32. W. Wendell Belew, *Churches and How They Grow* (Nashville: Broadman Press, 1971).

33. See n. 25, above.

34. In addition to the works already mentioned: Charles L. Chaney and Ron S. Lewis, *Design for Church Growth* (Nashville: Broadman Press, 1977); Vergil Gerber, *God's Way to Keep a Church Going and Growing* (Glendale, Calif.: Regal Books, 1973); Donald A. MacGavran, *Understanding Church Growth* (Grand Rapids: Wm. B. Eerdmanns Pub. Co., 1970); Donald A. MacGavran and Winfred Arn, *How to Grow a Church* (Glendale, Calif.: Regal Books, 1973); Donald A. MacGavran and Winfred Arn, *Ten Steps to Church Growth* (New York: Harper & Row, 1977); Donald A. MacGavran and George Hunter, *Church Growth: Strategies That Work* (Nashville: Abingdon Press, 1980); Donald J. MacNair, *The Growing Local Church* (Grand Rapids: Baker Book House, 1975); Charles Mylander, *Secrets for Growing Churches* (San Francisco: Harper & Row, 1979); Wilbert R. Shenk, *The Challenge of Church Growth* (Scottdale, Pa.: Herald Press, 1973); Ebbie Smith, *A Manual for Church Growth Sur-*

veys (Pasadena: William Carey Library, 1976); Bob Waymire and C. Peter Wagner, *The Church Growth Survey Handbook* (Santa Clara, Calif.: Global Church Growth Bulletin, 1980); C. Peter Wagner, *Our Kind of People* (Atlanta: John Knox Press, 1979); *The Global Church Growth Bulletin* (Box 66, Santa Clara, Calif.), published bimonthly.

35. Robert K. Hudnut, *Church Growth Is Not the Point* (New York: Harper & Row, 1975).

36. Dean R. Hoge and David A. Roozen, eds., *Understanding Church Growth and Decline: 1950–1970* (New York: Pilgrim Press, 1979); Carl S. Dudley, *Where Have All Our People Gone?* (New York: Pilgrim Press, 1979), a digest of material in the Hoge and Roozen volume.

37. Jackson Carroll, *Small Churches Are Beautiful* (New York: Harper & Row, 1977); Carl S. Dudley, *Making the Small Church Effective* (Nashville: Abingdon Press, 1978); Bernard Quinn, *The Small Rural Parish* (Washington, D.C.: Glenmary House Missioners, 1980).

38. Wagner, *Your Church Can Grow*, 159. See also Wagner's summary article in Hoge and Roozen, *Understanding Church Growth*, 270–87.

39. Wagner, *Your Church Can Grow*, 41.

40. Ibid., 31.

41. Robert H. Schuller, *Your Church Has Real Possibilities* (Glendale, Calif.: Regal Books, 1974).

42. Wagner, *Your Church Can Grow*, 27.

43. Lyle E. Schaller, "A Practitioner's Perspective," in Dudley, *Building Effective Ministry*, 160–74. See also Lyle E. Schaller, *Survival Tactics in the Parish* (Nashville: Abingdon Press, 1977); *Assimilating New Members* (Nashville: Abingdon Press, 1978); *Effective Church Planning* (Nashville: Abingdon Press, 1979); *Activating the Passive Church* (Nashville: Abingdon Press, 1982); and many other works. Note the mechanistic approach of another consultant in Roy M. Oswald, *Power Analysis of a Congregation* (Washington, D.C.: Alban Institute, 1981).

44. Many consultants and others who study the congregation are listed in Elizabeth Whipple, *The Study of the Local Church: A Directory of Participants* (Atlanta: Project Team for the Study of the Congregation, Rollins Center for Church Ministries, Emory University, 1983).

45. Lyle E. Schaller, "A Practioner's Perspective," in Dudley, *Building Effective Ministry*, 161.

46. Ibid., 162–64.

47. Ibid., 168.

48. "I have become convinced that the organizational structure, the size of the governing board, the frequency of their meetings, the nature of the room in which they meet, and the choice of who will preside at the meetings of the governing body have a significant impact on what happens in the life of a congregation. The design of the building has a great impact on the degree of 'friendliness' displayed by the members. In another setting I have argued that the importance of place may be the most neglected factor in church planning" (ibid., 164).

49. Some church consultants—for instance, those of the London-based Grubb Institute of Behavioral Studies—again use a mechanist approach to the congregation, but with more attention to organicist methods than Schaller employs. Bruce Reed, based at the Grubb Institute, and his American associate Barry Evans probe the psychology of members of a congregation and advance hypotheses about behavioral dynamics characteristic of a particular church to determine its "primary task—its normative function in the community" (Dudley, *Building Effective Ministry*, 38). Though the congregation is also understood as an "open system" functioning developmen-

tally, "the process of transformation is [itself] called a 'task' which is susceptible to analysis and definition" (ibid., 39). Bruce Reed, *The Dynamics of Religion: Process and Movement in Christian Churches* (London: Darton, Longman & Todd, 1978), analyzes a process of oscillation through which members and congregations regularly move. He also develops a theory of functional and dysfunctional behavior in church activities. The dominant image of the local church, the one that gives Reed's and Evans's findings much of their coherence and argument, is that of the congregation as a mechanistic field of traceable forces. See also Bruce Reed, *The Task of the Church and the Role of Its Members* (New York: The Alban Institute, 1976).

50. Wagner's *Our Kind of People* is a protracted argument for a homogeneous congregation. See also his fifth vital sign, in *Your Church Can Grow*, 33.

51. Robert C. Worley, *A Gathering of Strangers: Understanding the Life of Your Church* (Philadelphia: Westminster Press, 1976).

52. Ibid., 18. Worley goes on to clarify his use of "identity crisis," disclosing his organic bent by associating his use of the term with Erik Erikson's discussion of identity formation in late adolescence.

53. E. Mansell Pattison, *Pastor and Parish: A Systems Approach* (Philadelphia: Fortress Press, 1977), 6–12, notes three aspects of systems theory—holism, open synergy, and isomorphism—that correspond to the characteristics I describe.

54. Evelyn Eaton Whitehead and James D. Whitehead, *Community of Faith: Models and Strategies for Developing Christian Communities* (New York: Seabury Press, 1982), 21, 32.

55. Loren Mead describes parishioners who "feel trapped, unable to free their congregation from its hang-ups. . . . In its corporate life the parish often becomes an institution of frightened people. It becomes defensive, self-protective—the very antithesis of loving freedom proclaimed by the gospel and believed by many of its members" (*New Hope for Congregations*, 22–23). But, for Mead and the Alban Institute that he directs, such situations when squarely faced contain the seeds for resolution. "Congregations can change. . . . Purposeful people can determine much about the direction of a congregation's life" (ibid., 93).

56. Pattison, *Pastor and Parish*, 7.

57. James D. Anderson, *To Come Alive!*; John E. Biersdorf, *Hunger for Experience: Vital Religious Communities in America* (New York: Seabury Press, 1975); Paul Dietterich and Russell Wilson, *A Process of Local Church Vitalization* (Naperville: Center for Parish Development, 1976); James C. Fenhagen, *Mutual Ministry: New Vitality for the Local Church* (New York: Seabury Press, 1977).

58. Newton Malony describes how organization development enlivens the church body: "Organizations were hereby conceived as organic, systemic and alive entities that could be improved by intentional efforts. The goal is to improve the way they are organized, the jobs they provide and the relationships they engender, so that they function more efficiently and fulfill their members' lives more fully. It is important to note that organization development consultation assumes that the 'fulfilling of the members' lives' is just as important as increasing production. . . . More important, it assumes that participation in the organization is *the* way that the members' lives will become more satisfying. It is a mutually dependent and necessary relationship because nowhere else in modern society is it possible to increase life satisfaction so fully as in organizational life.

"When the church is perceived through this systems approach, it is seen as a place where the importance of fulfilling lives is probably *more* important than any program the church may produce or any building it may construct" ("Organization Development: A Framework for Understanding and Helping the Church," in Dudley, *Building Effective Ministry*, 179).

59. Pattison, *Pastor and Parish*, 8.

60. Robert C. Worley, *Change in the Church: A Source of Hope* (Philadelphia: Westminster Press, 1971), 93.

61. Wagner, *Your Church Can Grow*, 30.

62. Aidan Kavanagh, *The Shape of Baptism: The Rite of Christian Initiation* (New York: Pueblo Pub. Co., 1978); Gwen Kennedy Neville and John H. Westerhoff, *Learning Through Liturgy* (New York: Seabury Press, 1978); William H. Willimon, *Worship as Pastoral Care* (Nashville: Abingdon Press, 1979); Walter Wink, *The Bible in Human Transformation: Toward a New Paradigm for Bible Study* (Philadelphia: Fortress Press, 1975).

63. Don S. Browning, *The Moral Context of Pastoral Care* (Philadelphia: Westminster Press, 1976); Thomas Downs, *The Parish as Learning Community: Modeling for Parish and Adult Growth* (New York: Paulist Press, 1979); Thomas H. Groome, *Christian Religious Education: Sharing Our Story and Our Vision* (New York: Harper & Row, 1980); C. Ellis Nelson, *Where Faith Begins* (Richmond: John Knox Press, 1967); John H. Westerhoff, *Will Our Children Have Faith?* (New York: Seabury Press, 1976).

64. Stephen B. Clark, *Building Christian Communities* (Notre Dame: Ave Maria Press, 1972); Speed Leas and Paul Kittlaus, *Church Fights*, is representative of several works on church conflict (see chap. 10, n. 8). See also Jones and Wilson, cited in n. 15; Douglas Walrath, *Leading Churches Through Change* (Nashville, Abingdon Press, 1979).

65. Roger A. Johnson, *Congregations as Nurturing Communities* (New York: Division for Parish Services, Lutheran Church of America, 1979); Samuel Southard, *Comprehensive Pastoral Care: Enabling the Laity to Share in Pastoral Ministry* (Valley Forge, Pa.: Judson Press, 1975); Howard W. Stone, *The Caring Church: A Guide for Lay Pastoral Care* (San Francisco: Harper & Row, 1983).

66. James Gustafson, *Treasure in Earthen Vessels: The Church as a Human Community* (New York: Harper & Row, 1961), developed the concept of the church as a community of language, although he does not press the implication of language beyond its Christian symbols; nor does he argue that the community employing this language is either essentially or primarily the local church.

67. Earl Brewer, Theodore Runyon, and Harold McSwain, *Protestant Parish: A Case Study of Rural and Urban Parish Patterns* (Atlanta: Communicative Arts Press, 1967).

68. Nelson, *Where Faith Begins*. See also John H. Westerhoff and Gwen Kennedy Neville, *Generation to Generation*.

69. James E. Dittes, *The Church in the Way* (New York: Charles Scribner's Sons, 1967), 41. Clifford Geertz uses a similar notion of "bodied stuff" to distinguish the object of culture analysis from the abstractions that form nomothetic observations (*The Interpretation of Cultures*, 23). Like Geertz, Dittes further relates stuff to narrative style, and he sees, as I do, the implication of idiom for understanding the struggle of society at large.

70. John C. Harris, *Stress, Power and Ministry: An Approach to the Current Dilemmas of Pastors and Congregations* (Washington, D.C.: Alban Institute, 1977).

71. Samuel C. Heilman, *Synagogue Life*; Melvin D. Williams, *Community in a Black Pentecostal Church: An Anthropological Study* (Pittsburgh: Univ. of Pittsburgh Press, 1974). Melvin D. Williams, "The Conflict of Corporate Church and Spiritual Community," in Dudley, *Building Effective Ministry*, 55–67, and Michael H. Ducey, *Sunday Morning: Aspects of Urban Ritual* (New York: Free Press, 1977), study white Protestant churches from an anthropological perspective. Suggestions to students of congregations who wish to begin an ethnographic study of a church are offered,

largely in exercise form, in Dudley, *Making the Small Church Effective*, and in Neville and Westerhoff, *Learning Through Liturgy*, 71–88. See also William H. Anderson, "The Local Congregation as a Subculture," *Social Compass* 18 (1971): 287–91.

72. Urban T. Holmes's most extensive analysis of congregational culture occurs in *Priest in Community: Exploring the Roots of Ministry* (New York: Seabury Press, 1978).

73. Don S. Browning, "Integrating the Approaches, An Overview," and David S. Pacini, "Professionalism, Breakdown and Revelation," in Dudley, *Building Effective Ministry*, 220–37 and 133–52.

74. Heilman, *Synagogue Life*, xii.

75. In his study of Zion, a black Pentecostal church, Melvin Williams observes: "The system of symbolic expression in Zion validates this church community; the communication code . . . allows the members not only to belong to this religious community but also to be carriers of the community content wherever they find themselves in interaction with other members of Zion. . . . The members identify with Zion and one another. They embody the stuff of community. They reinforce, identify, and conceptualize in terms of images of whom that community represents. Thus their communication code, full of references to food, the farm, the rural landscape, human anatomy, death, the physical world, and the supernatural, contains messages and is indicative of a system of symbolic expression that validates and identifies these southern Black rural (peasant) migrants apart from a wider society" (*Community in a Black Pentecostal Church*, 175).

76. Heilman, *Synagogue Life*, xii. Cf. Frederika Randall, "Why Scholars Become Storytellers," *The New York Times Book Review*, 29 January 1984, 1, 31.

77. Cf. James F. Hopewell, "The Jovial Church: Narrative in Local Church Life," in Dudley, *Building Effective Ministry*, 68–83.

3

PARISH STORY

Most of us can probably remember participating, as student or teacher, in a course that died prematurely. I taught such a course, and I recall it here because from its ashes sprang the basic idea explored in this book. In the fall of 1977, Sammy Clark and I began work on a course designed to pursue an aspect of ministry in Sammy's congregation, the gifted Trinity Church in downtown Atlanta. Although congregation-based courses of this sort can be capricious, we felt we had this one under fair control. I had taught similar courses elsewhere; Sammy's experience in contextual training stretched back to his staff days in New York City's East Harlem Protestant Parish. We took on the present assignment with the easy confidence of veteran guides provisioning a familiar tour.

The course was to address the relative absence of racial diversity in many of the age groups at Trinity. Though substantial numbers of blacks and whites were active in this church, one or the other race tended to dominate each particular level of Trinity's youth and adult programs. Concerned about this layer-cake alternation, Clark as pastor and other church leaders decided to work with the seminary in which I was teaching to examine the problem and attempt some remedies.

My seminary accepted this responsibility because it believes that preparation for ministry requires participation in critical social situations. Therefore its faculty approved Clark's and my syllabus. The outline bristled with good readings. It projected the course's movement through phases of inquiry to those of theory making and experiment. We were careful to develop ways by which its twenty-four students—twelve seminarians and twelve Trinity laypersons—could themselves "own" the course and be supported in its stressful moments. Sammy and I felt that we had prepared for a worthy, sturdy undertaking.

The course began to disintegrate, however, in its first week. Several of the laypersons who had volunteered to participate never appeared; others soon dropped out; only four of the twelve persisted to the end. Their resistance paralyzed the course and puzzled the rest of us. Many of the same persons had collaborated fully in other courses that had dealt with difficult topics at Trinity. Why had this present course, then, provoked such massive truancy?

Those of us who remained in the course probed the resistance of our absent colleagues. As time passed, we became less convinced of the adequacy of the psychological explanations we had first offered. Instead, we began to discern in the words and actions of the truants a subtle and intricate pattern of values that seemed to transcend the motives of any single person. It began to appear that this course had violated a hidden code of worth and meaning that underlay the corporate life of this particular congregation. While each truant was a liberal Christian who gave private assent to the course plan, each was also a member of a body guided by a contravening set of norms and outlooks. As members, these persons guarded this corporate code by their absence, silence, and argument.

This code was embedded in what we came to call the "Trinity Story," the narrative that church members used to describe the recent history of their congregation. Founded before the Civil War and finally located across the street from Georgia's state capitol building, Trinity grew, as one of its ministers wrote, in "prestige, power, and people, and [became] one of the most influential Methodist churches in the South."[1] Nevertheless it lost both power and prominence after the Second World War. Its prestigious members died or transferred to other churches closer to their homes in the new suburbs of Atlanta. As a recent pastor put it, Trinity became a tomb. Some members and leaders of the Methodist conference advocated its relocation in an affluent suburb to reestablish its preeminent position.

Instead, Trinity chose a more adventurous path. In 1967, the year that segregationists put Lester Maddox into the capitol building as governor, the church next door decided to stay where it was and to recruit black and poor persons in the neighborhood as members. That costly decision alienated still more of Trinity's longtime members and aroused the anger of many outsiders. Fortunately, an exceptionally strong pastor was appointed to the church in time to guide it through its time of attrition and mistreatment. He remembers the bitterness of members when black teenagers began to worship at Trinity:

> Some of the previously saintly members took me to task verbally and to hell emotionally. Such terms as "niggerlover" and worse spewed out of the same mouths that sang, "In Christ There Is No East or West." Hate letters arrived. The journey from Sunday School to pulpit was lined by vicious comments.[2]

Trinity persevered through the corrosive attack, only then to be put to further tests of its will and capacity to help by the poor community itself. In response and at great cost, Trinity developed, in cooperation with some of its poorer neighbors, new modes of urban ministry: an employment project, a summer camp, an integrated high school group, a new parish house located next to the public housing project, visitation and food services for the elderly, a literacy program, parole referral, and overnight housing for the homeless. The high school group started a steel band which, to the group's delight, further irritated conservatives in the neighborhood.

Eventually Trinity gained new supporters. Some strong black leaders joined, and a number of suburban liberals, happy to find a church that really acted on the denomination's social principles, drove into town to work in Trinity's new ministries. By the mid-1970s Trinity had become an unusual but substantial community of diverse people. It had gathered into common worship "college professor and prison releasee, maid and manufacturer, young and old, black and white, male and female."[3] In late 1976 the church published its plan for a future ministry that would convey its experience to the wider church and society:

> Be a witness—Trinity has a responsibility to our community and our city to reflect the New South, the New America, the New Church.[4]

Older student and young adult members of Trinity who have since moved to other regions of the nation report that they carry on the church's vision in their new location.

During our course at Trinity, I heard its story told by its members with all the urgency of fresh news. Anecdotes that reflected the sharp pain and triumph of the early years were often repeated. The Trinity Story reached its climax, as I heard it told, in tales of the union of the two races, worshiping next door to a state capitol whose own policies bent toward integration in the same period. Out of this union was born Trinity's mission to witness human solidarity in a racist society and church.

The Trinity Story, however, contains not only a narrative of events but also a code that signals the identity and behavior of that congregation. The clue to that code, I believe, is the striking similarity of this story to a form of myth that has powered tales of many peoples, giving form to their self-concepts and strength to their standards. The myth is a very ancient story, one evident in the mythic patterns of many cultures and analyzed by Carl Jung[5] and Joseph Campbell[6] as the journey of the hero. Like the church that grew up around me, Trinity was an instance of a congregation working its way through a spontaneous and uncertain period of its life; yet it, like my own congregation, used structures of behavior and interpretation derived from the world's treasury of religious symbols.

In Trinity's case, the congregation's adventure implicates what Campbell argues are the most pervasive and fundamental of human mythic patterns.

Campbell displays the sequence of the hero journey in a diagram shown in Figure A.[7] The hero encounters a series of events that, though not all present in any single story, and though distinctive in their detail in each specific telling, nevertheless usually follow the sequence that Campbell outlines and function according to the purposes he describes. The pattern that Campbell found typifying hero myths thousands of years old is resonant in Trinity's re-

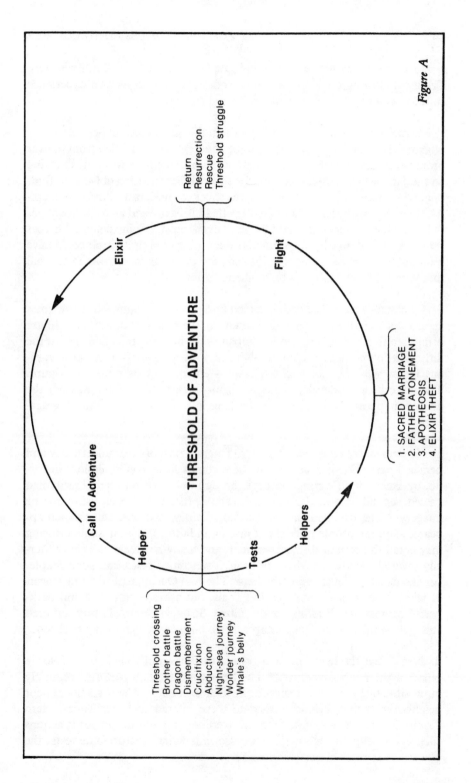

Figure A

43

cent experience. Trinity seems to replicate Hero's adventure. Trinity is Hero Trinity, following the sequence of episodes common to its own experience and, as an example, a sixth century B.C. religious figure.

a. *The call to adventure.* Before the journey, the once powerful hero is in a repugnant situation. In Trinity's case, the congregation had fallen from prewar prominence into a neglected tomb and was searching for a way out. Drawing on the Jataka Tales, Campbell describes the similar situation of Gotama Buddha, who, once a protected prince, was shocked by signs of illness, decrepitude, death, and austerity. The Buddha fled his palace and all its prerogatives to learn what existence shaped by these terrors meant. Some potential heroes refuse such a call to adventure and live out dull lives. Trinity itself could have built another palace elsewhere. Instead, the congregation answered the call that plunged it into its city's turmoil and suffering.

b. *A protective figure.* The hero is joined by a protective figure who sometimes appears as a guide or teacher. Representing the power of destiny, the figure brings amulets to the hero and accompanies the hero as protection against the difficulties about to be encountered. Trinity's new pastor—a big, hearty, pious fellow who did not frighten easily—emerged as its protective figure. Though critical to developments in Trinity's story, the pastor was not the hero. He appeared when needed and later left. The hero was the congregation.

c. *The threshold of adventure.* The hero enters a zone of great uncertainty and personal peril. Enemies attack; the hero comes close to annihilation, in battle, by execution or during journeys through water. (After Hero Trinity had passed beyond its own dangerous threshold, its pastor wrote, using marine imagery, "The troubled waters receded, the dry land of urban mission appeared, and the people walked out upon it in faith.") The threshold crossing may entail the pain of dismemberment, and many members of Trinity literally severed themselves when the church welcomed black and poor people. Antagonists ferociously beset the hero. The Evil One unleashed "nine storms of wind, rain, rocks, weapons, live coals, hot ashes, sand, mud and darkness"[8] against the Buddha in his Great Struggle. Hero Trinity suffered strangely similar abuse from antagonists in both church and neighborhood.

d. *Tests.* Next the hero "must survive a succession of trials, . . . a favorite phase of the myth-adventure."[9] The hero must agree to perform seemingly impossible tasks and must succeed in their execution. The suspicious, poor neighborhood that Trinity wished to serve offered such challenges. Hero Trinity had to prove that its faith involved not only routine domestic actions such as worship and fellowship but also unfamiliar, venturesome tests, the devising of programs to assuage hunger, despair, homelessness, and unemployment.

e. *Helpers*. Additional helpers come to aid the hero. After Buddha's triumph, a seven-day storm is unleashed on him, but the king of serpents protects Buddha with his expanded hood. As Hero Trinity undertook its tests it began to attract different sorts of church participants: persons from both the poor neighborhood and farther afield who strove for the same goals as Trinity. Mothers in the housing project, university teachers and students, city singles, and liberal families allied with Trinity in a now more popular cause.

f. *Sacred marriage*. At the bottom of Campbell's heroic circle is the goal of the quest, expressed in such images as atonement, deification, or the capture of a desired object. In his journey the Buddha here obtained supreme enlightenment. For Hero Trinity, the sacred achievement was a Christian union of normally polarized persons and classes, a coincidence of opposites. One pastor referred to Trinity's worship as a common table around which God gathered a marvelously diverse collection of human beings: rich and poor, black and white, privileged and outcast.

g. *Flight* and h. *Return*. The hero generally ends the adventure by returning to normal life. Sometimes the return passage requires escape or rescue. In other cases the hero emerges with divine blessing. Throughout the 1970s a number of younger people—college and seminary students, persons in their first adult jobs—were members of Hero Trinity. Now they have moved on to other places and tasks. Other persons blessed by the adventure have also departed. In fact, a standard rhythm of Trinity's present ministry is to accept persons attracted to its sacred banquet and then to help them on their way to their own ministries elsewhere.

i. *Elixir*. The hero returns to the world with a life-giving boon. What the hero has gained in the quest is not a private possession but to be shared with all. Although the Buddha experienced the bliss of enlightenment, by its nature not transferable, he nevertheless spent the rest of his long life not in withdrawn contemplation but in teaching. He acceded to visitors who pled:

> Now that you, O sage, have yourself crossed the ocean of the world of becoming, please rescue also the other living beings who have sunk so deep into suffering! As a generous lord shares his wealth, so may also you bestow your virtues on others! Most of those who know what for them is good in this world and the next act only for their own advantage.[10]

Hero Trinity likewise undertakes today a special mission "to our community and our city" to share its vision of God's kingdom. Had the congregation refused to embark on its journey, remaining set in its former ways, no special boon to humanity would have resulted. But because it launched out on its heroic adventure, it now helps a wider community understand how society might be healed.

If our preparations for the course at Trinity had been more sensitive to the Trinity Story, we might have avoided some of the consequences. As the course was constructed, however, it constituted a point-by-point repudiation of the story and its code. Instead of Hero Trinity bringing its boon to the world, we, the outside world, were bringing the boon to Trinity. Instead of celebrating Hero Trinity's sacred marriage of blacks and whites, we focused on their disunion. Rather than recall the congregation's heroic tales of trial and success, we focused on their antonyms, avoidance and failure. Our course plan implied that the heroic adventure of Trinity Church was only beginning, that it did not already exist as a story and a code that generated value and outlook. From a rational standpoint, the course seemed necessary and appropriate, but deeper matters were at stake in this venture than the purposes stated in the syllabus. The lessons this course taught were primarily the unintended ones that I, the professor, learned.

THE FUNCTIONS OF NARRATIVE

Through these introductory chapters I have stressed the idiomatic nature of parish culture, its thick networking of construable signs to form a dialect of signals and symbols. The most important lesson I learned from the Trinity course is that most parish idiom conveys and implies narrative. Story expresses the intricacy of congregational life. Though widely regarded as merely a form of entertainment or illustration, stories are an essential account of social experience. From the Hero Trinity story can be elicited three features of the fundamental relationship between congregational life and narrative:

1. The congregation's self-perception is primarily narrative in form.
2. The congregation's communication among its members is primarily by story.
3. By its own congregating, the congregation participates in narrative structures of the world's societies.

1. *The congregation's self-perception is primarily narrative in form.* Trinity used story to provide an account of itself, to itself and to others. Though our course was intended as a technical probe into certain issues, Trinity members, when pressed to account for their remarkable interracial identity, responded primarily by stories that described their past history, or by anecdotes that depicted the present state of affairs, or occasionally by scenarios that projected various futures for their fellowship. In each instance they apprehended their corporate existence by means of narrative. They found no

other adequate ways to communicate the richness and variety of Trinity's life. Only in storied form did explanations seem sufficiently comprehensive. Stories were required, to adapt terms used by Stanley Hauerwas, in order to give connection to contingent events.[11] The elaborate wholeness of Trinity's corporate existence, its passage through a thick diversity of events from past to future, required a narrative vehicle for its transmission.

A narrative can gather happenings that are not already substantively linked to each other. While formulas convey the regular sequences and synchronisms of actions, stories knit events that have a plausible but so far undetermined relation. The Trinity story is thickened by events that at first appear unrelated or are unforeseen. That is why, in listening to the story, we want to know what happens next: we cannot be sure what will next unfold. By building suspense through the incorporation of unpredictable actions—what Northrop Frye calls story's capacity to say "and then"—narrative enables its tellers to claim the association of separate happenings with a single life, personal or corporate. How does Trinity embrace in its own identity events as diverse as insults, steel bands, and a mission to racist institutions? It connects them by story. Other writers have attempted to explain the capacity of narrative to summarize the complexities of self-understanding: "Narrative history of a certain kind," says Alasdair MacIntyre, "turns out to be the basic and essential genre for the characterization of human actions."[12] Story is a device by which perceptions of corporate life are arranged in a telling way, but that is not its first or only function. Story is also the form by which corporate experience is in the first instance perceived.

In an intriguing if controversial article, Stephen Crites argues that experience itself is basically narrative in form, providing the essential order for human understanding.[13] The storied unity found in life is not, for Crites, a secondary result of human culture. Story is in a much more rudimentary way implicated in experience itself. Crites's argument is an attempt to account for human beings' innate sense of continuity among past, present, and future times. Earlier and forthcoming times at the moment do not exist, yet they are essential dimensions of the experienced present. Crites proposes that experience of the lived present must have a narrative character, because it necessarily ties the perception of the moment to the memory of past events and to the anticipation of the future. Thus, through its narrative character, experience contains the sense of both before and after as well as the distinctions among past, present, and future, enabling us to comprehend our persistence through time. Why do we warm to stories? In Crites's view, narrative does not merely order a chaotic world, it also provides the basic model that experience makes of life. Crites does not claim that reality itself is or has a story, but he places the presence of narrative at the very boundary of human knowing.

Story, then, may be more than a cultural response to prior perceptions. The awareness of personal and corporate existence is perhaps itself a nascent story. If so, to seek the story of the congregation, in its twists of plot and evolutions of character and circuits of setting, is to enter into the basic experience of corporate life. Story may be more than the mere play of children or the protoscience of primitives; it may relate the essential negotiation of the local church in realizing its own identity.

2. *The congregation's communication among its members is primarily by story.* Not only does narrative convey the experience of corporate existence, it also characterizes the continuing form of symbolic interchange among members.[14] The rich discourse that constitutes congregational life occurs almost entirely in story form. Members primarily tell, or allude to, stories. Congregational communication is seldom propositional. Members are less likely to speak in abstractions than in tales about their collective life. Think of the jokes, confessions, arguments, descriptions, explanations, memorials, objections, and intentions that compose parish discourse. Most are presented narratively. "We dream in narrative, daydream in narrative, remember, anticipate, hope, despair, believe, doubt, plan, revise, criticize, construct, gossip, learn, hate and love by narrative," says Barbara Hardy.[15]

Her point about the narrative nature of gossip is especially appropriate to an analysis of parish discourse. Gossip, the informal expression of stories about other people, constitutes a prevalent form of parish communication. Though conventionally viewed as destructive of community, gossip, Samuel Heilman demonstrates, is essential for corporate cohesion.[16] Telling tales about other members, even maliciously, is an important way of identifying and characterizing the congregation. Heilman demonstrates the presence of four layers of gossip in the congregation. One layer is parish news shared with even the most casual participant. The others, each increasingly private and more potent, provide more privileged information. The most secret layer harbors the confidences of a few central figures whose circle often does not include the ordained minister. All layers of gossip function to fortify activities and relationships within the congregation.

Narrative gives structure to other kinds of parish communication. In Trinity Church, the history of a congregation is taught and learned in story form. Narrative also appears to influence sequences of group behavior, such as fights, campaigns, and projects. The congregation's worship has a storied character. It comprises liturgical drama, formal metaphors, Scripture narratives, and sermons. In virtually every aspect of congregational expression, the discourse of members is in some manner narrative.

3. *By its own congregating, the congregation participates in narrative structures of the world's societies.* The individual actions caught up in the Trinity story were each irregular or apparently spontaneous, but the overall narrative form of the story is a pattern of meaning so regular that we term the pattern a myth. Myths are the primal and still powerful schemata by which a society

comprehends and signifies its corporate existence. They mark the essential structures of meaning and value in which that group participates. As Alasdair MacIntyre reports, "There is no way to give us an understanding of any society, including our own, except through the stock of stories which constitute its original dramatic resources. Mythology, in its original sense, is at the heart of things."[17] Myths provide the basic forms of signification by which a group perceives and expresses its identity.

The correspondence between the Trinity story and the hero journey does not necessarily argue for some deep archetypal reality upon which behavior and its signification is patterned. A more supportable claim is that the narrative behavior of a local church draws upon the treasury of symbolic forms that human groups have developed in all zones and eras to constitute themselves. In my view, the story that any particular church tells of itself necessarily participates in the imagination by which other societies have wrought their awareness of their own community.

The "house" (*oikos*) implied in the term "parish" (*paroikia*) is a way of envisioning that symbolic construction. The same *oikos* also characterizes the whole inhabited world (*oikoumenē*), suggesting the participation of the parish household as well in the structures that form all societies' dwelling. Although "parochial" today usually connotes an ingrown narrowness, *paroikia*, when understood as a narrative construction, participates in the *oikoumenē* of all groups' stories.

The reason for this is that stories are structurally interrelated. Literature in the vision of Northrop Frye constitutes a "big, interlocking family" of all themes, genres, and characters."[18] Any individual work, in Frye's view, is to be understood as a disclosure of particular images that reflect the whole world of literature:

> Thus the center of the literary universe is whatever poem we happen to be reading. One step further, and the poem appears a microcosm for all literature, an individual manifestation of the total order of words.[19]

As, for Frye, the symbolic construction of a literary work is a microcosm of all literature, so a congregation reflects the imaginative struggle of societies everywhere to congregate. Thus the *paroikia*, the local manifestation of the structures of the *oikoumenē*, emphasizes its participation in the frame of all social communication.

The congregation Trinity is also Hero because Trinity is a disclosure here and now of a narrative negotiation by which other societies have cohered. Human imagination as a whole provides the particular idiomatic construction of a local church story. The storied *oikoumenē* substantiates, apportions, and links the full multitude of parochial stories. Parish mission in this light springs from a solidarity with the world of struggling communities. The story each tells of its own mission is as well the world's story.

THE NEED FOR NARRATIVE

Stories and their mythic structures are the primary means employed in a symbolic approach to understanding the congregation. The other approaches, those outlined in chapter 2, also make use of narrative description, but they rely less upon story than upon other ways to characterize the parish. Contextual portrayals of a local church concentrate upon demographic features ("urban, middle class, white, elderly membership"); mechanist definitions frequently provide numerical and functional facts ("250 members, with a $100,000 annual budget and a darn good Sunday school"); organicist interpretations feature interpersonal and emotional attributes ("a big, usually happy family that enjoys its occasional fights"). Only within the symbolic approach does narrative serve an essential role, and this book, rooted in that approach, will depend upon narrative both to examine and to explain the life of a local church.

An emphasis upon narrative is overdue. Despite the narrative character of almost all congregational perceptions and talk, the temptation is to employ other, more solemnly theoretical modes of expression to explain the local church. Like doctors over a patient, congregational analysts reduce the object of their investigation to technical terms and procedures. Phrases derived from the contextual ("urban, middle class"), mechanist ("$100,000 annual budget"), and organicist ("enjoy occasional fights") approaches seem more analytical and precise. These empirical observations abstracted from corporate experience often become more persuasive than the experience itself. My survey in the preceding chapter documents how scant has been the attention paid in the last quarter century to the congregation's culture, idiom, or identity—its storied dimensions. In a catalog I recently edited of devices and instruments for congregational research, only a small minority of the hundred or so entries is designed to explore a congregation's narrative identity.[20] Most doctor of ministry programs continue the tradition: perusal of the theses and essays these programs produce strongly suggests that projects that employ contextual, mechanist, or organicist methods are more likely to be accepted than those that delve into congregational culture and story.

Crites speaks of our capacity to abstract ourselves from the ongoing press of corporate experience:

> Mind and imagination are capable of recollecting the narrative materials of experience into non-narrative forms. Indeed there seems to be a powerful drive of thought and imagination to overcome the relentless temporality of experience. One needs more clarity than stories give us, also a little rest.[21]

Essential as abstractions are to the analysis of the congregation, however, a greater use of story is today required to round out an understanding of the local church. Only narrative is sufficiently sensitive to amplify the unique accents of a congregation's idiom, sufficiently intricate to explain the congregation's constitutive power, and sufficiently comprehensive to link congregational events and meanings. As succeeding chapters of this book will demonstrate in detail, narrative underlies each congregation's view of the world, its assumptions about the setting or backdrop against which its actions are sequenced, and its unique ethos thrown into visible relief. Narrative also sharpens and illumines that ethos—the style, behavior, and values that constitute a congregation's character. And narrative provides temporal form for its plot, the sequence of events it selects and retells to confirm its identity. Finally, narrative knits together all these elements—setting, character, and plot—into a storied whole. In so doing, it defies the capacity of other approaches in their extreme forms to reduce the congregation to a series of abstractions. Narrative further reminds the researcher or observer of the limits of outside expertise: no matter how disciplined or detached, everyone is formed by corporate experience and dependent upon storied discourse for the sharing of meaning. Learning the parts and presentations of parish story, then, is a way of reasserting the lived nature of social experience.

In these introductory chapters, I have examined the remarkable nature of the congregation, notable today less for its accomplishment than for its communal discourse that at once particularizes a corporate genius and links it to the symbolic structure of all societies everywhere. I have noted several different ways of understanding congregations—as textures, machines, organisms, and idioms, all necessary approaches, and none diminished by the emphasis this book places upon the last image, that of the local church as a dialect. In the present chapter, I have argued that idiom is primarily conveyed in story form, as the parish apprehends its corporate experience and as its members communicate their common life and draw resources from the narrative structures of the world. I believe that telling such a story enables a congregation to comprehend its nature and mission and therefore I now set out to examine the major aspects of parish story: its setting, characterization, and plot.

NOTES

1. Kenneth R. Jones, "An Inner-City Experiment in Family Ministry" (S.T.D. thesis, Candler School of Theology, Emory University, 1975), 117.

2. Ibid., iii.

3. Ibid., ii.

4. *Report on the Desired Leadership Qualities for Pastor and Laity* (Trinity United Methodist Church, Atlanta, Georgia, 14 December 1976).

5. C. G. Jung, *Symbols of Transformation: An Analysis of the Prelude to a Case of Schizophrenia* (New York: Bollingen Foundation, 1956), 121–462.

6. Joseph Campbell, *The Hero with a Thousand Faces* (Cleveland: World Pub. Co., 1956).

7. Ibid., 245.

8. The *Buddha-Karita*, translated in Lucien Stryk, ed., *The World of the Buddha: A Reader* (Garden City: Doubleday & Co., 1968), 39.

9. Campbell, *The Hero*, 97.

10. The *Buddha-Karita*, trans. Edward Conze, *Buddhist Scriptures* (Harmondsworth: Penguin Books, 1959), 52.

11. Stanley Hauerwas, *Truthfulness and Tragedy: Further Investigations Into Christian Ethics* (Notre Dame: Univ. of Notre Dame Press, 1977), 75.

12. Alasdair MacIntyre, *After Virtue*, 194. Note Northrop Frye's similar estimation of the constructive function of narrative in Robert D. Denham, ed., *Northrop Frye on Culture and Literature: A Collection of Review Essays* (Chicago: Univ. of Chicago Press, 1978), 74–75: "Mathematics appears to be a kind of informing or constructive principle in the natural sciences; it continually gives shape and coherence to them without being itself involved in any kind of external proof or evidence. One wonders whether, in the future, when we shall know so much more about what literature says and how it hangs together than we now do, we shall come to see literary myth as a similarly constructive principle in the social or qualitative sciences, giving shape and coherence to psychology, anthropology, theology, history and political theory without losing in any one of them its own autonomy of hypothesis."

13. Stephen C. Crites, "The Narrative Quality of Experience," *Journal of the American Academy of Religion* 39 (1971): 291–311.

14. "Persons communicate and relate to each other by stories they tell. . . . There can be no community life, no consensus, and thus no common action without participation in a common understanding of the meaning of a common story, and without a common commitment to that story's nature" (John Navone and Thomas Cooper, *Tellers of the Word* [New York: Le Jacq Pub., 1981], xxiv).

15. Barbara Hardy, "Towards a Poetics of Fiction: An Approach Through Narrative," *Novel* 2 (1968): 5.

16. Samuel Heilman, *Synagogue Life*, 141–92. The function of joking, also often in narrative form, is described on pp. 193–209.

17. MacIntyre, *After Virtue*, 205.

18. Northrop Frye, *The Educated Imagination* (Bloomington: Indiana Univ. Press. 1966), 48f.

19. Northrop Frye, *Anatomy of Criticism*, 121. Frye depicts four levels of literary criticism, of which the most identifiably religious, the analogical level, conceives poetry in the manner described. Frye goes on: "Analogically, then, the symbol is a monad, all symbols being united in a single infinite and eternal verbal symbol which is as *dianoia*, the Logos, and, as mythos, total creative act. It is this conception which Joyce expresses, in terms of subject matter, as 'epiphany,' and Hopkins, in terms of form as 'inscape.'"

20. James F. Hopewell, ed., *The Whole Church Catalog: Where to Get Tools for Congregational Study and Intervention* (Washington, D.C.: Alban Institute, 1984), iv.

21. Crites, "Narrative Quality," 308.

PART TWO

THE SETTING OF PARISH STORY

4

THE STRUGGLE FOR
SETTING

Not long ago a tumor was taken from my chest and I was told that I carry an indolent but incurable form of cancer. What, I asked myself on my hospital bed, was a decent chap like me doing in such deadly circumstances? What on earth was going on? The threat of my death provoked for me an unprecedented search for meaning. I sought a plausible account of the world that explained my plight.

My friends joined the search. In the uncertainty of my sickroom we tried to find accounts that, in the face of dying, would disclose the point of my life. The accounts tended to be stories—personal recollections, tales of similar happenings, hopes, prayers, and resolutions about the future. Woven into their telling was the Christian faith that I and most of my friends subscribe to. That faith, plus other perceptions about our personal lives and the course of human history, provided a dimension to our stories that I call their setting: the world the story sets in which story's plot can credibly unfold and its character develop.

One of the major undertakings of narrative discourse is the establishment of settings, the conditions within which the events of a tale gain their reasonableness. Along with plot and characterization, setting is a principal element of storytelling. It describes the story's universe. So important is the development of setting in the narrative of a local church that three chapters will be devoted to exploring ways to analyze and understand the meanings implied in setting.

In an ethnographic analysis of a community the setting is termed its world view. In Geertz's words, world view is the "picture" a group shares "of the way things in sheer actuality are, their most comprehensive ideas of order."[1] A community over time develops a shared sense of what is really going on in the world. In traditional societies, world views may be more uniform and explicit than those we encountered in Western, technological ones, but the social need to construct a commonly satisfactory setting for our lives was also evident in the sophisticated encounters in my hospital room.

World views, both ancient and modern, are fragile and incomplete constructions, subject to damaging contradiction. No world view is irrefutable, even to its ardent supporters, and indeed it is often in conjunction with events that challenge its adequacy that it is most urgently expressed. It was when my own life was most pointedly threatened, for example, that stories about the world were told with greatest frequency. Both the strength and the frailty of setting are associated with crises that challenge its significance. Geertz describes the link:

> The strange opacity of certain empirical events, the dumb senselessness of intense or inexorable pain, and the enigmatic unaccountability of gross inequity all raise the uncomfortable suspicion that perhaps the world, and hence man's life in the world, has no genuine order at all—no empirical regularity, no emotional form, no moral coherence. And the religious response to this suspicion is in each case the same: the formulation, by means of symbols, of an image of such a genuine order of the world which will account for, even celebrate, the perceived ambiguities, puzzles and paradoxes of human experience.

Setting is a group's cosmic construction that accounts for crises. This working picture of reality often goes unexpressed until challenged. Then, in that tension, the plot thickens, and world view as story is related, binding even in the light of its contradiction the self to the Other, the finite frame to the world's outcome.

Anthropologists such as Geertz and Robert Redfield[3] make a distinction between the world view of a community and its ethos. World view indicates the universe that the group constructs; ethos, by contrast, reflects the values and dispositions that the group maintains. World view encompasses a community's perceptions and suspicions about what is happening in life. Ethos instead comprises its preferences and valuations of that life. I make a similar analytical distinction between the setting of parish story and its characterization. Character corresponds to the story's ethos, its wishes, style, and norms, elements to be examined in the next major section of this book. In the present section the focus is the setting of parish story, its world view.

One should not expect to encounter fully developed cosmologies in the settings of parish story. A congregation's thick description of its universe is expressed in local metaphors, not universal propositions. And a world view is more likely to be manifested, as it was in my hospital room, in stories about a personal life than in accounts about the world at large.

A personal story nevertheless dramatizes the way a community views itself and its total world. Mary Douglas has demonstrated how perceptions of the self mirror a society's interpretation of both its corporate nature and the larger cosmos. In her pioneering study of cosmologies of different peoples, she shows that the human body is our most accessible metaphor for figuring what we really suspect about our group's and the world's makeup. According to Douglas, the way a group perceives and regulates the personal bodies of members corresponds with their view of their collective body. The human body, for Douglas, is a "natural symbol" by which a people order the systemic nature of their corporate life.

> The human body is always treated as an image of society. . . . There can be no natural way of considering the body that does not involve at the same time a social dimension. . . . The social body constrains the way in which the physical body is perceived. The physical experience of the body, always modified by the social categories through which it is known, sustains a particular view of society. There is a continual exchange of meanings between the two kinds of body experience so that each reinforces the categories of the other.[4]

How a group sees and treats its members depends upon concepts that also articulate its corporate nature. However the members contemplate, heal, discipline, develop, pity, and finally commit their personal bodies is likely to coincide with the ways they understand and act on the corporate body of which they are a part.

The way a group understands the bodies of its members and its corporate body is also consonant with the way it views its world. Groups interpret the world by the same code that orders their individual and internal social activity. Thus there is a remarkable congruence among the three levels of bodied experience—personal, social, and cosmic—that a group identifies as systems within which life occurs. The shape of life at each level, its significance, and the stages of its development are frequently analogous. Any exploration of congregational world view therefore requires attention to the way a church sees and deals with its individual members, its corporate body, and the wider world. Since the belief system of a parish includes not only its formal creeds but also the meanings it assigns to itself and its members as finite bodies, to learn about a church's world view—what it believes is really going on in life—one must listen to the church's stories about its own body and those of the members who constitute it.

HOSPITAL STORIES

The tales told around my hospital bed illustrate what Geertz and Douglas have taught about world view. The stories were told at a time of acute crisis, in a situation that challenged the very world order the tales projected but that also required their telling. Struggling with me to establish an explanation of life that incorporated the fact of my condition, my friends put forward their images and experiences, knowing that none resolved the inevitable approach of my death, yet knowing even so that their tales were essential to our mutual quest for meaning and love.

The tales revolved around human bodies and their treatment. Illness, its course and possible cure, provided the metaphor by which we characterized our communities and universes. Although a number of my visitors held graduate degrees in theology and philosophy, our discourse seldom focused upon abstract propositions. In the urgency of my situation we projected our concepts of society and world through our narration of personal experiences.

The narratives we advanced were, however, remarkably varied in their outlook. They conveyed different senses of what life is about. While the tales all pictured the form and process of the world, the description each provided of the nature of that world conflicted with that of the others. And although all the stories addressed the evil of disease, each revealed one of several diverse suspicions about what the evil meant and thus posited a different world as the setting for its account, the meaning of each tale depending upon the distinctive nature of that world.[5]

To understand the interpretations of life and death proposed in our narratives requires an appreciation of the types of worlds those stories constructed. To distinguish these worlds I shall first use the four narrative genres identified by Northrop Frye.[6] Frye has laid out all of Western literature in a great imaginary circle that has four cardinal points much like those of a compass. The four points that orient the literary circle are, in clockwise order, comedy, romance, tragedy, and irony. The structure of a literary work, Frye argues, places it somewhere on the circle, if not fully within a particular genre, then somewhere between two adjoining types. The settings of the stories told about my illness can be seen in relation to the same circle of interpretation.[7]

Comic tales

Some accounts, notably those offered by some hospital chaplains and seminary students practicing hospital chaplaincy, conveyed primarily a comic sense of life. The essence of comedy, here and elsewhere, is not humorous incidents but a happy ending. (By my bed the tellers of comic tales were quite serious; they related, however, narratives that ended in the positive resolution of difficult situations.) Comedy projects a world that ultimately integrates its seemingly antithetical elements. Its direction is opposite to the disintegrative course of tragedy; it moves from problem to solution. In comedies as diverse as Shakespeare's and those on prime time television, life progresses from a state of crisis created by some illusion to a harmonious recovery brought about by discovering the true nature of the circumstances.

In countless situation comedies we enter a world that is at first misunderstood (e.g., a husband sees his wife with another man and mistakenly infers she is having an affair). The crisis deepens until the true knowledge, the gnosis, is uncovered (the husband finds out that the wife was using the other man to help buy the husband's birthday present). Comedies end in unions—pacts, embraces, marriages—that symbolize the ultimately trustworthy working of the world. Created in misinformation and convoluted by error, a comedy is resolved by the disclosure of a deeper knowledge about the harmonious way things really are.

The comic sense in some of my bedside narratives was based upon experiences of friends who as chaplains had had the opportunity to counsel cancer patients and to observe cases in which persons in dire situations actually had recovered from their immediate plight. In their stories that summarized these cases, the initial illusion was the terror a patient had of the cancer. According to the chaplains and such well-known cancer therapists as the Simontons (whose recent book bears the comic title *Getting Well Again*),[8] as long as the patient does not understand the relationship between person and cancer, the malignancy festers. As in comedy, a misunderstanding exists, here between one's mind and one's body. Not understanding their deep connection, cancer sufferers are unaware how their mental stress encourages the growth of disease and how cancer in turn affects their disposition.

What patients must discover is the gnosis, the deeper knowing, that can unite self and body and interrupt the malignant relationship. In the words of one of my chaplains, "You must get with your cancer." You must learn, according to the cover of the Simonton book, the "revolutionary life-saving self-awareness techniques" that envision the cancer and the manner in which the body overcomes it. None of my chaplain colleagues implied that I would live happily ever after, but their stories projected a longer and more harmonious life made possible by a comic gnosis.

Romantic tales

Other stories told at my bedside conveyed a romantic sense of the world. Like the comic tales, the romances foresaw my possible cure, but the way to recovery was not by new knowledge but through spiritual adventure. My friends who told romantic stories were charismatic seminary students and some members of my parish church. They saw in my sickness the opportunity, were I to seek it, for God to love me in a surprising and thrilling way.

In romance occurs a quest for the most desirable object—the distant planet in science fiction, the beloved in gothic novels, the lawful community in westerns. The hero or heroine leaves familiar surroundings and embarks on a dangerous journey in which strange things happen but a priceless reward is gained. Good and evil are sharply delineated in romance, protagonists and antagonists clearly displayed.

In their charismatic understanding of the world my friends who told romantic stories beckoned me to leave behind my domestic religious routine and wholeheartedly yield to the promise of God's healing love. Were I to believe that God really works miraculously within history, and specifically through that part of the world which is my own historical body, I would become a seeker, forsaking views of the world in which God, playing a more passive role, does not break into lives and circumstances to transform them. According to these romantic tales, God's Spirit would fill and empower me in adventure. I would persist in the face of evil, and my body through the Spirit would receive God's gifts and fruits, including the gift of healing. "The hero of romance," Frye writes, "moves in a world in which the ordinary laws of nature are suspended: prodigies of courage and endurance unnatural to us are natural to him."[9] I would become a hero in romance, venturing into the unknown, battling the evil, finding the good, and in the end gaining the prize, which, in my case, would be the release from my cancer as well as an experience of God's intimate presence. I would encounter God in a new, personal way, by the romantic indwelling of God's love and power. The wonders of the Bible still occur to those who seek them. I could expect a miracle.

Not all of my visitors, however, told stories of a world that promised healing. Comic and romantic narratives that envisioned cure were counterbalanced by tales of tragedy and irony that depicted settings in which I was to accept my body, and thus the world, as it is. Tragedy and irony do not, however, perceive the world's course in the same way. Tragic stories detect an underlying purpose in our setting; the ironies do not.

Tragic tales

Tragedy portrays the decay of life and the necessary sacrifice of the self before resolution occurs. The self in tragedy, as in romance, is heroic, but unlike the romantic hero, the tragic hero submits to a harshly authentic world. No *deus ex machina* breaks miraculously into the tragic scene. The divine is revealed largely as the eternal law or word made plain only to the self subject to it. In both great tragic works and tragic everyday life the protagonist submits to the Other. The fall of great tragic heroes is more monumental than our own, but final catastrophe is our mutual fate. One does not leave the familiar in a tragic plot. Without magic by which to escape, the hero is shaped by the pattern of the Other and is obedient to it in death. When portrayed as tragic hero, Christ accepts the cross, with the intervention of neither romantic miracle nor comic gnosis. Those who follow the way of Christ live their lives tragically in the shadow of the cross. They suffer; they die to self and gain justification only beyond, and through, Christ's death and their own.

Tragic stories told in my presence generally were offered by family members and fellow ministers. They stressed the importance of being honest about my condition. I was to be reconciled to my life and lot and even more to my God, bending my remaining time to God's will. I was not, as in a comic frame, to "get with my cancer," but to get right with God. My tragic friends and I would honestly mark changes in my life and track its heroic descent into darkness. Linda Bamber writes of the tragic world:

> It is a world that is separate from us who inhabit it; it will not yield to our desires and fantasies no matter how desperately we need it to do so. This means that in tragedy, recognition—*anagnorisis*, the banishing of ignorance—is a major goal. We question the tragic universe to discover *its* laws, since they are what we must live by. The worlds of comedy and romance, by contrast, are shaped by our hearts' desires and in history we are busy remaking the world to suit ourselves.[10]

What my family and clergy friends emphasized in their stories was not the sweet fulfillment of our own desires but our recognition of God's laws governing our own short lives.

In identifying ourselves with God's will, however, we would be saved. The reconciliation holds little likelihood of miracles. Death advances, but so does the promise of salvation through death. The law of God is revealed not only in the course of life but also in Scripture. By faith in the cross one is named to life eternal. The tragic hero is not cured but saved, by an identification with the transcendent pattern of tragic life. "Tragic heroes," says Frye, "are wrapped in the mystery of their communion with that something beyond which we can only see through them, and which is the source of their strengths and their fate alike."[11]

Ironic tales

My fellow faculty members were the primary purveyors of ironic stories. One is a hero neither in irony nor among faculty colleagues. In either circumstance, supposed heroes are shown to be all too human, and this sober incongruity marked the tales my fellow teachers told. In ironic stories, reputedly worthy persons come to naught and what seem to be good plans go sour. Irony challenges heroic and purposive interpretations of the world. Events that in other story genres have sacred significance in irony have a natural explanation. Miracles do not happen; patterns lose their design; life is unjust, not justified by transcendent forces. Trapped in such an ironic world, one shrugs one's shoulders about reports of divine ultimacies and intimacies. Instead of expecting such supernatural outcomes, one embraces one's brothers and sisters in camaraderie.

In an ironic setting one is freed only as one accepts the arbitrary working of life and reaches out to a humanity in common plight. The ironic tales related in my room recognized the absurdity of my situation and did not predict my cure. My visitors focused upon medical prognosis. We looked realistically at scientific therapies that might stave off death. We avoided the compulsory sadness of tragedy. Our sober assessment of empirical data was accompanied by an ironic defiance of any prescribed emotion. In our fellowship many touched me and some prayed. Their prayers were narratives that anticipated the skill of the medical staff and our emotional well-being. As a brother caught in an incongruous world, I was, by their efforts, loved but not led to healing.

Most stories in Northrop Frye's great literary circle blend two adjoining genres and are therefore identified by such double terms as comic ironies, tragic romances, or romantic tragedies (the noun in each phrase denotes the dominant type). Only the combinations of polar opposites—comedy and tragedy, and romance and irony—are structurally impossible.[12] Their worlds are contradictory: comedy moves from problem to solution, while tragedy moves from solution to problem; romance moves the self to the supernatural, while irony removes the supernatural from the self. The opposition of these types was evident in the reactions of my friends to stories other than their own. Least understandable to them were the opposite stories. Ironic interpretations were shocking to the tellers of romance. The ironists, in turn, had least patience with the miracles of the romantics. A similar antipathy existed between the comedians and the tragedians. Each saw the other as taking a liberty with the pattern of life. The tellers of tragedy identified the comic view as a shallow, godless trick; the tellers of comedies were quick to find in tragic narrative a legalistic, morbid obsession.

Many stories, however, partook of neighboring categories in the circle, and, possibly in consonance with the tale I came to tell myself, most told me tragic ironies. In tragic irony the characteristics of an empirical interpretation of the world dominate, but there is also evidence of some underlying pattern. The world in my own story is not entirely limited to what was experienced through my five senses; a pattern of meaning, beyond my empirical grasp but nonetheless demanding my submission, also had a claim on me.

THE STRUGGLE

Sometimes I want this illness of mine to be resolved by miracle. My desire comes less in night darkness or times of anxiety; then death seems fitting. It arises instead in moments of obvious goodness, on the cool day that follows a hot summer, in laughter among friends, or in a crisp paper of a good student. Then I want my whole self to resound the promise the moment reveals. Then sometimes I hope for a miracle.

But what would make up this miracle? Here I wrestle among world view options, pulled toward each by my desire for continuing identity but checked by suspicions about their descriptive adequacy. Is, for example, miracle best portrayed for me by Friedrich Schleiermacher's proposal that miracles are omnipresent signs that disclose the Infinite?

> What is a miracle? What we call miracle is everywhere else called sign, indication. Our name, which means a wonder, refers purely to the mental condition of the observer. It is only in so far appropriate that a sign, especially when it is nothing besides, must be fitted to call attention to itself and to the power in it that gives it significance. Every finite thing, however, is a sign of the Infinite, and so these various expressions declare the immediate relation of a phenomenon to the Infinite and the Whole. But does that involve that every event should not have quite as immediate a relation to the finite and to nature? Miracle is simply the religious name for event. Every event, even the most natural and usual, becomes a miracle, as soon as the religious view of it can be the dominant. To me all is miracle. In your sense the inexplicable and strange alone is miracle, in mine it is no miracle. The more religious you are, the more miracle would you see everywhere. All disputing about single events, as to whether or not they are to be called miraculous, gives me a painful impression of the poverty and wretchedness of the religious sense of the combatants.[13]

Were I to follow what I would call the comic or gnostic vein in Schleiermacher's thought, I would gain the assurance that I, like any other single entity, am actually resolved in the eternal.[14] All things, including my cancer, are really signs, miracles in themselves that signify the encompassing One. Instead of considering my condition a frustration of life, I could, by the gnostic negotiation, work to see the inherently miraculous nature of my state, and rest upon its indication of being in God.

Or I could accept an opposing, tragic understanding of miracle that identifies the world's life itself, not its signifiers, as the wonder. Listen to Karl Barth:

> God does not grudge the existence of the reality distinct from Himself; He does not grudge it its own reality, nature and freedom. The existence of the creature alongside God is the great puzzle and miracle, the great question to which we must and may give an answer, the answer given us through God's Word; it is the genuine question about existence, which is essentially and fundamentally distinguished from the question which rests upon error, "Is there a God?" That there is a world is the most unheard-of thing, the miracle of the grace of God. Is it not true that if we confront existence, not least our own existence, we can but in astonishment state the truth and reality of the fact that I *may exist*, the world may exist, although it is a reality distinct from God, although the world including man and therefore myself is not God? God in the highest, the Triune God, the Father, the Almighty, is not arbitrary; He does not grudge existence to this other. He not only does not grudge it him, He not only leaves it to him, He gives it him. We exist and heaven and earth exist in their complete, supposed infinity, because God gives them existence.[15]

My life is the object of God's sovereign grace, not the sign of God's reality. The marvel for Barth is that we exist at all, not that we reflect an ultimate Being. Were I to follow such an understanding, I would submit to the sure sign, the Word, that discloses the created nature of my life and its unapparent, unmerited, redemption. The miracle is not inherent in my illness; it is that my life depends upon a transcendent God who promises my eternal salvation.

Then there is the more individuated perception of miracle advanced by the romantic world view. Michael Harper represents the perception of those who witness personal encounters with a healing God.

> There are few greater thrills for the Christian than to see people touched by the power of God and healed in their bodies and minds. One has been present when a paralyzed arm has straightened and received its natural strength again, when the darkness of massive depression has rolled away, and so on. One now knows something of the kind of excitement which ran through Palestine when Jesus ministered there to so many sick people two thousand years ago. . . . We are living in a day in which there is a welcome resurgence of faith in a God who performs miracles. The working of miracles is one of the gifts of the Holy Spirit. It is not the only one. But it does have an important place in the overall strategy of the Holy Spirit, and it does glorify Christ.[16]

Romantic miracles are both a gift and a sign from God. As the Spirit's spontaneous gift, they are not the omnipresent metaphors of a comic world. Romantic miracles also differ from the tragic acknowledgment of the miracle of life itself. More than simply accepting my existence as miraculous, if I take the romantic part I might expect a charismatic miracle of specific healing.

Ironic world views also countenance miracles, ones that cause our senses to marvel. Willa Cather writes:

> Where there is great love there are always miracles. . . . Miracles . . . rest not so much on faces or voices or healing power coming to us from afar off, but upon our perceptions being made finer, so that for a moment our eyes can see and our ears can hear what there is about us always.[17]

Miracle occurs when through love we gain the finer sense of things. In an ironic world those things require neither ultimate referent nor grand design. They exist wondrously in themselves, about us always, but usually obscured by our selfish, loveless blindness.

All four world interpretations acknowledge miracles, the wonders that refract the world in different figures, and all four views are to some extent available and attractive to me. My own need for cosmic order, however, cannot tolerate an acceptance of all their contradictory claims. Instead, I engage in a negotiation, in my case a primarily ironic one, that confirms my understanding of the inherently miraculous in part by rejecting a romantic vision of the occasional blessing. As much as I would welcome my personal release from my imprisoning illness, I cannot believe in a world that offers selective solace to a privileged few. Much closer to my sense of life is the proposition that it contains within itself the extraordinary. I gain a glimpse of its wonder, when, in a communion of love, the scales fall from my eyes and I am amazed by the intricacy of the ordinary.

But I hedge a bit. I am suspicious of the way an ironic outlook lyricizes the dull, given matter of life. And I am frightened of a position that promises no significance beyond the way things now are. I do not want to be merely intricate; I want also to participate in some pattern that transcends the course of my feeble life. I therefore supplement my essentially empirical understanding with what logicians call subalternation, by a secondary reliance upon a tragic viewpoint. My world displays, in Frye's terms, a tragic irony.

The tragic irony that I tell about my mortal body reflects something of the approach I make to understanding the congregation. From neither bodily nor congregational habitation do I see miraculous escape, either by comic recognition that will give the church a special knowing at a higher stage of development or by a romantic quest that turns the parish outward into God's undomesticated presence in the larger context. Rather, the setting of my story and the congregation's portrays my own body and that of the local church essentially in human terms, but my factual portrait of the world is darkly shaded by the tragic inevitability of God's inexorable plan.

In the following two chapters, I shall examine more precisely the various forms that parish stories assume and show how by observation and inquiry one can explore the setting of a congregation's narrative. These steps are best taken with the giant circle of literary genres in mind. Within this circle are the local churches we know, each arranging its view of the world by stories whose structure links them to a certain section of the horizon.

NOTES

1. Clifford Geertz, *The Interpretation of Cultures*, 89.
2. Ibid., 107–8.
3. Ibid., 87–141; Robert Redfield, *The Little Community* (Chicago: Univ. of Chicago Press, 1955), 85–98. Other anthropologists employ a third analytical dimension similar to what I call plot. Ethel Albert calls the three aspects the "focal values" of a group. For her, the three are the "entities" (objects, feeling states, situations, activities) that I would term the group's setting; the "directives" (actions to be done or avoided) I term its plot; and its "character" (qualities of personality approved or disapproved, rewarded or punished) to which I give the same name (Ethel Albert, "The Classification of Values," *American Anthropologist* 58 [1956]: 251ff.).
4. Mary Douglas, *Natural Symbols*, 99, 93. See also Ernst Cassirer, *An Essay on Man: An Introduction to a Philosophy of Human Culture* (New Haven: Yale Univ. Press, 1944), 23–26.
5. "We allocate conversations to genres just as we do literary narratives. Indeed a conversation is a dramatic work, even if a very short one, in which participants are not only the actors but also the joint authors, working out in an agreement or disagreement the mode of their production" (Alasdair MacIntyre, *After Virtue*, 196).
6. Northrop Frye, *Anatomy of Criticism*, 158–239. See the use of Frye's genres in analyses of historiography in Hayden White, *Metahistory: The Historical Imagination in Nineteenth-Century Europe* (Baltimore: Johns Hopkins Univ. Press, 1973); of psychoanalytic method in Roy Schafer, *A New Language for Psychoanalysis* (New Haven: Yale Univ. Press, 1976); and of the growth of secularity in Robert W. Funk, *Parables and Presence: Forms of the New Testament Tradition* (Philadelphia: Fortress Press, 1982), 124–37.
7. Mary Douglas is herself reluctant to transpose ethnographic categories into literary analogues, but her observations nevertheless invite literary interpretation. In her book *Natural Symbols* she identifies, for example, four distinctive attitudes toward the physical body that are remarkably similar to the narrative modes of Northrop Frye. In her typology of basic stances toward life that societies take, the body may be seen as essentially the organ of communication (and, hence, comically integrating all meaningful action), or as the vehicle of life (body and spirit romantically joining), or as purely spiritual (its life tragically awaiting its release), or as very practical (ironically defeating other interpretations). Persons in societies that reflect one of these representations of the body, moreover, certainly convey its image primarily by their stories.
8. O. Carl Simonton, Stephanie-Matthews Simonton, and James L. Creighton, *Getting Well Again: A Step-by-Step Self Help Guide to Overcoming Cancer for Patients and Their Families* (Toronto: Bantam Books, 1978).
9. Frye, *Anatomy*, 33.
10. Linda Bamber, *Comic Women, Tragic Men: A Study of Gender and Genre in Shakespeare* (Stanford: Stanford Univ. Press, 1982), 22.
11. Frye, *Anatomy*, 208.
12. Ibid., 162.
13. Friedrich Schleiermacher, *On Religion: Speeches to Its Cultured Despisers*, trans. John Oman (New York: Harper & Brothers, 1958), 88–89.
14. Ibid., 99–101.

15. Karl Barth, *Dogmatics in Outline* (New York: Harper & Row, 1959), 54.

16. Michael Harper, *None Can Guess* (Plainfield, N.J.: Logos International, 1971), 137, 140.

17. Willa Cather, *Death Comes for the Archbishop* (New York: Alfred A. Knopf, 1927), 50–51.

5

PARISH SETTING

The building that was constructed by the church community that I helped to start is small but walled with windows that permit those inside to gaze out in all directions. Because the structure sits on the top of a hill, we could arrange our worship furniture to face virtually any point on a distant horizon.

Now imagine the horizon of Northrop Frye's great circle of Western literature. Orient the genres of literature according to the cardinal points of a compass. To the east, with its promise of dawn after a dark night, envision works of comedy. Comedy, like the eastern horizon, manifests the regular return of light and renewal. Move around the circle through romantic comedies and comic romances until reaching the south and its pure romantic interpretations. In the bright sun and sharp shadows of a southern exposure, romance pits innocent good against obvious evil in high noon adventure. Then arrange the tragic romances and romantic tragedies on the arc between south and west. The pure tragedies meet the setting western sun. There in the inevitable decline of light occur interpretations that follow life to its certain obliteration. Put the ironies in the northern night and cold. What gives life in the ironic north is not cosmic certainty but a sense of common unheroic humanity.

Surrounding the congregational house is what Frye portrays as a total quest myth that circles from romantic adventure through tragic despair and ironic darkness into a comic dawn, there to begin the whole round again. Any single work of literature is a recognizable bit of the gigantic circle of human interpretation. No human being sees the whole. Each instead is oriented, by a story, toward some direction within the total horizon.

Congregations adopt a similar orientation. Were any of them to be situated in our windowed church building surrounded by the total horizon of the Western world's literary interpretation, they would arrange themselves to face a particular point on the circle. Different congregations would face different ways.

I first became aware of the structure of the narratives that express world view several years before the discovery of my cancer, when I began during my sabbatical year to study congregations systematically. Part of my activity in the two churches I studied was to interview as many members as possible to determine what themes each group employed to organize the world. Almost immediately I found I had to discard several firmly held assumptions about the nature of parish world view. This chapter may help other students of the congregation to avoid my mistakes and to dig deeper into a field whose intricacy extends well beyond even the lines of inquiry and interpretation I finally adopted.

After only a few conversations it was evident that a catechetical approach —one in which I would ask what an informant understood about some credal tenet such as the Trinity or salvation—did not plumb the richness of that member's perception of life. It was not that Christian beliefs were superficial aspects of the person's world view. The problem rather lay in the way my questions were posed. When I would ask respondents to describe some theological topic in their working picture of reality, I translated their ongoing portrayal of life into abstract categories. Not only was abstraction a different operation from the narrative manner by which they usually interpreted their existence, it was also a game that I, their theologically trained interviewer, was by reputation better equipped to play than they. They usually answered questions about the nature of God and redemption in an embarrassed, defensive, or ingratiating way. When I decided to study congregations, I had imagined an idealized field scene in which native informants would satiate the anthropologist with information about the local religion. That never happened in my interviews. In a local church, members participate in religion more readily than they explain it.

I had to find an approach other than the catechetical one to encourage conversation about beliefs. What worked best, it developed, were sessions in which members recalled a crisis in their own lives and went on to tell what they suspected was happening "behind" the event. When members would talk about a death or a trying family circumstance, for example, they would often augment the account with other stories that, like the ones in my hospital room, interpreted the crisis by introducing other metaphors.

Most of the remainder of this chapter categorizes these interpretations, and the next chapter details the guided interviews and other methods I used to examine the setting of parish story. But before moving into these matters, I must confess the other mistaken assumption I had made about the nature of world view.

I did not adequately anticipate the complexity of the views that church members hold. I had once thought that I could employ a bipolar scale in characterizing belief, one that assumed that the views of persons might be located at some position between orthodoxy (or conservatism) and modernism (or liberalism). But those simple two-pole distinctions were not much help in my analysis of interviews of members. I needed four basic categories to differentiate the range of beliefs expressed in the interviews. Although one type, which I call canonic, did express a kind of conservative standpoint, and although another, which I call empiric, conveyed the outlook of many liberals, those two categories did not exhaust the interpretive options that members employed in their stories. I also found orientations that I came to call the gnostic and the charismatic categories. The four categories can be differentiated in the following manner:

Canonic   Reliance upon an authoritative interpretation of a world pattern, often considered God's revealed word or will, by which one identifies one's essential life. The integrity of the pattern requires that followers reject any gnosis of union with the pattern but instead subordinate their selfhood to it. Characteristics of the canonic orientation are similar to those of Frye's tragic genre.

Gnostic   Reliance upon an intuited process of a world that develops from dissipation toward unity. The ultimate integrity of the world requires the deepening consciousness of those involved in its systemic outworking and their rejection of alienating canonic structures. Characteristics of the gnostic orientation are similar to those of Frye's comic genre.

Charismatic   Reliance upon evidence of a transcendent spirit personally encountered. The integrity of providence in the world requires that empirical presumptions of an ordered world be disregarded and supernatural irregularities instead be witnessed. Characteristics of the charismatic orientation are similar to those of Frye's romantic genre.[1]

Empiric   Reliance upon data objectively verifiable through one's own five senses. The integrity of one's own person requires realism about the way things demonstrably work and the rejection of the supernatural. Characteristics of the empiric orientation are similar to those of Frye's ironic genre.

Further themes and concepts that characterize each category are listed in the table on pages 70-71. Before we delve into these, it is important to ponder how the orientations were employed in actual discourse.

I found from the beginning that, though one of the categories might best describe an informant's interpretation, that person was actually engaged in a more complex negotiation that used two or three of the types in different ways. The stories I heard were constructed in the manner that structural analysts of literature propose. Students of narrative semiotics, those who investi-

WORLD VIEW CATEGORIES

	Canonic	Gnostic	Charismatic	Empiric
Narrative Features				
Motif	Sacrifice	Integration	Adventure	Testing
Movement	Union toward subordination	Subordination toward union	Uniformity toward variation	Variation toward uniformity
Body Scenarios (1. *Situation*, 2. *Response*, 3. *Resolution*)				
Personal	1. Hubris 2. Surrender 3. Justification	1. Ignorance 2. Enlightenment 3. Peace	1. Weakness 2. Tarrying 3. Empowerment	1. Bondage 2. Honesty 3. Love
Social	1. Vice 2. Righteousness 3. Judgment	1. Discord 2. Wisdom 3. Harmony	1. Conventionality 2. Charism 3. Transformation	1. Oppression 2. Justice 3. Community
Cosmic	1. Principalities and powers 2. Passion 3. Kingdom	1. Illusion 2. Process 3. Union	1. Perpetuity 2. Signs 3. Day of the Lord	1. Absurdity 2. Science 3. Regularity
Cognitive Features				
Authority	God's revealed word and will	Intuition, esoteric wisdom	Personally manifested evidence of God's immanence	Data objectively verifiable through one's five senses
Focus of Integrity	Scripture	Trustworthy cosmos	Providence of God	One's person
Valued Behavior	Obedience	Inner awareness	Recognition of God's blessings	Realism

WORLD VIEW CATEGORIES (continued)

Concepts	Canonic	Gnostic	Charismatic	Empiric
God	Father	Ground/Force	Spirit	Ultimate concern
Jesus	Savior	Living Symbol	Lord	Teacher
Evil	Devil	Ignorance	Demons	Demonic
Time	Linear	Cyclical	Premillennial	Amillennial
Bible	Word	Allegory	Program	History
Minister	Messenger	Guide	Exemplar	Enabler
Eucharist	Memorial	Sacrament	Presence	Agape
Church	Covenant	Pilgrimage	Harvest	Fellowship
Gospel	Salvation	Consciousness	Power	Freedom

gate the internal logic of a passage of literature, often use a "semiotic square" to describe a story's relation to a series of four opposing propositions. They find that a text gains its meaning by rejecting one of the propositions, accepting its opposite and implicating a third assertion. I have not engaged in such studies and my four categories are not the deep structures that semioticians find in literature, but common assumptions about narrative structure probably prompt both their observations and mine.[2] In any case, a square of opposition gives dimension to the kinds of negotiation that people undertake among the four world view categories (see Figure B).

When persons are encouraged to address critical situations, they respond in narratives that tell of a complex negotiation among several categories of world view. The setting of their own story often gains its force of argument from an opposite position that is rejected, and is supplemented by reference

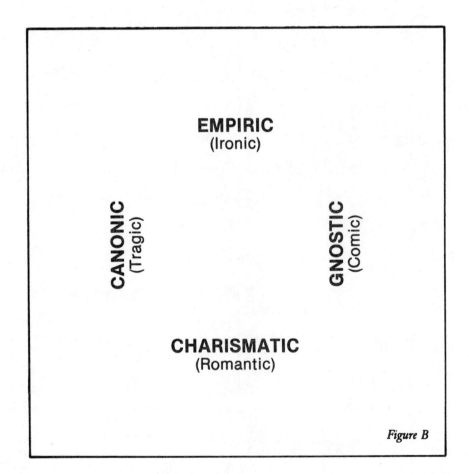

Figure B

to attributes of still a third standpoint. The negotiation once again shows how dependent personal belief is upon the larger imaginative process of humanity. One's singular position expresses and requires the total struggle of humanity for meaning. It simply does not stand alone or outside, in judgment of the whole. One finds in any person's world view, as does Frye in a single poem, the full range of human imagination. Using the actual words of church members recorded during my sabbatical year and after, the four categories as negotiations for world view are illustrated below.

THE GNOSTIC NEGOTIATION

A newspaper editor explains his ambivalent feeling about his church:

I was raised a very strict Methodist; never even thought to rebel against its ways. Only when I was in college did I learn to think, and I started to ask questions. . . . It used to bother me that I was thinking for myself, and I then totally rejected organized religion. . . . Today I just don't feel that I have to go to church. I suppose I take part as much as I do because of [my wife].

Having opposed his strict canonic upbringing, the editor's story moves toward gnostic unity:

Anyway, in looking for something for me, I became friends with [another editor] who was a major force in the Methodist church but also a strong believer in reincarnation. . . . Two or three other friends would end up going to her house in the evenings. So I am not a gung-ho Methodist; I have my own beliefs which [my pastor] understands. My religion makes me at peace with myself. Its strength is that it answers all my questions; it gives the reasons and answers for being here. By understanding karma I understand the laws of cause and effect.

He recounts his consciousness of a world in which stress is resolved:

Late at night—I am a night person—I get into . . . my mind, blocking out everything else, doing deep thinking. No vision, only a mind voice. And life makes sense. Everybody has that power. There is a lot about it we don't know, but on three or four occasions I almost reached the force itself. . . . We are going toward perfection, to join God. Actual union with God is the ultimate goal. It is to be perfect.

At another point in our interview the editor drew secondary support from a more charismatic argument about spiritual entities different from the gnostic flow toward unity.

After I really got into meditation, I made contact with my "contact" who showed me what my past two lives were. The contact gives me signs from God.

Such a secondary alliance with a neighboring category exists in many accounts of world view struggle. Attention shall be drawn to it in the statements that follow, though my primary purpose is to describe the four types in themselves.

Reality in the gnostic negotiation is ultimately dependable. Narratives that relate a gnostic outlook usually begin with a depiction of estrangement but end with the integration of all that was once alienated. The critical point in the story is, of course, the reception of gnosis, the inner knowing, which confers an awareness of the way things really are. In the end the cosmos not only proves true to the reality revealed in consciousness but finally itself becomes that consciousness.

The gnostic journey begins in bafflement and first looks for ultimate meaning in the wrong places. This, said one person, is the source of fear: "At the time my dad was ready to die, he was almost totally paralyzed, but he had this terror-stricken expression. He knew that he was about to die, but I couldn't figure out why he was afraid. I was already into reincarnation at that time and said to myself, 'Why should he be afraid?'" In this instance the gnosis that freed the respondent from the terror of death was his knowledge that the body, whether personal or cosmic, has an inner nature that cycles its way through time and death toward the blissful pleroma of all that is.

For many, the gnosis is nothing as exotic as reincarnation; it may be, rather, a sense of abiding power. Listen to a city church member committed to supporting the rights of the poor:

> God made a very logical, ordered world, and I don't believe it to be as hostile as some think. We are just beginning to see beyond the hurt, into the power and strength of the nonphysical, into our minds. This is what God intended, that we fulfill the potential of our minds.

She states her opposition to the canonic and charismatic sides:

> I have problems with born-again Christians. The things they feel to be interventions, the product of prayer, are, in fact, the work of the mind. God is there; he is active, but I am not sure doing what—certainly not changing rules. God may be the original creator but the undefined, imperishable power may also be God: the stuff that flows between human beings. . . . Yes, if you would press it, God is the world. . . . Whatever is God in us continues. When our bodies die, then the unknown creative forces within us go on being. . . . I don't understand the worry about what's going to happen to us.

She speaks of how such a comforting idea impels her to work among the urban poor:

> We're making the world a more equal place. Our equality with God requires this. Our community best happens when we live in conjunction with each other.

Many quite different scenarios support the movement toward cosmic unity. Over 20 percent of Americans, half of them churchgoers, today practice the gnosis of astrology as a method of self-realization.[3] And smaller numbers seek, or are influenced by, experiences of clairvoyance, telepathy, precognition, and other extrasensory perceptions that provide clues to their views of the personal as well as the cosmic mind.[4]

A more pervasive form of gnosis today is the "possibility thinking" of Robert Schuller. Possibility thinking and its predecessor, positive thinking, set the world aright and promise a complete, harmonious life. Schuller's television program is a tireless reiteration of the comic story of life that begins in frustration and discord but through enlightenment ends in beautiful harmony. The Crystal Cathedral, with its fountains and flowers, catches—as other major religious television programs holding different world views do not—the awareness that the world and its inhabitants are good and that in such recognition the world moves toward wholesome fulfillment.

As it moves from illusion through gnosis, the story line of the gnostic negotiation ends in a final order and solution to life.

> I am not going to jump in and say "No" if asked whether or not I am actually God. I have a feeling of God's presence in us. It's more a feeling of a power than of a person. . . . There are so many joys of life that I cannot believe that life is basically a chaos. I experience all the problems of the city and I can understand grim lives, but the world is essentially a good place. God is the comfort to people, all that is beautiful. Although I find it hard to come to terms with there being a heaven or hell, I know the spirit doesn't die. I could almost buy the Hindu idea that we become part of the One.

The passages cited in this section are also characterized by their positive, optimistic tone, a tone less familiar to readers who frequent congregations with certain other orientations. Both gnostic and charismatic narrative can be distinguished from the other categories by what scientists call spontaneity. Its opposite is entropy. (Some scientists now find evidence for both forces in the universe.[5]) Gnostic and charismatic approaches assume the spontaneous inner energy of the known world, whether in the cosmos itself (the gnostic view), or by active spirit, as the charismatic view has it. At my bedside, the comic and romantic tales were stories of the cure to be found in the spontaneity of faithful life.

Most church members and physicists, however, think the world is moving toward entropy, its static equilibrium. Denying an inner energy in life, the tragic and ironic stories told about my cancer spoke instead of decline into the dissolution of death. Only a minority in mainline churches sustain a sense of the world's spontaneity required to continue gnostic or charismatic negotiations of the world. But still the arguments of those categories are present, since the other positions, more common at least in the main line, are formed in relation and opposition to them.

THE CHARISMATIC NEGOTIATION

A teacher:

> You really have to believe, to have faith. There really is a higher being to whom we can go when there is nowhere else to turn. He spearheads things; he turns things around in my life.

That estimation of Spirit spontaneously active in the world is based upon personal experience.

> I have had a vision of Christ. It was like a ray of light in my living room, and it came at a point of great desperation. I had been told that I had a malignancy, and

that life would be short, no more than five years. For many hours I talked to God, in the darkness of my room, and then a great big light came to me. I heard a voice that said, "Life will be different." And as fast as the problem came it went, like a great big miracle dream. Three weeks later no trace of the cancer could be found. The vision of Christ was just like a glow, and it came right into the corner of my living room.

Heroically the self in the charismatic negotiation works out a romantic, not a comic, story. The setting for the charismatic narrative is a more frightening and thrilling place than the gnostic world. The calm serenity of gnostic process disappears. The world instead gives paradoxical signals: souls are eternally damned in it, yet God does not fail those who trust in him. In a charismatic world, the source of integrity is not an evolving cosmos but the constancy of God. The world in which the charismatic lives is fundamentally equivocal and dangerous, challenging the believer to seek its blessings amid the peril of evil forces and events. God's steady providence, however, accompanies the self who launches out toward God in an exciting, romantic adventure. Though like the gnostics their goal is a happy ending, charismatics distinguish their sense of empowerment by God's Spirit from a gnostic trance in which the self gains mystic union with God. Charismatics maintain a persistent dualism of spirit and body.[6] God surely enters and transforms the body, but does not merge with it.

What differentiates the charismatic and canonic approaches to the world from gnostic and empiric negotiations is their sense of transcendence. Both God and the human soul are ultimately distinct from the world. In contrast, the gnostic and empiric understandings find God and self ultimately embedded in the experienced world, finally indistinguishable from its nature. Figure C shows this two-way division, and the division between entropy and spontaneity, explored above, that crosscuts it.

The charismatic story begins with discomfort about conventionality. Routine, domestic life is judged inadequate, and the self yearns for a more immediate, direct experience of God's power. "I wanted Jesus to be my Lord and not just my Savior," recounted one charismatic, noting characteristically that the redemption that all Christians can claim was only a first step in the "walk" of the faithful.

> Salvation is wonderful, but there was just something missing. I wanted very earnestly to do God's will. I wanted to glorify him. I realized that there was a deeper depth where I could get into the Lord. I hungered and thirsted for this.

Oral Roberts, whose television programs typify the romantic world view, paraphrases Eliza Doolittle to express the disdain with which the charismatic approach views conventional Christianity:

> Words, words, words, we're sick of words. We've heard your theologies. We've listened to your sermons. Will you please now give us a demonstration. We want to see. Show us.[7]

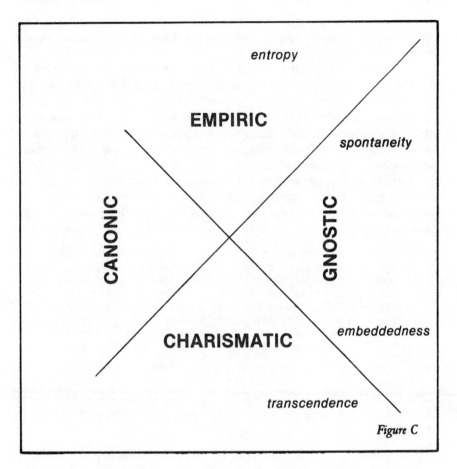

Figure C

Leaving behind daily routine, the self ventures into an uncertain world. As romantic hero, the self enters what Frye calls "the stage of the perilous journey."[8] There it tarries, like the disciples in Jerusalem, awaiting the Spirit's power. Audaciously the self lifts both its sense of personal impotence and also its expectation of God's invading grace. Evil is encountered, even demons themselves:

> With the removal of the Bible and prayer from our schools and homes, the Devil has gained much strength in our land. Many people are being oppressed and possessed by demon forces all over the USA. I believe there is a definite connection between demons and the spreading of such drugs as LSD, speed, amphetamines, etc. There is also a connection [among] the crime wave, violence, homosexuality, long hair on males and demon activity. . . . The main reason for the present day move of the Holy Spirit is to restore the body of Christ to the supernatural power of its early days so as to raise up a standard against the flood of the enemy.[9]

For many, the evil occurs in an affliction of the personal or family body. Dissatisfied with, or distrustful of, conventional therapy, the charismatic seeks evidence of Pentecostal power.

God rewards the search; the romantic adventure ends in the triumph of God's love. The hero becomes the home of God's Spirit. Evil is vanquished (7 percent of all Americans report that they have healed by faith[10]) but, even more important, the floodgates of God's blessing are thrown open wide to those who venture beyond religious convention. In a second baptism the indwelling Spirit brings gifts, fruits, and miracles. The person directly experiences what one recipient called "the liquid love" of God poured through her, profoundly altering her sense of life and the sacred.

Glossolalia also mark the charismatic sense of a divinity that indwells yet nevertheless distinguishes itself by the act of language. Oral Roberts tells the story of tongues:

> The Holy Spirit is down here inside, and down inside is the desire of our hearts which is often bottled up . . . which is often formless and seemingly void. There it is inside. We are bottled up with our emotions, our frustrations, the goals that we desire that seem to be impossible. We have this deep earnest desire to communicate with God and we try it with our minds, with our understanding, and sometimes it works. Sometimes it doesn't. But when we go down deep into the inner man, the Holy Spirit and our spirit join together, creating a new language ability, a new power of communication with God, and we speak directly with God.[11]

The romantic story culminates in the exaltation of the hero.[12] In the charismatic world view, the self is similarly honored, not by comic *ekstasis* but by the romantic *enthousiasmos* of indwelling spirit.[13] An airline pilot's wife tells her story:

> I really knew all *about* Jesus for years but really didn't *know* him. Carried him around in my pocket, and go from crisis to crisis and only then pull him out. But I began to realize that he didn't want to be in my pocket but wanted to be lord of my life. He really is concerned about what I was going to cook and how I was cleaning the bathroom. God was concerned with everything in my life, and he was trying to tell me this, and finally I began to listen. . . . Then I was filled with his spirit. The spirit was down in there all these years but was not then to control me. It was given me at age twelve, but I did not let it become active in my life. . . . As we activate and use the Holy Spirit in our lives . . . we gain power and love and joy and peace. . . . There is more out there and we want more.

As must now be evident, the charismatic orientation may be cloaked in the style of those groups which call themselves charismatic or Pentecostal, but it is important to note that the charismatic negotiation is primarily a *structure* and as such may give form to the world views of persons and groups that do not adopt any of the features or practices of what is conventionally called charismatic religion. Indeed, the charismatic outlook need not be dramatic at all. Here is a more cautious story but one that nevertheless hews to the romantic line of a charismatic world view:

As dyed-in-the-wool Episcopalians, only a few years ago both of us would have found writing about Christ's effect on our lives a bit ridiculous. . . . Life was full, but it was also remarkably empty. . . . The Lord saw fit to put a local evangelical department store manager squarely into our lives. In his office the manager asked Lew, "Have you ever asked Christ into your heart and life?" . . . Life has not been the same since. No thunder clapped. No lightning flashed. . . . But little by little, day by day, imperceptibly, without conscious effort on our part, our lives began to change, not always better in the short run, but definitely different and unquestionably better in the long run. . . . We truly met Christ for the first time at Cursillo. We met him in the chapel, in the music, in the people, in the unutterable that poured out of every door. . . . Once you've seen Christ, you'll never be the same again. Oh, you'll still be fat . . . gray . . . short. You'll still swear (but you'll hear it), you'll still sin (but you'll suffer), but now you'll seek and search and struggle and strive for more glimpses of Him. Your spiritual world will become a vacuum sucking up anything and everything that looks as though it might be your salvation.[14]

THE CANONIC NEGOTIATION

A businesswoman:

When my husband died on Christmas Day in an automobile accident, leaving me with two small children, I just knew that I could get through with God. All of a sudden the world just crashed around me: everything inside was gone, but we knew we could get through. There was God's plan. I had a feeling that things were going to be all right. I knew real suffering but not despair. I had no vision or speaking from God. Just a plan that I knew was there.

Like tragedy, the canonic negotiation asserts the inevitable decline of the self. The charismatic story portrays an escape from the conventionality of life; the canonic story claims instead the certainty of life's pattern. Born in sin, one is capable of no career but failure, no other end but death. Only by realizing the certainty of one's fault and by submitting to the total sovereignty of the God who controls life does one resolve the decline. And even that resolution is postponed until after death, in the next world.

In this negotiation, the controlling canon provides integrity, functioning here as dependably as does God's providence in the charismatic negotiation and the harmonious cosmos for gnostics. For canonic Protestants the inviolable canon is God's word, the Holy Scripture. The Bible in their canonic eyes is completely reliable and authoritative. Roman Catholics who are canonic may find a similar integrity in the church's traditional teaching authority. In the charismatic outlook, God's pattern is tested by the spirit within oneself,[15] but for the canonic, the canon is the final decree. "Whether the context is Greek, Christian or undefined," says Northrop Frye, "tragedy seems to lead up to an epiphany of law, of that which is and must be."[16] The canonic Christian beholds a world fated for catastrophe, fulfilling the pattern laid down in Holy Scriptures and ancient teachings.

Although the canonic narrative develops along a tragic course, its beginning may give no forecast of catastrophic outcome. The self initially glorifies itself, thinking erroneously that it is autonomous, perhaps divine. Its hubris, or arrogance, seduces the self to claim its own freedom and goodness. The error of that claim is, however, quickly exposed in both great tragedies like *Macbeth* and canonic musings like that of a Southern Baptist:

> What I have noticed in different pastors and preachers is that some preach a sermon and read Scripture and it doesn't sound like the gospel. What I need and what I like is to have Scripture really read and have it interpreted from the pulpit. That is, that such-and-such is sin, and the Bible says so. I don't hear that often from the pulpit these days. I need somebody to convict me, not just say, "Janet, you're free and a good girl. . . ." I have an unfulfilled feeling. I could be a better person if someone would present to me the right way and teach me how to live.

One is not free and good. One is lost and sinful, and one's story develops the costly consequences of one's depraved nature. If the self remains disobedient, refusing to recognize the sovereignty of God, then life continues to deteriorate and ends in hell. If, however, one repents and accepts the lordship of Christ, one takes on a different yoke, of suffering love and obedience.

As Jerry Falwell maintains in his tragic television productions (which stand in opposition to the comic presentations of Robert Schuller), society slips toward its destruction. The moral fiber of the nation is decaying; families, schools, cities, and entertainment are close to disaster. Only by a massive mission can this nation be saved. Churches must become obedient, "Bible-centered, Bible-believing, Bible-teaching churches."

"The Christian is characterized," says a local pastor, "by humility and willingness to serve in whatever capacity or place Christ has given him." Narrative movement in the canonic world view thus directly contradicts the gnostic, its polar opposite. The canonic story traces a self that declines tragically from a state misunderstood as apotheosis to total subordination, while the gnostic story elevates the self from a state misunderstood as bondage to union with God.

Accepting the cross and its mortification is, in the canonic view, a joyful and often exciting event, supremely important to life and happiness after life ends. That joy is based, however, in the knowledge that the self is submissive to God's will and is following God's plan. "Until people," reports a pastor,

> begin to discover God's plan for their lives and how much he has to offer them, they will miss most of the lasting joy and sense of fulfillment that God desires to give them, not to mention the power and grace to meet the unexpected and tragic of life.

Ultimate happiness is deferred to an afterlife "on the other side" of present existence. "Home" has a different connotation for canonics than for charismatics. In the charismatic world view, the Holy Spirit makes its home within the present body. In canonic understanding, the "blessed home" is "beyond this land of woe, where trials never come, nor tears of sorrow flow." The pattern for life in the present land is that of Christ, who was willing to take the cross and, in the words of the famous evangelistic hymn, willing to suffer all of life's misery:

> Willing to go to Calvary,
>   Laying his glory aside,
> Willing to hang there on the tree;
> Willing to bear the agony,
> Willing to die for you and me,
>   Jesus the crucified.[17]

In canonic pattern, Christ lays aside his prior glory and accepts the tragedy of life. A canonic follower of Christ in a nursing home makes sense of her own story by that model:

> Yes, I don't mind being here. You know, the Bible tells us we're going to have suffering and pain. So I don't bother about worrying what's happening to me. I think it's a blessing just to be around. I believe that my affliction was given to me so that doctors can learn more about this rare disease. . . . I never married. Devoted my life to my family. But I'm not sorry. When I die I'll go to heaven to be with the Lord and my family.

Sin and its consequences rule the person, making it imperative to achieve personal faith in Jesus Christ as savior from that sin and also a commitment to Christ as Lord. The canonic story in its personal mode begins in hubris and its deadly effects. To avoid the hell of one's own sin one surrenders to Christ, dying to self, to be born again, as today 48 percent of all American Protestants report they have been.[18] The rebirth that comes from conversion, however, is not an antinomian release from duty but an entry into a new life controlled by the canon. "So much of our life has been out of control," reflects an older Baptist:

> Our oldest son was brain damaged. He is still with us, and we have to live our life a day at a time. . . . He is thirty-five and we never know whether he'll have a high or a low. A very pathetic thing. He is not retarded. He realizes his limits but he has never accepted them. I relate to Job through the experience of my son. I also like to take Proverbs, beginning on the first day of the month, and move through its thirty-one chapters simultaneously with the month's days. Some point in that chapter will strike me right between the eyes. . . . You've got to get involved in the Bible. Find your place in God's word.

THE EMPIRIC NEGOTIATION

A social worker:

> I don't know what I believe, and I am resentful of people who claim they understand what's going on. There is certainly a life force of incredible variety and color and function, all interrelated, but I can't say it's going anywhere. What I can't get are those people who feel the actual presence of God. My father felt this, and I did not dare doubt it when I was young. Now I understand that a lot of faithful people like myself doubt. But I never felt God's presence. I actually feel he is unfair. I get mad at God a lot; I can't understand the misery here at the housing project. They deserve better. I have to share what I have with them. If

I've got it, I've got to share it. It's a sin not to. Religion is made by man to help man.

Although empirical observations of the world can be reduced to scientific propositions, their form in community discourse is narrational. A story as emotionally compelling as the romances and tragedies of other world views can be told in the ironic vein of the empiric view. The story may begin with some example of numinosity and then show counterevidence of its absurdity. An affirmation of ordinary human worth provides the conclusion. The setting of the empiric story shows an often anomalous world in which signs of the sacred are belied by their link to folly and injustice. It is by repudiating situations in which spirit power is said to dwell miraculously that true human stature emerges. In contradicting sacred explanations, one finds within human community itself the true mystery of life.

Truth emerges in empirical observation, not in revelation. The world is perceived through the senses, and by means of the senses the world's regularity is demonstrated. The charismatic world view romantically draws one away from the conventionality of life into the contention of the sacred and the profane. The empiric sense of reality moves ironically in the opposite direction, away from assertions about divine presences and powers and toward the scientific understanding of the world's regularity. The integrity that other negotiations discover in cosmic wholeness, or in God's providence, or in canonic Scripture, is suspect in an empiric understanding. Here alleged processes and evidences of spirit are investigated and subjected to rational scrutiny. Mystic wisdom and miracles must be tested. Holy Scripture cannot be accepted as revealed truth but must be analyzed as historical data. For the empiric, the locus of integrity is within human society itself. Only in rational observation of reality, observation that others through their own senses can replicate, can reliable indication of the nature of the world be found. And only as human society frees itself from a thralldom to concepts, leaders, and structures that draw on supernatural assumptions can that integrity manifest itself in honesty, justice, and equality.

No television preacher of national renown orients his or her program from a strictly empiric viewpoint. Coming closest to that outlook is probably someone like Walter Cronkite, who, with good heart and human fellowship, displayed the world's anomalies—starving children, wars, and crimes—and then concluded his show with ironic summary: "That's the way it is."

In local churches the empiric negotiation appears in a mitigated manner that Wade Clark Roof characterizes as "cosmopolitan religion."[19] Thoroughgoing empirics tend to avoid organized religion altogether, but many whose outlook is dominated by this orientation are in fact faithful church members. As Roof points out, their religion affirms: (*a*) the centrality of ethical principles in their meaning systems; (*b*) a parsimony of beliefs, few attributions of numinosity; (*c*) breadth of perspective; (*d*) piety defined as a personal search for meaning; and (*e*) license to doubt.

An empiric story rejects examples of supposedly superior piety and proposes instead a reasonable loyalty to God and fellow human beings.

> No, God does not speak to me. I discussed this with [my husband] recently. His niece and nephew were here a week ago, about twenty-two years old, but they behaved like silly teenagers. They spent two days praying to the Lord about buying a car. Now when Bob and I sit down and give some thought to something— maybe that's how God speaks to us. He must be guiding us, but I don't know. But God doesn't worry about what you put on every morning.

Contradicting a charismatic understanding of spontaneous divinity within the person, the empiric self opposes those who behave as if they were "holier than thou" and is anxious to deny any special sanctity conveyed in his or her person. "The main lesson," reports a woman troubled about religious hypocrisy,

> is learning how to be honest with myself, that I didn't think I was something that I wasn't. I am disappointed when I don't get that honesty back from another person. I am not fooled. I try not to bear false witness, even though you can really take swipes at people. One person I know is very active in church, but she has a razor-sharp tongue. She delights in taking swipes at people for no reason.

An empiric person finds, having purged the self of spiritual presumption, how much one has in common with other persons, none now superior or subordinate, and all deserving love.

> I think we got to keep up with people. We got to know about the world and what's going on. We have to help people live in this world. Can't just talk about what Jesus did a long time ago. We have to know the facts about here and now and apply the teachings of Jesus to these.

Empirically oriented literature, says Frye, "takes for granted a world which is full of anomalies, injustices, follies and crimes, and yet is permanent and undisplaceable. Its principle is that everyone who wishes to keep his balance must learn first of all to keep his eyes open and his mouth shut."[20]

CONGREGATIONAL
WORLD VIEW

A differentiation among the world views of various congregations such as I have laid out here is not widely employed. Most observers of the parish would readily acknowledge a bipolar categorization of congregations that distinguishes liberal parishes from conservative ones, and some differentiate parishes according to three interpretations (such as literal, antiliteral, and symbolic)[21] of Christian doctrine. But few advocate a more complex typology, and thus my quadripolar analysis of parish world view is unusual.

In fact, the capacity of a contemporary congregation to sustain any unified, sharply defined world view has been more frequently questioned than confirmed in recent studies of church life. To many observers, the outlooks and expectations of mainline congregations evince a bland uniformity indistinguishable from that of their surrounding society. In their investigation of churches in a Midwestern county, for example, W. Widick Schroeder and Victor Obenhaus describe as a major finding the absence in each of "informing cognitive structures."[22] Jeffrey Hadden has held that "Christians join together in a common experience of faith when in reality there is no shared consensus regarding the nature of that faith."[23] "It can be safely said," states Thomas Luckmann, "that within Protestantism doctrinal differences are virtually irrelevant for members of the major denominations."[24] And the suburban church proved for Gibson Winter to be a middle-class enclave possessing little capacity for coherent belief distinct from that of the society that holds it captive.[25]

Investigators who cite the amorphous nature of parish beliefs base their findings on responses that parishioners give to lists of credal statements (e.g., "Jesus is the Son of God," with scaled responses ranging from "strongly agree" to "strongly disagree"). They find that members of a parish, especially one with liberal leanings, show little uniformity in their replies. One member may prize an orthodox interpretation of faith; the next may hold a looser interpretation. My own investigation does not center on responses to credal assertions, because I find that members build their world views from many more materials than Christian doctrine. As I reported earlier, I found it almost useless to ask direct, "Do you believe in . . . ?" questions in the manner of Gallup. People are too ready to assent to anything that sounds worthy and to deny anything that might possibly be perceived as silly or disloyal. And the symbols employed in such questions themselves dampen thought. Symbols have great stopping power for the nontheologian. In effect they "say it all," do not encourage reflection, and instead command mute allegiance.

I therefore framed my questions around what Peter Berger calls the "marginal situations of human existence [which] reveal the innate precariousness of all social worlds."[26] My intention was to encourage respondents to ponder various crises so that I might understand their interpretation of them. The consideration of death, the uncanny, life crises, and nonsense should evoke a concept of world order, a world view that accounts for them.

What I found in Corinth (the name I have given elsewhere to the town whose two principal churches—Baptist and Methodist—I spent my sabbatical year studying) is that most of the stories I heard in a particular congregation were similar in genre. Their settings, in other words, were the same. In the Methodist church, most of the stories were empiric, though many were also shaded by a strong canonic tinge. Least often heard were tales that countered the predominant empiric view, that is, charismatic ones. By contrast, in the Baptist church a canonic view predominated, leaning somewhat toward the empiric. Again, any echoes of the gnostic view—the structural opposite of the canonic position—were difficult to identify in members' accounts of crises.

In the next chapter, further ramifications of and conclusions about congregational world view will emerge. For the moment, I want simply to report that my research in Corinth and studies since strongly suggest that even mainline congregations—the type most observers have had most difficulty distinguishing from one another—do maintain distinctive world views. In Corinth the manner in which one congregation framed its understanding of reality differed consistently from the outlook of the other. Such differences were denied by the participants in these parishes who, if they countenanced distinctions at all, would confine them to matters of practice (worship patterns, frequency of Scripture reading, baptism) and not faith. The majority of members of each church, nevertheless, gave different meanings to similar events and crises, and each group treated evidence of evil or the numinous or nonsense in a distinctive manner. From this I conclude that world views reflect and give a focus to group experience, providing a map within which words and actions make sense. The setting of a congregation is the order by which its gossip, sermons, strategies, and fights—the household idiom— gain their reasonableness. What is expressed in daily intercourse about the nature of the world is idiomatic, responsive to a particular pattern of language, expressing a particular setting for narrative. Tales in a local church tend to travel in packs: one good story evokes another, one member's account of an illness, for example, is usually reciprocated in kind. In comradeship and commiseration members top each other's stories, building up the world setting that they together inhabit.

NOTES

1. ED. NOTE: See pp. 78–79, where the author explains, as he did in oral presentations of this material, that his use of the term "charismatic" refers to a general orientation to the Spirit, not to the specific religious groups called "charismatics." He also frequently noted that "gnostic," as he used the term, referred to a general orientation, not to specific historical groups or their teachings.

2. Similar to the traditional square of opposition used in formal logic, the semiotic square is used in Algirdas J. Greimas, *Du sens: Essais sémiotiques* (Paris: Editions du Seuil, 1970), 136–50, and by the Entrevernes Group, *Signs and Parables: Semiotics and Gospel Texts* (Pittsburgh: Pickwick Press, 1978). The square points two semantic axes of contradictories, permitting operations among four elementary units of signification distinguished as contraries. An inference of opposition marks the relation between semes on either pole of one axis, with implication for the other two poles in the square. Analysts of semiotics would not designate, as I do, the axes by four specific poles. Brian Wicker, *The Story-shaped World: Fiction and Metaphysics: Some Variations on a Theme* (Notre Dame: Univ. of Notre Dame Press, 1975), designates the axes but not the poles; so do Lévi-Strauss and Roman Jakobson in the analysis of discourse. In all instances, however, utterance gains its significance from the tension marked by the axes; and the pattern of rejection of one pole in a unit of signification accompanied by an assertion of relation between two others, used by the semioticians, is similar to the narrative expression of setting found in a local church.

3. Gallup Opinion Index, *Religion in America: Report No. 145* (Princeton: American Institute of Public Opinion, 1978).

4. Morton Kelsey, *The Christian and the Supernatural* (Minneapolis: Augsburg Publishing House, 1976).

5. Ilya Prigogine, *From Being to Becoming: Time and Complexity in the Physical Sciences* (San Francisco: W. H. Freeman & Co., 1980).

6. Ronald A. Knox, *Enthusiasm: A Chapter in the History of Religion* (New York: Oxford Univ. Press, 1961), 581. Knox distinguishes the gnostic and charismatic approaches as two distinct types of enthusiasm. A similar distinction obtains in Quincy Howe, *Reincarnation for the Christian* (Philadelphia: Westminster Press, 1974), 58.

7. Oral Roberts, *The Holy Spirit Now* (Tulsa: Oral Roberts Associates, 1976), 44.

8. Northrop Frye, *Anatomy of Criticism*, 187.

9. Ken Sumrall, *What's Your Question?* (Monroeville, Pa.: Whitaker Books, 1969), 33.

10. Gallup Opinion Index, *Religion in America: Report No. 145*, 52.

11. Roberts, *The Holy Spirit Now*, 63.

12. Frye, *Anatomy*, 187.

13. The charismatic experience is a "sensation of surrender to an immersion in a larger reality: an experience perceived as self-fulfillment and enhancement of individuality rather than the loss of it" (Luther P. Gerlach and Virginia H. Hine, *People, Power, Change: Movements of Social Transformation* [Indianapolis: Bobbs-Merrill Co., 1970], 124).

14. Dee Feuerstein and Lew Feuerstein, "No Thunder, But Life Changed After Accepting Christ," *The Episcopalian* 147 (1982): 13.

15. Richard Quebedeaux, *The New Charismatics: The Origins, Development, and Significance of Neo-Pentecostalism* (Garden City, N.Y.: Doubleday & Co., 1975), 111.

16. Frye, *Anatomy*, 207.

17. Floyd W. Hawkins, "From His Celestial Abode Jesus Came," in *Triumphant Service Songs* (Chicago: Rodeheaver Co., 1934), no. 16.

18. Gallup Opinion Index, *Religion in America: Report No. 145*, 43.

19. Wade Clark Roof, *Community and Commitment*, 182ff.

20. Frye, *Anatomy*, 226.

21. Sociological analyses of beliefs occasionally use a tripolar model of world view. The LAM scale (Liberal, Antiliberal, and Mythological) is demonstrated in Richard A. Hunt, "Mythological-Symbolic Religious Commitment: The LAM Scales," *Journal for the Scientific Study of Religion* 11 (1972): 42–52. Andrew M. Greeley, "Comment on Hunt's 'Mythological-Symbolic Religious Commitment: The LAM Scales,'" *Journal for the Scientific Study of Religion* 11 (1972): 287–92, proposes a fourth nonliteral but transcendent category for the scales but argues only for its legitimacy as an autonomous position, not, as I do, for its role in completing a quadripolar approach to world view.

22. W. Widick Schroeder and Victor Obenhaus, *Religion in American Culture: Unity and Diversity in a Midwestern County* (New York: Free Press of Glencoe, 1964), 94.

23. Jeffrey K. Hadden, *The Gathering Storm in the Churches: The Widening Gap Between Clergy and Laymen* (Garden City, N.Y.: Doubleday & Co., 1969), 34.

24. Thomas Luckmann, *The Invisible Religion* (New York: Macmillan Co., 1967), 34.

25. Gibson Winter, *The Suburban Captivity of the Churches*, 82–104.

26. Peter L. Berger, *The Sacred Canopy*, 24.

6

EXPLORING WORLD VIEW

This chapter describes some methods for the study of the world view of the congregation. Some people who have already used these methods have, however, missed critical points of the undertaking. Before presenting the techniques, I therefore issue some warnings about the possibility of distortion or misuse.

a. *My four categories do not exhaust the richness of parish world view.* I devised the categories as a more adequate way to acknowledge variables of belief than a two-point liberal-conservative categorization permits. But even a fourfold typology does not delineate the full picture of self and world that the congregation sees. To discover that a parish has, for example, an empiric-gnostic orientation may be a helpful recognition, but that finding alone does not identify the whole range of motifs and images by which a local church understands its world.

Use of the techniques of participant observation and guided interviews, introduced in the present chapter, will help to prevent facile classifications of parish beliefs according to the fourfold scheme. Remember that the congregation is idiomatic; it constitutes itself by a very distinctive language whose indicative aspect identifies a world in some ways allied with metaphors widely employed in the culture but in other ways peculiar to that group alone. The four world view categories may help organize the interpretation of idiom elements, but they do not describe the full richness of parish settings.

b. *World view is not adequately conveyed in quantitative measures.* The test instrument described among the methods in this section is comparatively easy to use and score, and it provides a helpful way to compare the outlooks of both different churches and different people within a single church. But the instrument is essentially a confirmatory device to give a quantitative indication of the belief patterns that participant observation and guided interviews examine more adequately and accurately.

The temptation is to use the test as a free-standing indicator of parish world view. Its packaged approach and numerical conclusion appeal to mechanist leanings in all of us, and, especially for time-pressed consultants, it produces a quick payoff by summarizing world view in percentages and diagrams. Reducing to a statistical dot a member's deep struggle to apprehend the world can, however, pervert the interpretive task of ministry. More necessary than the calculus of people's scores is a disciplined sensitivity to the narratives they construct in the face of death and absurdity. What expresses the faith of a congregation is not numerical data but rather the stories that the numbers only grossly approximate.

c. *The world view categories are nonhierarchical and nondevelopmental.* As their graphic arrangement in a square suggests, they do not indicate a layered progression in value or a staged progress toward maturity. All categories are interdependent: holding a world view involves a negotiation that requires the presence of several available and attractive categories.

Having issued these warnings about possible misunderstandings of the methods offered to ascertain and measure world view, I now present three vehicles: participant observation, guided interviews, and a test instrument.

PARTICIPANT OBSERVATION

The fullest and most satisfying way to study the culture of a congregation is to live within its fellowship and learn directly how it interprets its experience and generates its behavior. That approach is called participant observation. As the term suggests, the analyst is involved in the activity of the group to be studied but also maintains a certain detachment. Participant observation has not always been an accepted way of learning about a social group. Throughout history most of what was known about a people came from accounts of travelers or from persons who, though resident within the group, were paid to do some task other than observe its culture. Only in the past century have the discipline and resources been developed to enable substantial numbers of anthropologists and ethnographers to go "into the field" to study cultures as diverse as those of hill peoples and hospital wards.

Some participant observers have studied congregations,[1] but in general the art of congregational observation is still at the travelogue stage. Most accounts of parish culture are loosely anecdotal or motivated by mechanist or contextual goals. Very seldom has anyone within a local church treated it as a field of study and reported out its patterns of culture because they constitute an important disclosure of the symbolic nature of the group. Several good reasons underlie the paucity of observations about parish culture. One goes to church for purposes quite different from, even opposed to, analysis. And observation within one's own church is more difficult than the study of a distant culture. As Melvin Williams points out, a church member must become more of an "observing participant" than a participant observer, because the member is already an insider and accustomed to the values and behavior that he or she must now study objectively.[2]

But Williams reports that being an observing participant is both possible and rewarding.[3] Diligent members of a local church can learn a great deal about its language and story. Though members can never achieve the detachment of an ethnographer who comes from the outside, they can become their own best informants, because they already participate in the structures that the outsider has to learn. The trick is that members must learn to function and observe *as if* they were outsiders so that they see afresh the myriad matters about the congregation that they now take for granted. Pastors and members can begin to see extraordinary aspects of common church happenings if they consider themselves visitors from another culture or time. They learn to ask what common things mean, why ordinary operations work.

A persistent curiosity nags observing participants. They look at routine events and hear common expressions as if for the first time. They now take nothing for granted. They listen intently to both formal and spontaneous discourse; they examine signs and gestures; they read all that is written; they do not avoid embarrassing episodes and fights. Shortly after any observation they must write down the details of what they have experienced, because the act of recording the event is critical to its understanding. As their notes (I use $5'' \times 8''$ cards) accumulate, they begin to pore over them for evidence of themes that seem to organize the congregation's behavior and give meaning to its perceptions. They become not only specialists in construing the parish story but also its literary critic, gaining enough distance to assess what the story means, to explore its setting, trace its plot, and consider its character.

Detailed instructions about participant observation are readily available,[4] and much can be learned about the method by reading the congregational studies of Melvin Williams and Samuel Heilman. One learns best, however, by doing it oneself, perhaps starting out with a limited inquiry focused on one of the following elements in parish culture:

jokes, stories, lore	lines of authority and influence
the written material of the parish	use of time
conversations that follow	ritual
administrative meetings	social class
sermons, classroom presentations	demographic features
use of space	history
organizations	conscious and unconscious
social groupings	symbols
processes of becoming a	conflict
nuclear member	

The list could be several times longer. Once launched in a particular direction, participant observers seek occasions that present an object of inquiry and try to uncover the object's function and meaning. Again writing down what is observed is absolutely essential. It trains the eye for subsequent encounters and it begins the process of interpretation that ultimately brings new understanding to the congregation.

Within the information gathered are, of course, data about the congregation's world view. Certain objects of inquiry, such as sermons and histories, will probably yield a higher proportion of world view data, but important insights may also be gained from other elements. Fights, parish bulletin boards, even the litter of closets, may also disclose what the parish suspects is really happening in life. Such information is especially helpful when used in conjunction with the results of guided interviews, described below.

GUIDED INTERVIEWS

Some of the data for understanding the world view of a parish come, as we have shown, from overhearing the parish's conversations and speeches and from observing its behavior. Other, more structured, information must come from guided interviews, which are dialogues in which the inquirer directs predesigned questions to an informant. The result is open-ended conversations with members of a congregation who, as informants, respond to these questions designed to evoke pertinent answers. Concentrated information about the setting of the congregational story can be obtained through such conversations.

To encourage an essentially theological discussion with parishioners not given to that sort of talk, I base my questions in guided interviews upon crises experienced by the informants. A number of social scientists—Peter Berger, Mircea Eliade, Clifford Geertz, Wade Clark Roof, Philip Slater[5] —note the link between the threat of chaos and the construction of world view. Relying upon the narrative idiom of their community, people address their understanding of the universe in response to crisis. Part of the function of parish story is to keep the congregation's ontology in repair. When crisis threatens one's sense of order, the community works, often by narrative, to reassert the circumstances that can accommodate even the threat. Thus by using questions that help church members speak about crises, something can be learned about the way they apprehend reality.

Members must be told in advance about the searching nature of the interview, but care should also be taken not to frighten people by portentous descriptions of what is about to happen. In fact, the conversations are usually rewarding for both the member and the interviewer. They often release thoughts that have long been bottled up. In inviting a member to an interview, the interviewer might first clarify the nature of the study and its purpose for the church. Then the interviewer might say, "Part of the study is to learn how members feel about critical problems now facing our lives, and I would like to get your ideas about them."

Usually lasting about ninety minutes, interviews seek responses to a limited number of questions. Interviewers approach the conversation without a hidden purpose, using the interview neither to argue with the informant nor to diagnose his or her problems. Instead, the interviewer treats the member's answer as a disclosure of meaning important within itself, a symbolic construction that the interviewer must try to understand. While interviewers try to ask the whole series of predesigned questions, they also guide the conversations by spontaneous inquiries that pick up on particular avenues of thought advanced by the informant. The interviewer attempts, of course, to keep the discussion focused on the ideas of the informant and avoids personal responses that disclose the inquirer's own views.

Informants are frequently anxious before the interview starts, persuaded that they know little of value to the interviewer and perhaps wary because of earlier experiences in which they were the objects of a catechism or experiment. Most, however, quickly sense the open spirit of the conversation— that they are not being judged and that their answers are in fact useful and interesting—and many grow enthusiastically articulate. Though the questions bring to mind crises, the freedom to address threatening topics in a friendly atmosphere often encourages informants to relate rarely shared parts of their own story. Some express surprise at the end of the interviews that they have had so much to say. Pastors who have used this method report that some interviews are among their most satisfying pastoral calls. So accustomed are members to being told what they *should* believe that to be asked what they in fact *do* believe may prompt unprecedented communication.

At some point in the session three questions are asked that portray crises related to person and group:

—Think of the death of a friend or a relative. What do you suppose was going on?
—Tell me about the way your faith has changed throughout the years.
—What is happening with someone who is senile?

Although these questions may be asked at any appropriate moment in the interview, I have generally begun with the one about death. The question often releases an extraordinary number of ideas and suspicions that the informant has seldom shared, and the exchange sets the tone for the rest of the conversation.

To understand other aspects of the world view of the informant, I ask some further questions about crises in larger contexts:

—Remember a time when life in your family seemed out of control. What was really happening?
—What is God doing with our nation?
—What would a new pastor do to the life of your church?

And some questions that deal with supernatural crises:

—Has God spoken to you? Given you a sign? Have you felt God's presence?

—Tell me about any experiences in which you have sensed a spirit or spiritual force.

—How do you get in touch with God?

A record of the conversation is essential. Write down as much as possible of the informant's answer as it is spoken, and later fill in the gaps. The interview may be tape-recorded, but manuscription has several advantages: (1) The act of writing signifies the importance of what is being said and encourages the informant to elaborate; (2) no later transcription is needed; and (3) the interviewer can ponder the text while clarifying and advancing the conversation. Use 5″ × 8″ cards. They permit easy comparison and rearrangement of notes. Mark the source and sequence of each card.

About half of the persons interviewed should be those who give formal and informal leadership to the congregation. The other half should be a sample of membership varied according to sex, age, education, and intensity of participation. Interview people individually, not as couples or groups. When questioned together, spouses or friends tend to settle for compromise statements rather than to search their own souls.

Steps in interpretation

1. After you have collected the results of several interviews, begin to read your notes as if they were spoken by inhabitants of a recently discovered village. Your task is to find out, with as little preconception as possible, how your informants describe what is going on in life, where it seems to be headed, and why. Explore how they perceive themselves as persons and how they typify their church, their world, and their God.

2. Underline phrases that characterize the nature of things and events.

3. Note recurrent themes: images that organize the ideas of several informants, similar phrases, common solutions, reiterated stories, repeated symbols. Put each theme on a separate card.

4. Arrange the cards in a spatial pattern that suggests the affinity of each to the four world view categories. The closer the card to the cardinal point, the greater the consonance between its language and the world view type (see Figure D).

5. Note features of the pattern. Start writing an account of the world that employs the themes and frequent phrases of the community.

From this base further inquiries could:

—*thicken* the description of world view by a second round of interviews (some with the same informants) and by the information you have gathered from participant observation and analysis of documents written by members of the congregation.

—*test* the picture by a survey instrument (such as the one described next) that asks similar questions, and by inviting members of the congregation to review and comment on the results of your observations.

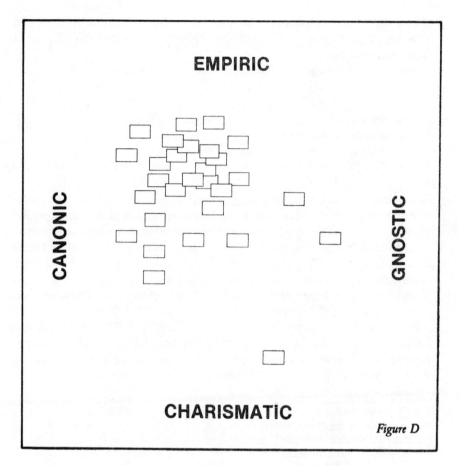

Figure D

—*determine* whether the picture is more characteristic of nuclear than marginal members.

—*compare* the view with that of another congregation. Because much of a congregation's expression is already familiar to its churchgoing observer, the contrast between the patterns of two churches may lend a deeper appreciation of the variables in world view that each employs.

A WORLD VIEW
TEST INSTRUMENT

One's perception of a congregation's world view gained from participant observation and guided interviews can be verified by a relatively simple device, a questionnaire that poses questions similar to those asked in the interviews. The instrument is a forced answer test that requires its takers to choose one of four responses. The responses, which I derived from phrases collected in interviews with church members, reflect each of the four world view categories.[6]

We can see how the questionnaire works by examining one of the questions:

In the worst times of my life I find:
    a. the divinity within me makes my troubles less crucial
    b. comfort in Bible stories like that of Job
    c. patience to work for better times
    d. God blessing me in new ways

Respondents are asked to choose the response closest to the one they themselves would make. A few, often the more sophisticated members of the church, complain that none of the answers expresses their sentiments. They may be cajoled into choosing the answer that is the least offensive to them. Even in its constricting format, however, each item encourages the member to construct a small story of his or her life, imagining the tension created by a particular crisis and then resolving it by subsequent explanation chosen from among the several alternatives.

Printed below are several questions from the early (1979) version of the test instrument. The scores of different congregations that used this version are reported in the next section. Next to each response is the category it represents: canonic (Ca), charismatic (Ch), empiric (Em), and gnostic (Gn).

1. I see my religion as:
    (a) not "holier than thou"   (Em)
    (b) filled with the Holy Spirit   (Ch)
    (c) born again in Christ   (Ca)
    (d) insight into my own spark of divinity (Gn)

2. When I die:
    (a) I keep the blessings God has already begun to give me (Ch)
    (b) I shall then be with Christ (Ca)
    (c) I may later be reincarnated (Gn)
    (d) I may or may not live afterward (Em)

3. When I see a picture of a starving child I think:
    (a) if everyone did God's will, this would not happen (Ca)
    (b) the child is living out a phase of his many lives (Gn)
    (c) why does God permit this? (Em)
    (d) God is with him and easing his troubles (Ch)

4. I feel that I mature as I:
    (a) grow in the presence of Christ (Ch)
    (b) follow God's plan for me (Ca)
    (c) learn to love (Em)
    (d) realize the divine potential in me (Gn)

A revised version of the complete, 27-question test and its scoring key are printed in the Appendix.

In most instances, the questionnaire was distributed, after a verbal introduction that included the assurance that there were no "right" answers, on a single Sunday morning to those who attended the worship services of the church. Those who received the test, therefore, were a sample of the active church membership. In some cases, members completed the test before leaving the church; in others, they later returned the document in a stamped, addressed envelope.

The instrument provides a quantitative assessment of the general belief orientation of a congregation. Because guided interviews with a large proportion of church members would take a great deal of time to conduct and analyze, an analyst may wish, after conversing with, say, twenty or thirty informants, to test the drift of findings by using the instrument. By displaying respondents' scores graphically in the manner described in the next section, the test offers, moreover, a way by which members can see how their answers compare with those of the rest of the church.

As I warned earlier, *the instrument is not a substitute for searching conversation with church members.* When used by itself, it reduces to a numerical figure the tentative, complex negotiation a parish makes in a whole universe of interpretations to construct a specific world plausible to itself. In so doing, it can confirm the all too prevalent impression that the congregation is mainly a machine, described by numbers and oriented by forces. Thus it should be used with care, *never* as the sole analytical instrument.

FUNCTIONS OF
CONGREGATIONAL WORLD VIEW

As I learned in my study of Corinth, persons tend to cluster with others who see the world as they do. By that participation, they come to align their own outlook even more with that of fellow members.[7] In the household of a local church dwell mostly members whose idiomatic discourse projects a mutually recognizable world.

Like the sociologists who study mainline churches, leaders of large or liberal congregations are sometimes persuaded that their members together hold an incoherent plurality of beliefs. "We have all kinds here," says one pastor, "a real Heinz 57 Variety parish." Recognizing no consistency in world view, they explain membership solidarity in their churches by personal and programmatic factors, and they shape their ministries around such means. They are mistaken. In no congregation studied so far are world views of members so diverse that one could consider that church a mere aggregate of miscellaneous believers. A single setting is common to most members, and for a minister to preach, teach, or counsel as if beliefs were private and optional fancies is both insensitive and irresponsible. Large churches may be structured to accommodate minor variations in world outlook (a 1,200 member congregation that was recently examined had four adult Sunday school classes, each of whose discourse favored by a slight margin a different world view category) but church story even there unfolds in a recognizable setting.

Through the discourse of its members the congregational story establishes its world setting. It is possible to demonstrate, using the results of the world view test instrument, the way that different congregations, even apparently inclusive mainline ones, have distinctive world views. Shown in the table below, in percentages, are the quite distinct patterns of response according to world view categories:

Church			Ca-nonic	Gnos-tic	Charis-matic	Em-piric	Total*
A. United Methodist, CT	(n =	71)	17.6	15.8	8.6	57.8	100.0
B. United Methodist, OH	(n =	92)	16.0	16.4	11.5	56.1	100.0
C. Episcopal, GA	(n =	71)	14.4	19.7	10.7	54.7	100.0
D. United Methodist, GA	(n =	97)	25.2	11.1	17.0	46.8	100.0
E. United Methodist, GA	(n =	99)	24.8	15.5	13.3	46.4	100.0
F. United Methodist, GA	(n =	155)	32.6	11.2	23.8	32.4	100.0
G. United Methodist, OH	(n =	105)	33.2	13.1	22.2	31.5	100.0
H. United Methodist, GA	(n =	48)	39.4	9.3	17.5	33.8	100.0
I. Southern Baptist, GA	(n =	114)	43.8	8.5	19.2	28.6	100.0
J. Church of God (Cleveland, TN), GA	(n =	53)	47.4	2.1	31.1	19.3	100.0
K. United Methodist, TN	(n =	63)	24.8	28.8	25.3	21.2	100.0

*Totals may vary slightly from 100.0, due to rounding.

A number of United Methodist congregations are included in this table to show the variations among churches in a single denomination. Denominations do not determine world view. A similar divergence could be shown among the scores of churches in other denominations. What the scores demonstrate is that congregations view their lives and act out their stories within distinctive settings. Some, like churches A and B, undertake a largely empiric negotiation. Others modify that perception by a secondary use of gnostic and canonic categories. Charismatic negotiations are more significant for churches F, G, and J. Church K is guided by a gnostic orientation.

Because the canonic and gnostic sides function both conceptually and statistically[8] as opposites, as do the charismatic and empiric sides, it is possible to display the world view pattern of a congregation in graphic form according to the x and y axes of a coordinate system. The horizontal x axis in Figure E

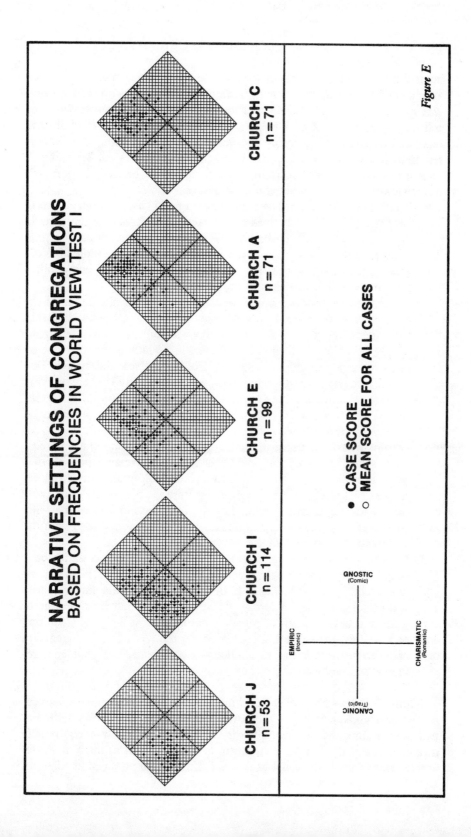

NARRATIVE SETTINGS OF CONGREGATIONS
BASED ON FREQUENCIES IN WORLD VIEW TEST I

CHURCH J
n = 53

CHURCH I
n = 114

CHURCH E
n = 99

CHURCH A
n = 71

CHURCH C
n = 71

● CASE SCORE
○ MEAN SCORE FOR ALL CASES

GNOSTIC
(Comic)

EMPIRIC
(Ironic)

CHARISMATIC
(Romantic)

CANONIC
(Tragic)

Figure E

holds in binary opposition the canonic and gnostic sides, while the vertical y axis has as its poles the charismatic and gnostic sides. Dots on the grid indicate scores of individual members of the congregation. One can see both the collective negotiation of a congregation within the interpretive field of story represented by this instrument and also the internal linking of members within each church. A blank copy of the grid is supplied in the Appendix.

In my research to date, certain correlations appear between a member's world view position and other church activities.

a. Parishioners who attend worship services nearly every Sunday seem to have scores closer to the mean orientation of the congregation than do those who participate in worship irregularly. Frequency of participation in other church programs, however, does not show the same high degree of correlation, suggesting a special, if not surprising, communicative link between worship and world view.

b. Pastors whose personal scores are close to the mean orientation of the congregation seem frequently to enjoy a more satisfying relationship with their congregations than do pastors whose own scores differ significantly from those of their flocks. Pastors in the latter situation must expend more interpretive energy to make themselves understood. Few congregations and pastors, however, understand why they are working so hard. Pastors and congregations whose world views differ significantly may instead express their discomfort with each other in *ad hominem* conflicts.[9]

c. Persons whose scores are on the periphery of the cluster of a congregation's scores are often marginal to the life of the congregation in other respects as well. Those in one congregation who were interviewed because their scores deviated so decidedly from the norm were also dissatisfied with the behavior of that church. They did not express their discontent in terms of divergent beliefs; rather, they found fault with the leadership and conduct of the church's programs.

d. Lay leaders of the congregation, however, do not necessarily have scores that approximate the mean orientation of the church. In a number of churches the scores of leaders are more canonic and/or charismatic than the congregational mean, suggesting that it is the role of leaders to bear in tragic or romantic heroic fashion the great tradition[10] of a stylized orthodox Christianity while the rest of the congregation may carry on a little tradition, a household wisdom, less beholden to religious stereotypes.

Within the broad horizon of world interpretations are individual congregational households, negotiating their own relation to the four modes. Different parishes circumstantiate themselves in different ways, a few unequivocally dwelling within the narrative structure of a certain genre, many more favoring one category but using as well the interpretive power of another. In every instance, however, whatever cast its story takes, a congregation derives its world view from the struggle of the entire field of human interpretation. No church, no person, identifies the world merely by self-held beliefs. The world gains its meaning only because human imagination accounts for the world in an interwrought narrative texture of many views. The storied world substantiates, apportions, and links the full multitude of idiomatic parochial stories.[11] To locate all beliefs on a single line between liberal and conservative poles is to succumb to a conceptual convenience that limits and flattens what people actually say they perceive and overlooks the larger symbolic struggle in which all people participate. One's peculiar belief is a privilege wrought by the intricate labor of all humanity.

NOTES

1. See chap. 2, n. 74.

2. Melvin Williams acknowledges that the concept of "observing participant" was earlier used by Bennetta Jules-Rosette in her study of an African independent church that she herself joined: *African Apostles: Ritual and Conversion in the Church of John Maranke* (Ithaca, N.Y.: Cornell Univ. Press, 1975).

3. Melvin D. Williams, "The Conflict of Corporate Church and Spiritual Community," in Carl S. Dudley, ed., *Building Effective Ministry*, 56.

4. James P. Spradley, *Participant Observation* (New York: Holt, Rinehart & Winston, 1980), and *The Ethnographic Interview* (New York: Holt, Rinehart & Winston, 1979), are careful introductions to ethnographic field work, although the procedures they set forth may be more elaborate than "observing participants" may want or need to follow. Less painstaking procedures are found in Julia G. Crane and Michael V. Angrosino, *Field Projects in Anthropology: A Student Handbook* (Morristown, N.J.: General Learning Press, 1974). See also Morris Freilich, ed., *Marginal Natives*, and the introductory treatments mentioned in chapter 2, n. 74.

5. Peter L. Berger, *The Sacred Canopy*; Peter L. Berger, *A Rumor of Angels: Modern Society and the Rediscovering of the Supernatural* (Garden City, N.Y.: Doubleday & Co., 1969); Mircea Eliade, *Myths, Dreams and Mysteries: The Encounter Between Contemporary Faiths and Archaic Reality* (London: Harvill Press, 1960), 19; Clifford Geertz, *The Interpretation of Cultures*, 107; Wade Clark Roof, *Community and Commitment*, 156; Philip E. Slater, *Microcosm: Structural, Psychological and Religious Evolution in Groups* (New York: John Wiley & Sons, 1966).

6. To determine whether the responses were in each case adequate reflections of the world view types, a panel of judges consisting of one professor and four graduate students in religion at Emory University rated each answer. No set of answers for a question received less than 80 percent agreement, and 18 of the 27 items were rated with 100 percent agreement. A table of the results of this process and certain other statistical tests of the world view instrument are reported in James F. Hopewell and G. Melton Mobley, "Identification of Congregational World Views: Measurement of Myth and Belief," paper presented at the Annual Meeting of the Society for the Scientific Study of Religion, Baltimore, Md., 29 October—1 November 1981.

7. Alasdair MacIntyre's concept of the accountability of the self in social discourse is one way to explain the growth of consonance between a personal and a group story (*After Virtue*, 203).

8. Factor analysis confirms that the sides function as opposites. See Hopewell and Mobley, "Identification."

9. ED. NOTE: In oral presentations, James Hopewell warned against the use of the world view test as a device to "match" congregations and potential pastors. As he wrote earlier in this chapter, any use of the test as "a substitute for searching conversation" about world view/setting and the other dimensions of narrative explored later in the book was in his view more likely to yield a mechanist reduction than a deepened symbolic understanding.

10. Elites in a society generally represent and uphold a designated orthodoxy which Redfield calls the Great Tradition. Others in the community are permitted to pursue the Little Tradition, a less defined wisdom passed on unofficially through families and friends. Robert Redfield, *Peasant Society and Culture* (Chicago: Univ. of Chicago Press, 1956), 67–104.

11. The world view differentiations seem to me to function in other religions. Islam possesses a canonic orientation in its Sunni form, a charismatic version in some Shi'ite sects and a gnostic side in Sufism. In Hinduism there are the canonic mode of karma yoga, the charismatic understanding of bhakti yoga, and the gnostic orientation of jnana yoga. Various developments in Buddhism reflect the same distinctions, such as the shift from a gnostic to a charismatic orientation required in the development of Mahayana from Thervadin sources. Buddhist sects in the United States today range from Jodo Shin-Shu (canonic) to Soka Gakkai (charismatic) to Zen (gnostic).

PART THREE

THE CHARACTERIZATION OF
PARISH STORY

7

PARISH GENIUS

Recall the course I helped to organize that became an unfortunate experience for Trinity United Methodist Church in Atlanta. Remember how, despite its promising syllabus and experienced leadership, the course collapsed almost as soon as it began. Readers of this book can no doubt propose cogent reasons for the breakdown, not least the remnants of racism and classism even in Trinity, a church splendidly accomplished in its quest for human solidarity. We who remained in the course acknowledged that theory and others, but still it seemed that there were particular local factors in Trinity's resistance. The church members who absented themselves from the church were, after all, sturdy veterans of other projects in racial bonding. The ground rules of the course had seemed, at least in prospect, fair enough to them. They were not bigots or fainthearted liberals. They just did not like the course. It contradicted Trinity's character.

It was when those of us who were left in the course sought to talk with the absentees about what had gone wrong that the story of Hero Trinity began to emerge. The dissenters felt that we did not understand Trinity's authentic nature. The best way they had to present the identity of the parish was to relate incidents that demonstrated the parish's character. The hero narrative provided the vehicle. It recounted, as laid out earlier in some detail, a harsh call to adventure, the appearance of a protective guide, a painful crossing of a threshold into adventure, then trials and the arrival of allies, followed by a union of races and a boon brought to the larger world. In age after age, epic singers have sung a structurally similar tale to identify a group's moral fiber: its hopes and trials, its accomplishments and crises. In telling both us and themselves about Hero Trinity, members were representing their character in one of the most forceful portrayals devised by humankind.

Stanley Hauerwas devotes the first part of *A Community of Character* to demonstrating the intimate connection between character and story.[1] "Every community and polity," he writes, "involves and requires a narrative,"[2] actually a constellation of stories, that acts to indicate and to inculcate a society's collective character. Using Richard Adams's story of an intrepid group of rabbits in *Watership Down*, Hauerwas demonstrates how narrative acts doubly to describe and provide the identity of a group. In persisting against great odds, the rabbits exemplify their own myth, and, in exemplifying their own myth, they persist against great odds. Hauerwas's point is to show that, because Christian churches are also "story shaped communities," the account of Christ's kingdom both describes and transforms the character of ordinary Christians in our congregations.

Hauerwas thus introduces several different aspects of the link between social character and story. Functioning descriptively, story expresses a narrative coherence among the disparate states and events that constitute the identity of the community. In this way, story primarily *recounts* social character. But narrative in its telling also changes group identity, modifying self-understanding and altering corporate behavior; so story also *informs* character. Further, narrative structures shape the basic ways a society values and interprets its life; story as paradigm here *accounts for* social character. To these descriptive and operative functions of community narrative, Hauerwas adds another action that is normative: in the Christian community is embedded the Christian story that judges and redeems the other actions of narrative. By so doing, story *transforms* group character.

In telling us the story of Trinity Church, the persons who had left the course were primarily *recounting* their social character, knitting into narrative form its significant elements. Our noting the association of the Trinity story with the Hero journey was an attempt to *account for* Trinity's character, to find its structural associations. Both we and the truants also witnessed to evidence of the *transforming* Christian story at work as well in Trinity's character. Thus in characterizing Trinity, the absentees recounted its story as its history, the rest of us accounted for its story as its metaphor, and both we and they witnessed the story transformed as gospel. Had the course progressed in the manner we had hoped, we would probably have also employed the *informing* aspect of narrative, sketching the story as a scenario for action.

Our course ran aground because it repudiated one of these links between narrative and character: the metaphorical link, the representation of the Trinity story by the Hero story. Our study, we ruefully discovered, had approached the Hero cycle from the wrong direction. As earlier confessed, the course had usurped from Trinity itself the role of bearer of a blessing to the larger community: we had tried to impose such a boon on Trinity and to ignore what Trinity had labored through great peril to deliver. We had also failed to celebrate the other phases of Trinity's heroic journey: its trials, its alliances, its "sacred union" of the races. We had, in other words, systematically ignored the metaphorical aspect of Trinity's storied character. In retrospect, it appears that though we may have been sensitive to parts of Trinity's identity, we had, to our peril, ignored Hero, its spirit.

THE SPIRIT OF THE
CONGREGATION

When pastors refer to the "unique personality" of a congregation, they engage in an ancient practice of representing a community's character by a singular spirit. The spirits associated with a community's masks (*personae*) were early "persons" that symbolized the particular ethos of a society. Until recent decades, for example, Liberian people in Poro Society masks both represented and regulated corporate life in the West African interior.[3] In donning a mask and a concealing costume, a Poro member joined the mask's spirit to perform stylized tasks and movements that not only governed much of community behavior but also impersonated the hopes and values that shaped the society's character. Spirits that identify and guide the nature of a community also appear in the New Testament. Angels of individual churches are vividly addressed in the second and third chapters of Revelation. The angels both personify the churches—Laodicea's, for instance, is accused of lukewarmness (3:14–17)—and speak to them.

But the assiduous advocates of community spirit were the Romans. Armed with the earlier Greek understanding of *daemon* (the tutelary spirit of an individual), the Romans so institutionalized the concept that virtually any social group could claim an associated sacred being. This being was called the group's *genius*. Families were identified and protected by the *genius familiae*, and Rome itself was personified by the *genius Populi Romani*. "The Genius," reports Georges Dumezil, "is no doubt an expression of the originality, of the distinctive personality, and, occasionally of the esprit de corps of these various collective bodies."[4] Some evidence suggests that the naming of a particular saint as patron to an early Christian congregation built upon the concept of *genius domus*, the spirit of the household. If so, "St. Mark's Church" would have signified not merely its members' high regard for the evangelist but also their confidence that the spirit of Saint Mark actually personified and oversaw the congregation.

In neither centuries past nor today, however, was a parish genius such as Hero Trinity considered a free-standing independent deity. Instead, genius is an immanent spirit, standing for the church, its mythic story a metaphor that echoes the congregation's story, giving it a resonant identity and augmenting the church's power of self-reference. To be able to say "We are St. Mark's" is to adopt a powerful narrative that in turn characterizes its parish.

Attempts to describe the character of a congregation by means other than narrative have not been very successful. Some have attempted to assess by questionnaire the "climate" of a church. These inquiries ask members to scale their corporate propensities, such as their tendency to emotional display or their attention to administrative order. The problem with such approaches is that they yield measurements of disparate traits but no framework for understanding the relation of the traits to each other or to a coherent whole. Narrative supplies such a framework. It is primarily in narrative that the character of the congregation emerges as an authentic figure that embodies and historically enacts a variety of traits. A storied *persona* best suggests the "unique personality" that pastors sense that their congregations possess.

The use of mythic figures to distinguish individual societies has continued, though many of the figures have long since lost any social or religious power. Nietzsche, for instance, found it helpful to distinguish Apollonian (aesthetic, ordered) from Dionysian (emotional, spontaneous) cultures.[5] Nietzsche's distinction has since been employed by both anthropologists[6] and sociologists.[7] Other figures are similarly employed: Meyer Fortes, in his ethnography of the Tallensi, uses the Oedipus and Job stories to characterize local custom and outlook.[8] Myths are the fascinating, evocative, succinct metaphors by which societies throughout all times, including our own, catch sight of themselves.

Note the extraordinary susceptibility of the local church to interpretation by myth. Earlier we showed how modern concepts of the congregation were based upon four arguments that Stephen Pepper termed root metaphors: contextual, mechanist, organicist, and formist or symbolic. But metaphors, as Victor Turner avers, are also "a species of liminal monster . . . whose combination of familiar and unfamiliar features, or unfamiliar combination of familiar features provokes us to thought, provides us with new perspectives."[9] We can find not only monsters but also ghosts, leviathans, and totems inhabiting the four metaphorical concepts of local church.[10]

Half close your eyes and glimpse the mythic creatures lurking within our four quite sober, disciplined interpretations of the parish. Consider first the contextual depiction of the parish, common in the 1960s, which portrayed it as imprisoned within its physical structure. Only insofar as the church could escape such confines would it assume its true purpose: to pervade the context of larger social surroundings and there to serve the political and economic needs of the world. In this it may be likened to a ghost. In ghost stories the present physical body entombs the spirit. To fulfill its essential nature the ghost must escape its material nature and, disembodied, haunt its context. There it makes its numinous contribution. The spirit of the contextual church is a vaporous ghost, and thus the form and identity of the contextual church are elusive.

Contradicting the contextual interpretation of the congregation is the mechanist understanding that seeks to revive the physical, tangible church by scientific techniques. Once revived, the church is set to work and grow. Within the image of a mechanist congregation is the figure of a monster. Monsters are different from ghosts. They are mechanistic, while ghosts are animistic. Like the figure created by Dr. Frankenstein, the monster comes to life by a scientific manipulation of inert forms. Now daunting readers for over 160 years, Frankenstein's monster expresses the promise that life is not an elusive, ghostly spirit but the result of the combination of mass and energy subjected to expert knowledge. Thus by consecrated pragmatism a congregation can, in the monstrous view, be given life. It grows efficient and productive, as Frankenstein's monster might have done had he not frightened everybody. Mechanist interpretations of the church are powered by monstrous images.

Still another creature inhabits the organicist conception of the local church: the leviathan. According to Thomas Hobbes, the leviathan is the huge "mortal god" whose like is not upon earth.[11] Its system organizes the organicist hope for the parish, that disparate sorts of humanity will by covenant be brought to a wholeness greater than any of its parts. For both Hobbes and Herman Melville the leviathan arises in the midst of antagonism, but when human beings finally comprehend its harmonious system, the highest of human hopes are fulfilled. For Hobbes, the prior antagonism is a poor, nasty, brutish, and short life; through social contract, the commonwealth is established as a remedy. *Moby Dick* begins with the antagonism that fires the heart of Captain Ahab but is concluded in the sweet fellowship of the whalers. "Inner Leviathan," says Robert Zoellner, "becomes a vigorous antidote for the alienation from others and separation from self which are the consequence of an astringent New England Puritanism and an Ahabian view of the world as antagonist."[12] Within organicist notions swims the giant reconciling leviathan.

The fourth approach to the congregation, the symbolic, is figured by the totem, the most potent of metaphors. Totems are to anyone else quite ordinary beings—rabbits, dogs, even plants, but to the people whom they represent they encapsule the group's identity. For Emile Durkheim they were the elemental symbol of the community. Totem imputes a different concept of church, not one monstrously efficient, or spiritually pervasive, or whalishly inclusive. It argues that any community reflects a structure and peculiar idiom within which the meaning and identity of its members are expressed.

ETHOS AND MYTHOS

What might account for the descriptive connection that I persistently uncover between the features of myth and those of a congregation's character? Myth is a primal account of the world, a classical representation of reality. Local character, by contrast, refers to the distinctive values, preferred style of behavior, and mood that together identify a contemporary group's ethos. A connection between myth and world view would at first glance seem easier to argue, because both deal in ultimate meanings. The link between the perceptions of myth and the preferences of character is not immediately apparent: myths employ the indicative language of belief, while character involves the subjunctive language of value. And myths, moreover, primarily refer to the past, often to a time before history, while character has a purchase on the future. To have character, as Hauerwas points out, means that one possesses not only particular traits but also the moral strength to respond tomorrow in ways contrary to prevailing custom. Character "denotes not only what is distinctive but also what is in some measure deliberate, what a man can decide to be opposed to what he is naturally."[13] On the face of it, the role of myth in representing character is difficult to establish.

Yet the Hero journey characterized Trinity Church, and from preliterate times mythic beings in the forms of masks, angels, genii, and saints have served to identify the local community. As noted above, post-Enlightenment students of human culture have continued to use mythic figures like Apollo and Dionysius to distinguish in trenchant form the ethoi of particular cultures. And ghosts, monsters, leviathans, and totems seem each to dwell in a root metaphor that shapes consciousness of the nature of the congregation. How, then, might this unlikely linkage between myths and ethos be explained?

Others who have observed the connection have advanced two theories. The first is that a deep archetype controls the expression of both myth and ethos. Advocating this view, followers of Carl Jung propound a specific, interactive engagement with archetypal entities. "The Gods grab us," David Miller says in animistic hyperbole, "and we play out their stories."[14] Miller's polytheism springs from a psychology in which a number of mythological figures populate a collective unconscious that patterns the behavior of both individuals and their societies. Especially on the occasion of ritual action or stylized behavior, the archetypal images give structure and meaning to the way people act and value their lives.

Miller employs the archetypal theories of James Hillman. Hillman himself writes:

> Archetypal psychology envisions the fundamental idea of the psyche to be the expressions of persons—Hero, Nymph, Mother, Senex, Child, Trickster, Amazon, Puer and many other specific prototypes bearing the names and stories of the Gods. These are the root metaphors. They provide the patterns of our thinking as well as of feeling and doing. They give all our psychic functions—whether thinking, feeling, perceiving or remembering—their imaginal life, their internal coherence, their force, their necessity, their ultimate intelligibility.[15]

In archetypal theory, myth is defined as the story that tells the congregation. In this argument, if the character of a particular local church were found to be Dionysian, the explanation would be that a deep paradigm of Dionysian norms and dynamisms informs the way the parish values and acts.

Other observers argue in a similar vein for the existence of deep structures that shape the character of a group. Victor Turner proposes the presence of root paradigms that function as mental models of acceptable conduct, guiding the performance of people during a community crisis.[16] And Don Browning, looking specifically at congregations and their moral decisions, uncovers five levels of symbolic and instrumental action, the most fundamental a metaphorical basement that harbors myths and symbols that fashion more obvious congregational norms and behavior.[17]

By using arguments that affirm the existence of archetypes or root paradigms, one might reason that the consonance between myth and social character is a result of their mutual dependence upon deep cultural templates that shape their distinctive appearance. Hero and Trinity resemble each other because both are funded by a common deep structure. In such an understanding, the archetype or paradigm persists through time almost independent of its observable manifestations. Turner compares a root paradigm to a strand of DNA, which profoundly influences the cellular structure of its host but nevertheless keeps its autonomy. The archetypes of a collective unconscious likewise continue through countless generations of societies that display their shaping power.

The other major argument holds that the myth is itself a product of the struggle of a community for the particularity of its character. This approach does not attribute the similarities between a myth and a society's ethos to an influential but independent paradigm, but posits instead the similarities as the direct result of a community's labor for, in Alasdair MacIntyre's term, its moral particularity.[18] To survive, a community must develop and maintain a specific, and therefore particular, constellation of outlooks and values. Unless it possesses a distinctive character recognizable to its members, the community dissolves in anomie. A group needs to identify "who we are" in order to embody its otherwise amorphous sentiments and actions. Myth quite literally characterizes the community.

In this second approach, myths and the struggle for social character fit together in two ways. First, the establishment of moral identity requires both narratively shaped world view and propositionally shaped ethic.[19] The development of group ethos demands images and stories perhaps even more than a code of abstract prescriptions. A group more often follows a pattern of behavior because it is story-shaped than because it responds to a set of norms. Myth, then, helps to fashion community values and also reflects their formation.

Rejecting the archetypal origin of myth, Walter Burkert writes:

The phenomena of collective importance which are verbalized by applying traditional tales are to be found, first of all, in social life. Instructions or presentations of the family, clan, or city are explained and justified by tales—"charter myths" in Malinowski's term—or knowledge about religious ritual, authoritative and absolutely serious ritual, and about the gods involved, is expressed and passed on in the form of such tales; then there are the hopes and fears connected with the course of nature, the seasons, and the activities of food supply; there is the desperate experience of disease. But also quite general problems of human society, such as marriage rules and incest, or even the organization of nature and the universe, may be the subject of [myths]; . . . it is only philosophical interest, both ancient and modern, that tends to isolate the myths of origin and cosmogony, which in their proper setting usually have some practical reference to the institutions of a city or a clan.[20]

For all of their seemingly exotic features, myths in this view are closely associated with maintaining the corporate life of the community, typifying it, exploring it, enforcing it.

A second feature of the struggle for community character that links it to myth is that it results in a selection from among several behavioral and descriptive options. Individual character, by Hauerwas's reckoning, is "the qualification of our self agency, formed by our having certain intentions (and beliefs) rather than others. . . . Our character is our deliberate disposition to use a certain range of reasons rather than others."[21] A group gains moral particularity in its local and immediate appropriation from a universe of values and their interpretations. In becoming accountable, a community selects particular accounts that specifically portray and inform the group's character.

It can be argued, therefore, that a twentieth-century church like Trinity can echo a millennia-old Hero pattern because both group and myth participate in the process of self-qualification: the reduction of the group's potential traits, connections, and moods from a full panoply of possibilities to a particular pattern of values. The ethos of Trinity is the result both of choices it has made, some unconscious and some conscious (such as its decision not to move to an Atlanta suburb), and of matters beyond its control (the attitudes of legislators across the street), each giving Trinity's character its qualification. The process of character modification continues; it develops or deteriorates, but always in relation to the particular choices Trinity makes and the particular circumstances the church encounters. Though Trinity's story is distinctive, it is not unique. Through the centuries, other groups have met with (or hoped for) structurally similar adventures. And these have been represented in the many versions of the Hero journey. The myth interprets the desires and experience of communities that have qualified their ethoi in forms similar to those which characterize Trinity Church.

Hence the perennial argument about the nature of myth offers us the two not entirely antithetical explanations of the consonance of myth and ethos. Hero Trinity may be authentic because a deep metaphor generates both the narrative and societal patterns. Or Hero Trinity may represent the current ethical configuration of a congregation because the myth brings interpretive power to that pattern, the myth itself the product of congruent social situations. Though neither explanation is easy to discount or verify, I find myself—as must be evident—drawn to the second because it permits the characterization of a church by myth without suggesting that the church is indelibly imprinted with a particular pattern of behavior. That accords with my observations and experience: powerfully descriptive and formative as myth and ethos may be, for congregations that authentically "have character" the future is not preternaturally determined. Character may in specific ways limit the range of future choices a congregation is equipped to make. But character also provides the moral power for a congregation to make its own choices.

FACTORS IN CHARACTER

There are several different ways to interpret to a congregation its particular character, the most helpful of which are narrative in form. A written history of the parish, if it can be propelled beyond names and dates to explore the church's identity, can reveal the richness of character. So can vignettes that disclose certain congregational traits and dispositions. The stories adumbrated in responses of members to interviews or to questionnaires that focus on preferences and dislikes may also be suggestive, although the usual reduction of this data to statistics ("47.5 percent want a new adult group; 22.3 percent do not; 11.2 percent did not care, and 19.0 percent did not answer") actually says surprisingly little about parish character ("more people agreed with the 'new adult group' answer than with any other answer, but more people avoided this answer than favored it"). Pastors considering a call to a congregation often complain about how little they learn about the church from a "parish profile" in which answers of members to long questionnaires have been quantified. What prospective pastors want to hear is the church's inside story, the drama within which they might become a principal actor.

The final chapter in this section on characterization will examine methods by which a congregation can come to terms with its history and other stories, deal with problems of narrative distortion, and contemplate the possibility of character transformation. Before then, I want to advocate what I consider a more difficult but rewarding channel to understanding congregational ethos: the task of apprehending the parish genius, the myth that recounts and accounts for a congregation's character.

This unusual undertaking benefits a congregation in several ways but also poses some difficulties. Myth enables a community, now as it did in the past, to speak concisely about its complex cultural character. To say, for example, that a society is narcissistic is to report a descriptive mouthful in a single mythic word. For a congregation to be able to refer to itself as Valhalla, as one I know now does, permits it to recall an intricate self-portrait that features (a) absentee warrior-salesmen who return bruised to the household, (b) subordinate women, (c) an emphasis upon alcohol and boisterous games, and (d) an Odinesque style of leadership. But not only does a church gain in myth a metaphor by which to model the features of character, it also finds a way to address publicly and corporately features, such as drinking and male dominance, that heretofore were explained as the problems of individual members, and then only in private conversation.

The metaphorical power of a myth also gives members a poetic jolt. One sees one's church in fresh terms, as I did in exploring the disastrous conclusion of the Meleager myth that I think characterized the Episcopal congregation I served as founding pastor. Understanding a congregation to be participant in a mythic structure also helps a leader understand how the pattern of its corporate action may override his or her personal influence. In one of the stories that we shall examine in the next chapter, a pastor with high ideals was dismissed because of the way he tried to insert into parish life his personal convictions. In the period that the vote against him was taken and he served his last months, he, I, and a group of the church's leaders were exploring the congregation's character and mythic pattern. The myth we discovered in part gave symbolic form to the dismissal incident, helped the pastor to see his personal plight in a larger contextual scheme, and gave the members some images by which to discuss the deeply embarrassing incident with their pastor.

Most of all, the use of myths helps a congregation affirm its juncture with the human race. To discover that a local church's most intimate and intense activities do not at their base reflect a withdrawal from the world but rather a participation in public, mythic structures can be a liberating perception about the symbolic depth and breadth of church activity. Things that seemed to be household routines and petty indulgences in the parish are by myth lifted to the mystery of the whole storied world, the *oikoumenē*.

There are also dangers in mythopoesis. Unless the congregation is itself actively involved in the steps and reasons for mythic characterization, the result will probably appear to the congregation strange and even repulsive. Members not used to having their congregation depicted in terms other than Christian or traditional metaphors (such as family and fortress) can easily miss the point. Comments on, say, the Orphic quality of their common life, unless carefully developed, may be misunderstood among the very people whose life together the mythic concept might illuminate; if this happens, the myth's contribution to congregational self-understanding and self-transcendence will be lost.

A myth can also stereotype a congregation, implying that the tale exhausts all that is worth knowing about the church and its future. It is precisely this danger of reducing the thick description of a parish to a Procrustean myth that makes me wary of theories about deep mythic paradigms as archetypes that would grab a parish and force it to work out a mythic story. A more helpful and I think accurate understanding of myth portrays it as a story by which groups qualify their character and catch sight of themselves in doing so. The myth of a congregation binds neither behavior nor the description of behavior. Rather, myth is the companion story, the genius, that gives corporate life a metaphorical resonance.

Myths also present major hermeneutical problems in their relation to the Christian gospel. It is easier for most people to understand the complex link between, for instance, Christian stories and an individual person with Oedipal tendencies than it is to comprehend the interpretive nexus of the gospel and a congregation characterized by the Oedipal tale. We are, on the whole, willing to believe that individuals may have distinctive, mythically resonant personalities and yet be saved in, even through, their characteristic fullness. But to learn that the genius of one's local church approximates some deity such as Demeter may stir up an inquisitorial zeal to purge the corporate ethos of its non-Christian characteristics.

Such a purge is of course culturally impossible, and it misses the point of an incarnational gospel. The servant form that Jesus assumed was not culture free. It participated in the mythic structures of a specific time and people; indeed, the message thus conveyed is that it is within such human finitude that the redeeming love of God occurs.

Does this mean that biblical stories might be the myths that best characterize the congregation? I do not draw from the rich resources of the Bible for mythic patterns by which to frame a congregation's life, and I am frequently asked why. Two basic reasons account for my reluctance, the second more significant than the first. The first reason is that Bible stories are standard fare for Christian congregations. A comparison of the life of a congregation with that of the Children of Israel, or the parish with a parable, is a common device, often superficially employed in the church today. Even if powerfully presented, such comparisons seldom awaken a fresh self-understanding of the church's corporate nature. Nonbiblical myths are different. Members are not used to comparisons with Daedalus or Oedipus. They pay attention, argue, repeat what they hear, and sometimes enrich the comparison with further examples. That seldom happens with biblical comparisons.

The second reason stems from, and I think explains, the fact that in none of my studies has a biblical story seemed to me adequately to identify the ethos of a particular congregation. For the Christian congregation, biblical narrative is different from other mythic stories. It serves a different function and, as Northrop Frye contends, provides a structurally different message from the other myths of the world. Frye argues that the Bible, although full of metaphors, is not essentially metaphorical but rather rhetorical, a "concerned address" in which Christians (and, in Frye's view, Western culture as a whole) find themselves to be the object, not the topic. For Christians, the Bible does not function as an anthology of likely tales with descriptive implications:

> The linguistic idiom of the Bible does not really coincide with our three phases of language, important as these phases have been in the history of its influence. It is not metaphorical like poetry, though it is full of metaphor, and is as poetic as it can well be without being a work of literature. It is really a fourth form of expression, for which I use the now well-established term kerygma, proclamation.[22]

To use biblical narrative as a descriptive tool by which to picture the local church is to reduce its meaning to that of a companion image, a metaphor that reflects and enriches careful self-understanding. Eviscerated from such a use of the Bible is its prophetic, challenging, always elusive message which often defies self-understanding. The church canonizes the Bible not because it provides a mythical picture of congregations but because it contends with the self-characterizations that Christian households are wont to construct. But the kerygma does not void the myths by which society characterizes itself. The kerygma instead gives them radical, critical, and finally redemptive meaning.

In chapter 9 I shall suggest methods and devices for "finding" a myth that has interpretive significance for a particular congregation. Here I want to demonstrate, by telling a congregational story in the light of its myth, the four features of both story and myth to which I pay special attention in the search for character. When I find correspondence between myth and ethos at each of these points, tale and congregational character seem to illuminate each other. The four points for correlation are remarkably similar to a typology of four elements of character that Richard Bondi developed independently and by a different method.[23] In his investigation of how story influences personal character, Bondi undertakes a phenomenology of the self to discover the various aspects by which the self exists in relation to the world. My own study is aimed at the rationale for the consonance of a particular myth with a particular ethos, but our corresponding results suggest their mutual utility in further analysis.

I look at four elements—each a moment or quality in which character tells:

1. *Crisis and integration*: In a loss or dislocation, what is the characteristic response and reintegration that is sought?
2. *Proficiency*: What is the characteristic skill, the chosen manner of doing things, the reliable pattern of behavior?
3. *Mood*: What is the characteristic temperament, the emotional atmosphere?
4. *Hope*: What end is characteristically expected and sought?

Note how these four elements point to the character of a church that began its ministry not too far away from Trinity Church.

DAEDALUS CHURCH

On the surface the story of this congregation is familiar enough. It is the ambiguous history of a middle-class, white church in the last decade, during which its mainline denomination declined in membership and influence. In the late 1960s members of the church sold their building on a busy metropolitan corner to purchase property in a growing suburb to which most of them had already moved and from which they hoped to gain further members. An alert and active group, they designed their new building in a way that would make it distinctive. They paid special attention to the welcoming of newcomers, and, in the early 1970s, they called to their pulpit a talented pastor who they felt would attract young people and those in the neighborhood searching for a church home. Although several churches around them grew substantially in size, theirs did not. As the 1970s passed, they concentrated upon the development of their corporate worship life and a deeper understanding of the covenant they sought to share. Except for nagging concerns about losing their own young people, they now consider themselves a reasonably secure and involved, though not a popular, congregation.

The story of the congregation gains character and moral significance as it unfolds in greater detail. The congregation's own genius emerges, distinguished from the field of other forms, but empowered by a resonant association with other stories that throughout history have related the same design. The story, when further rendered, echoes the myth of Daedalus.

Visitors complain that Daedalus Church is hard to find because its building is invisible from the road and its driveway entrance sandwiched between a shopping mall and a woods through which its road winds. A meandering footpath surrounds the building, and the building by architect's plan is a further labyrinth. Because the structure is unlike most churches and does not have spires and doors to direct a visitor to the sanctuary, a newcomer is first puzzled about how to enter the building and, once inside, must decide from among three corridors which one might lead to the worship area. In the words of its designers, the building "unfolds" as people move through it. "You work your way in, and it keeps on opening." Having entered the sanctuary, worshipers find themselves, however, back in the woods, because the area is a small auditorium facing a huge glass proscenium that brings the woods inside. The woods captivate the worshipers. "If that sanctuary were not dominated by a twenty-seven foot cross," says the pastor, "I would be worried by its window."

Mood

The clever craftsman who designed the labyrinth for King Minos was Daedalus, an Athenian immigrant who came south to serve the Cretan kingdom. "We are all outsiders of one sort or another," says a Jew who became a member of the congregation. A hundred years earlier the founders of the church were northerners who came to this southern city to teach in the region's first black college, an institution their denomination had helped to establish. Since then the congregation has attracted primarily other northerners and clever people—academics and other professionals—disaffected from their childhood denominations. More than a dozen Baptist and Methodist clergy sympathetic to black causes in the 1960s left their own denominations and now make Daedalus Church their home. Members in general consider themselves "enlightened, . . . a one percent among ninety-nine percent with different views." The labyrinth was created by Daedalus to house the half man, half bull borne of Pasiphaë, wife of Minos, who lusted for the white bull given Minos by Poseidon of the Sea. She had persuaded Daedalus to fashion the shell of a cow that she could enter. In unnatural love the bull mounted her and Minotaur was born. In the years since Reconstruction the members of the congregation have frequently been called Yankee nigger-lovers.

Proficiency

Daedalus is the clever artist and inventor, his work on display in temples throughout the Mediterranean. He creates a cunning honeycomb, a magic sword, toys, lifelike statues, and wings. The church's daily life celebrates the originality of its members. Local artists hang their work in its halls; art, craft, and bread-baking classes are held each week. A mark of membership is to possess a work fashioned by another parishioner: "We need to own something—a rug, metal sculpture, or painting—made by another member."

Crisis and integration

Every ninth year, seven Athenian boys and seven Athenian maidens were sacrificed to the Minotaur. The problem at Daedalus Church is the children. Perhaps because the church must coax the adults, it leaves the needs of youth less tended. Although the present pastor was selected a decade earlier with the hope that he could do something for the young people, and elaborate schemes are made each year to involve the youth, the younger members do not participate as they do in nearby Methodist and Baptist churches. Many members think their children will not succeed them in the pews; the off-spring of the pastor do not participate.

Icarus, son of Daedalus, flew with him but so close to the sun that the wax in his wings melted and he fell into the sea. "A lot of our kids are not going to be part of this in the future." "The future generation may not be our children, but other people who have since grown up."

Hope

"This is the church of the last resort," says one of its members, a university professor who struggles for faith in a secular era. "For us it is not a question of which church but whether church at all." The church serves those who want a spirituality although they "are afraid of being and appearing pious, holier than thou." Were this congregation not to offer a way by which the religiously disaffected can find spiritual help, this group would leave the organized church altogether.

Unlike the protagonists of many myths, Daedalus and the other actors are not divine. As a human being, Daedalus creates his own mortal means of transcendence, showing Theseus how to thread his way out of the maze, but chiefly by fashioning for himself and his son the wings by which they escape the land and surrounding seas of Crete.

Each Sunday the pastor makes wings for the congregation. Fighting the natural drama of squirrels and birds and swaying branches that flood the worship service through the giant window, the pastor, beginning nonchalantly, slowly reintroduces the God of history, the deity of Israel. His sermons and patter throughout the service brilliantly coax the congregation into reconsidering Christian terms and acts they long ago discounted—heaven, Sabbath, baptism. "Hey, folks," the pastor later imitates his own style, "this language is yours as well as that of the fundamentalists." The congregation assists him at the several points in worship where they add their own thoughts, and, for an hour, they together fly beyond the confines of their present earthbound character.

Daedalus is neither god nor hero. He survives by his human ingenuity in a world of threats. Daedalus' story foreshadows the account of outsiders throughout history who create mazes to involve themselves in, and wings to extricate themselves from the mystery, and who lose their children in the process.

NOTES

1. Stanley Hauerwas, *A Community of Character*, 9–35. See also Alasdair MacIntyre, *After Virtue*, chap. 15.

2. Hauerwas, *Community of Character*, 4.

3. George W. Harley, *Masks as Agents of Social Control in Northeast Liberia*, vol. 32, no. 2, Papers of the Peabody Museum of Harvard University (Cambridge, Mass.: Peabody Museum, 1950); *Notes on the Poro in Liberia*, vol. 19, no. 2, Papers of the Peabody Museum of Harvard University (Cambridge, Mass.: Peabody Museum, 1941).

4. Georges Dumezil, *Archaic Roman Religion*, vol. 1 (Chicago: Univ. of Chicago Press, 1970), 362. A study of the word "genius" is found on pp. 357–63.

5. Friedrich Nietzsche, *The Birth of Tragedy* (New York: Random House, 1967), 33–144.

6. Ruth Benedict, *Patterns of Culture* (Boston: Houghton Mifflin Co., 1934).

7. Andrew M. Greeley, *The Denominational Society: A Sociological Approach to Religion in America* (Glenview, Ill.: Scott, Foresman & Co., 1972).

8. Meyer Fortes, *Oedipus and Job in West African Religion*, with an essay by Robin Horton (Cambridge: Cambridge Univ. Press, 1983).

9. Turner, *Dramas, Fields and Metaphors*, 31.

10. James F. Hopewell, "Ghostly and Monstrous Churches," *The Christian Century* 99 (1982).

11. Thomas Hobbes, *Leviathan* (London: Collins, 1962), 176.

12. Robert Zoellner, *Salt Sea Mastodon: A Reading of Moby Dick* (Berkeley and Los Angeles: Univ. of California Press, 1973), 158.

13. Stanley Hauerwas, *Vision and Virtue: Essays in Christian Ethical Reflection* (Notre Dame: Univ. of Notre Dame Press, 1981), 52.

14. David Miller builds upon the archetypal psychology of James Hillman. "The Gods and Goddesses live through our psychic structures. They are given in the fundamental nature of our being, and they manifest our behaviors. . . . The Gods are Powers. They are the potency in each of us, in societies and nature. . . . By calling for an *impersonal* dimension in our psychology, Hillman reaches below or beyond the merely personal and discovers that the Gods and Goddesses are worlds of being and meaning in which my personal life participates" (David L. Miller, *The New Polytheism: Rebirth of the Gods and Goddesses* [New York: Harper & Row, 1974], 59–61).

15. James Hillman, *Re-Visioning Psychology* (New York: Harper & Row, 1975), 128. Elsewhere Hillman describes the functioning archetypal complexes of fifty-seven Greek, Hebrew, Chinese, and Indian deities.

16. Root paradigms are "certain consciously recognized (though not consciously grasped) cultural models in the heads of the main actors. . . . These have reference not only to the current state of social relationships existing or developing between actors, but also to the cultural goals, means, ideas, outlook, currents of thought, patterns of belief, and so on, which enter into those relationships, interpret them, and incline them to alliance or divisiveness. . . . Paradigms of this fundamental sort reach down to irreducible life stances of individuals, passing beneath conscious prehension to a fiduciary hold on what they sense to be axiomatic values, matters literally of life and death" (Turner, *Dramas*, 64).

17. Don S. Browning, "Integrating the Approaches: A Practical Theology," in Carl S. Dudley, ed., *Building Effective Ministry*, 220–37.

18. MacIntyre, *After Virtue*, 205.

19. Clifford Geertz, *The Interpretation of Cultures*, 87–141. See also Steven Tipton's study of ethical configurations in a Christian sect, a Zen center, and a human potential movement, in Steven M. Tipton, *Getting Saved from the Sixties: Moral Meaning in Conversion and Cultural Change* (Berkeley and Los Angeles: Univ. of California Press, 1982), 244–77.

20. Walter Burkert, *Structure and History in Greek Mythology and Ritual* (Berkeley and Los Angeles: Univ. of California Press, 1979), 23.

21. Hauerwas, *Vision and Virtue*, 59.

22. Northrop Frye, *The Great Code: The Bible and Literature* (New York: Harcourt Brace Jovanovich, 1981), 28.

23. Richard Bondi, "The Elements of Character," *Journal of Religious Ethics* 12 (December 1984). Addressing the unresolved question of how story influences personal character, Bondi undertakes an analysis of the aspects by which the self through character exists in relation to the world. He develops four elements: (*a*) "the capacity for intentional action" (which is similar to my category of proficiency); (*b*) "involvement with the affections and passions" (my category of mood); (*c*) "subjection to the accidents of history" (crisis and integration); (*d*) "the capacity of the heart" (my category of hope).

8

THREE CONGREGATIONS

The intent of this chapter is to observe how in each of three instances a myth helps express and explore the genius that characterizes a congregation. The subjects are three ordinary congregations, two from the same denomination and two drawing their membership from the same neighborhood. In spite of their similarities of affiliation and context, however, each of the churches displays a remarkably different ethos. For each a myth will be related that seems to catch up the special sort of crisis, proficiency, mood, and hope that individuates that church. Myth, as argued earlier, is a way of catching sight of one's corporate self. A good myth, from the perspective of this study of parish story, would be one that leads us into the thick of local church characterization.

BACKGROUND INFORMATION

The community I call Corinth,[1] the town in which I spent my sabbatical year, has changed during the last thirty years from a rural, rather backward county seat town into a satellite community for a large metropolitan area. Its population has doubled once and a half since 1960, the growth due to the influx of families of persons who work in the large city or in new local industries and service agencies, or who retire in Corinth, attracted by its extensive recreational facilities. The two "first churches" in town, Baptist and Methodist, both constituted at Corinth's founding nearly 150 years ago, have been profoundly altered by the newcomers. Membership in each has more than doubled since 1970, First Baptist now numbering 900 and First Methodist 400. Surprisingly few current members are county natives; only 5 percent of the Methodists have lived there from birth, and about 30 percent of the Baptists. The natives go to church elsewhere. They feel more at home in smaller churches farther away from the courthouse square, and frequently voice their suspicion of the modernist, watered-down religion of the first churches. Although some farmers are prominent and many politically significant in the county that surrounds Corinth, no farmer is a member of either First Baptist or First Methodist. The first churches serve instead white, middle-class business and professional families. Since they are close neighbors and business associates, the worshipers in the first churches find little religious or theological distinction between the two congregations, and some of them expressed discomfort with my attempt to discuss with them whatever differences there might be. Older members preferred to recall the period prior to 1940 when neither congregation had a full-time pastor and they would all attend one church on one Sunday and the other on the next, and in the same way attend together the staggered meetings of the Epworth League and the Baptist Training Union.

The third congregation described in this chapter is also United Methodist, but a younger church built to accommodate a major white population shift in the 1960s to a new suburban region within the metropolis itself. Lyle Schaller would term Bigelow Methodist a "teenaged church," because it is roughly that old and also because, after a spectacular growth to 1,250 members, it suffered an adolescent malaise that afflicted both its spirit and its program. The church is only now recovering. Bigelow serves primarily the families of business executives, many of whom travel throughout the week but live less than a ten-minute automobile ride away from its nondescript architecture. Two nearby Methodist churches enjoyed better fortune during the time of Bigelow's affliction, and the people of Bigelow frequently base their self-assessment upon their sense that the programs in the two other churches are livelier and church life more opulent.

World view test scores for the three churches were the following:

		Canonic	Gnostic	Charismatic	Empiric
Bigelow Methodist	(n = 97)	25.2%	11.1%	17.0%	46.8%
Corinth Methodist	(n = 99)	24.8	15.5	13.3	46.4
Corinth Baptist	(n = 114)	43.8	8.5	19.2	28.6

Differences between the world views of the two Methodist churches are relatively minor. The Baptist church is, as we shall see, far more distinct.

MYTHIC CONSONANCE

The character of each church is illumined by a myth. Corinth Baptist follows the pattern of Oedipus. The *New Larousse Encyclopedia of Mythology* summarizes the Oedipal myth as follows:

Laius, son of Labdacus, king of Thebes, had married Jocasta. Having been warned by an oracle that his son would one day kill him Laius carried the child to which Jocasta had just given birth to Mount Cithaeron. He pierced the infant's feet with a nail and tied them together solidly, hoping thus to be rid of him. But a shepherd found the child and took him to Polybus, King of Corinth, who adopted him and named him Oedipus because of his wounded foot. When Oedipus had grown up he learned his destiny from an oracle who told him that he would kill his father and marry his mother. Oedipus believed that he could escape this fate by exiling himself for ever from Corinth, never again seeing Polybus and his wife whom he assumed to be his true parents. This scruple was his own undoing. He went to Boeotia and on the road quarrelled with an unknown man whom he struck with his staff and killed. The victim was, indeed, Laius, his own father. Oedipus continued on his journey without suspecting that the first half of the oracle's prediction had been fulfilled. He arrived in Thebes where he learned that the region was being devastated by a fabulous monster with the face and bust of a woman, the body of a lion and the wings of a bird. Guarding the road to Thebes the Sphinx—as the monster was called—would stop all travellers and propose enigmas to them; those who were unable to solve her riddles she would devour. Creon, who had governed Thebes since the recent death of Laius, promised the crown and the hand of Jocasta to the man who delivered the city from this scourge. Oedipus resolved to attempt the feat. He was successful. The Sphinx asked him: "Which is the animal that has four feet in the morning, two at midday and three in the evening?" He answered: "Man, who in infancy crawls on all fours, who walks upright on two feet in maturity, and in his old age supports himself with a stick." The Sphinx was vanquished and threw herself into the sea.

And thus, still without realising it, Oedipus became the husband of his mother, Jocasta. From their union two sons were born, Eteocles and Polyneices, and two daughters, Antigone and Ismene. Oedipus, in spite of the double crime he had innocently committed, was honoured as a sovereign, devoted to his people's welfare, and appeared to prosper. But the Erinnyes were waiting. A terrible epidemic ravaged the land, decimating the population, and at the same time an incredible drought brought with it famine. When consulted, the oracle of Delphi replied that these scourges would not cease until the Thebans had driven the still unknown murderer of Laius out of the country. Oedipus, after having offered ritual maledictions against the assassin, undertook to find out who he was. His inquiries finally led to the discovery that the guilty man was none other than himself, and that Jocasta whom he had married was his mother. Jocasta in shame and grief hanged herself and Oedipus put out his own eyes. Then he went into exile, accompanied by his faithful daughter Antigone. He took refuge in the town of Colonus in Attica and, at last purified of his abominable crimes, disappeared mysteriously from the earth.[2]

In the same town, Corinth Methodist presents a character shared with the myth of Orpheus, here told by Edith Hamilton:

A few mortals [were] so excellent in their [music] that they almost equaled the divine performers. Of these by far the greatest was Orpheus. On his mother's side he was more than mortal. He was the son of one of the Muses and a Thracian prince. His mother gave him the gift of music and Thrace where he grew up fostered it. The Thracians were the most musical of the peoples of Greece. But Orhpeus had no rival there or anywhere except the gods alone. There was no limit to his power when he played and sang. No one and nothing could resist him. . . . Everything animate and inanimate followed him. He moved the rocks on the hillside and turned the courses of the rivers.

Little is told about his life before his ill-fated marriage, for which he is even better known than for his music, but he went on one famous expedition and proved himself a most useful member of it. He sailed with Jason on the *Argo*, and when the heroes were weary or the rowing was especially difficult he would strike his lyre and they would be aroused to fresh zeal and their oars would smite the sea together in time to the melody. Or if a quarrel threatened he would play so tenderly and soothingly that the fiercest spirits would grow calm and forget their anger. He saved the heroes, too, from the Sirens. When they heard far over the sea singing so enchantingly sweet that it drove out all other thoughts except a desperate longing to hear more, and they turned the ship to the shore where the Sirens sat, Orpheus snatched up his lyre and played a tune so clear and ringing that it drowned the sound of those lovely fatal voices. The ship was put back on her course and the winds sped her away from the dangerous place. If Orpheus had not been there the Argonauts, too, would have left their bones on the Sirens' island.

Where he first met and how he wooed the maiden he loved, Eurydice, we are not told, but it is clear that no maiden he wanted could have resisted the power of his song. They were married, but their joy was brief. Directly after the wedding, as the bride walked in a meadow with her bridesmaids, a viper stung her and she died. Orpheus' grief was overwhelming. He could not endure it. He determined to go down to the world of death and try to bring Eurydice back. . . .

He dared more than any other man ever dared for his love. He took the fearsome journey to the underworld. There he struck his lyre, and at the sound all that vast multitude were charmed to stillness. The dog Cerberus relaxed his guard; the wheel of Ixion stood motionless; Sisiphus sat at rest upon his stone; Tantalus forgot his thirst; for the first time the faces of the dread goddesses, the Furies, were wet with tears. The ruler of Hades drew near to listen with his queen. Orpheus sang . . . [and] no one under the spell of his voice could refuse him anything. He

> Drew iron tears down Pluto's cheek,
> And made Hell grant what Love did seek.

They summoned Eurydice and gave her to him, but upon one condition: that he would not look back at her as she followed him, until they had reached the upper world. So the two passed through the great doors of Hades to the path which would take them out of the darkness, climbing up and up. He knew that she must be just behind him, but he longed unutterably to give one glance to make sure. But now they were almost there, the blackness was turning gray; now he had stepped out joyfully into the daylight. Then he turned to her. It was too soon; she was still in the cavern. He saw her in the dim light, and he held out his arms to clasp her; but on the instant she was gone. She had slipped back into the darkness. All he heard was one faint word, "Farewell."

Desperately he tried to rush after her and follow her down, but he was not allowed. The gods would not consent to his entering the world of the dead a second time, while he was still alive. He was forced to return to the earth alone, in utter desolation. Then he forsook the company of men. He wandered through the wild solitudes of Thrace, comfortless except for his lyre, playing, always playing, and the rocks and the rivers and the trees heard him gladly, his only companions. But at last a band of Maenads came upon him. They were as frenzied as those who killed Pentheus so horribly. They slew the gentle musician, tearing him limb from limb, and flung the severed head into the swift river Hebrus. It was borne along past the river's mouth on to the Lesbian shore, nor had it suffered any change from the sea when the Muses found it and buried it in the sanctuary of the island. His limbs they gathered and placed in a tomb at the foot of Mount Olympus, and there to this day the nightingales sing more sweetly than anywhere else.[3]

And, as might befit a teenaged church, Bigelow Methodist is described in the fairy tale of Briar Rose, here told by the brothers Grimm, translated by Francis Magoun and Alexander Knappe:

In days of yore there was a king and a queen who every day used to say, "Oh, if we only had a child!" yet they never had one. Once when the queen was bathing, it happened that a frog crawled ashore out of the water and said to her, "Your wish will be fulfilled: before a year's out, you'll give birth to a daughter." What the frog said came to pass, and the queen gave birth to a girl; she was so beautiful that in his joy the king didn't know what to do and arranged a great feast. He invited not only his relatives, friends, and acquaintances, but also the wise women, that they might be gracious and well disposed toward the child. There were thirteen of them in his kingdom, but because he had only twelve gold plates from which they might eat, one of them had to stay home. The feast was celebrated with all splendor, and when it came to an end, the wise women presented the child with their marvelous gifts. One gave it virtue, the second beauty, the third riches, and so on, with everything the heart desires. When eleven had finished bestowing their gifts, suddenly the thirteenth came in. She wanted to revenge herself for not having been invited, and without greeting anyone or so much as looking at anyone, she cried out in a loud voice, "In her fifteenth year the king's daughter will prick herself with a spindle and fall down dead." Without another word she turned about and left the hall. Everybody was frightened. Then the twelfth, who still had her wish left, stepped up and because she couldn't undo the evil gift but merely temper it, said, "It won't be a real death; the princess will fall into a hundred years' deep sleep."

The king wanted to guard his dear child against this misfortune and issued a decree that all spindles throughout the whole kingdom should be burned. The gifts of the wise women were, however, quite fulfilled in the girl, for she was so beautiful, well mannered, friendly, and intelligent that whoever looked at her couldn't help loving her. On the very day she became fifteen the king and the queen happened not to be at home, and the girl was left all alone in the palace. She went all about, looking into rooms and chambers to her heart's content, and finally even got to an old tower. She climbed up the narrow winding stairs and came to a little door. There was a rusty key in the lock, and when she turned it, the door flew open and in the little room was sitting an old woman with a spindle and spinning her flax industriously. "Good day, Granny," said the king's daughter, "what are you doing there?" "I'm spinning," said the old woman, bobbing her head. "What sort of thing is it that's jumping about so gaily?" asked the girl. She took the spindle and wanted to spin too, but no sooner had she touched the spindle than the spell started working and she pricked her finger with it.

The very moment she felt the prick, she fell down on the bed there and lay in a deep sleep. This sleep spread over the whole palace: the king and the queen, who'd just come home and had entered the great hall, fell asleep, and the entire court with them. The horses in the stable also fell asleep, the dogs in the courtyard, the pigeons on the roof, the flies on the wall, even the fire that was flickering on the hearth died down and fell asleep, and the roast stopped sizzling, and the chef who was about to pull the scullery boy's hair because he'd done something wrong let the boy go and fell asleep. The wind died down and not a leaf stirred on the trees in front of the palace.

Around about the palace a hawthorn hedge began to grow. This grew higher every year and finally surrounded the entire palace and even grew out beyond it, so that nothing more was to be seen of it, not even the flag on the roof. The legend of the beautiful sleeping Briar Rose—for such was the name of the king's daughter—went about the country, so that from time to time kings' sons came and tried to break through the hedge and reach the palace. They found it impossible, however, for the hawthorn bushes held together as if they had hands, and the young men remained stuck in them, couldn't get free, and died miserable deaths. Once again after many, many years, a king's son came to the country and heard an old man telling about the hawthorn hedge: a palace was said to be behind it, in which a most beautiful king's daughter, named Briar Rose, had already been sleeping a hundred years, and the king and the queen and the whole court sleeping along with her. From his grandfather the old man also knew that many kings' sons had already come and tried to break through the hawthorn hedge but had remained stuck in it and had died miserable deaths. Then the youth said, "I'm not afraid; I'll go out and see the fair Briar Rose." No matter how hard the good old man tried to dissuade him, he wouldn't listen to his words.

Now the hundred years were just up, and the day had come on which Briar Rose was to wake up again. When the king's son approached the hawthorn hedge, there were nothing but beautiful big hawthorn blossoms that moved aside of themselves and let him through unharmed, closing again behind him like a hedge. In the palace courtyard he saw the horses and spotted hunting dogs lying asleep; on the roof were perched the pigeons with their heads under their wings. When he entered the house, the flies were asleep on the walls. In the kitchen the chef was still holding his hands as if about to take hold of the scullery boy, and the kitchen maid was sitting in front of the black chicken which she was supposed to pluck. Then he went on and in the great hall saw the whole court lying asleep, and up near the throne lay the king and the queen. He went on still farther, and everything was so quiet that one could hear oneself breathe. Finally he got to the tower and opened the door of the small room in which Briar Rose was sleeping. There she lay and was so beautiful that he couldn't turn his eyes away and stooped down and kissed her. As he touched her with his lips, Briar Rose opened her eyes, woke up, and looked at him in friendly fashion. Then they went downstairs together, and the king woke up and the queen and the whole court, and they all looked at one another in astonishment. The horses in the courtyard got up and shook themselves; the hounds jumped about, wagging their tails; the pigeons on the roof drew their heads from under their wings, looked about, and flew out into the country. The flies on the walls went on crawling; the fire in the kitchen came up, blazed, and cooked the meal; the roast began to sizzle again; and the chef boxed the scullery boy's ears so that he cried out; and the maid finished plucking the chicken.

Then they celebrated the wedding of the king's son with Briar Rose in all splendor, and they lived happily until their death.[4]

To compare the distinct characters of each of the three churches we shall treat each story four times. In succeeding rounds we shall note: (1) how each church finds an integrity in crisis, (2) its manner or proficiency, (3) its mood, and, finally, (4) its expectation.

1. THE THEME OF CRISIS
AND INTEGRATION

"Violence," says René Girard, "is the heart and secret soul of the sacred,"[5] yet its presence in congregational life in expressions other than Christ's crucifixion is frequently ignored.[6] But the character of each of the three parishes examined here develops in relation to a specific, if symbolic, death, making a virtue of it and knitting its consequence into the patterned behavior of that church. Samuel Heilman reports a similar phenomenon, which he calls "symbolic murder," in a study of a synagogue.[7]

1a. *Threshold death.* At Corinth Methodist the death that became a symbol was that of a small child. Three years earlier the infant son of Sam Singer, the pastor, had died suddenly, and this tragedy had become critical to the church's self-understanding. "I'm frankly up to here with the death of his baby," muttered one parishioner recently, but in spite of several muted objections, the frequent representation of that innocent death altered the manner in which the parish comprehended and behaved itself. A member recalls:

Before he died, for a short time we didn't have a unifying thing. His death unified us in sadness, but we began to live on a caring basis. It was a time of massive compassion; group compassion. And it made a difference in Sam. In his own spiritual growth. He had not been touched by grief personally, but now Sam knows personally what he is saying. He is better able to minister. And see the things that have happened.

The things that happened after the death included the increase of membership and worship attendance to the extent that the church later won the conference evangelism prize. After the death, more laity volunteered for church posts than there were positions, and Sam's perception of his own ministry notably deepened:

I always knew the mechanics of ministry, what is expected of a minister, but there is a tremendous difference in the gut level feeling and in the way you do that ministry. I have been around death all my life and was told "You do good funerals," but now I think I have a new understanding. . . . [I now have a] ministry in the midst of death. And this is why we stay here in Corinth. You know I'm on the move list, but we're going to stay.

The child's mother, Sam's wife, refers to:

the strength we found and the strength [the church] found. Not just lip service. God is really here. For the first time in my Christian life I really had to grasp that strength. It was kind of like John Wesley: no blinding light, but I was strangely warmed.

From the sudden death of a child came an unprecedented cohesion, strength, purpose, and exertion to Corinth Methodist.

Orpheus also signifies the potent promise beyond death. He crosses the threshold, charms the powers of death with sublime music, and wins from them the right to bring his beloved Eurydice back to life. He nearly succeeds but loses her at the last step before the threshold. When the head of Orpheus was ripped from his body by the Maenads of Thrace, it survived to deliver oracles from a fissure of rock on Lesbos. A principal teaching of the Orphic mysteries was that death was but a threshold to another, more powerful life.[8]

On the Sunday following the death of his son, Sam preached a sermon.

> The kingdom of God has already begun in Corinth. It is a long way from being fulfilled, but it has begun. God has promised that he will work through everything for those who love him, and as I have viewed the experience of the life of [my little son], I can see how the kingdom has come. . . . Oh, my friends, I have been through the valley of the shadow, but I have been to the mountain!

Sam also survives the ritual death of the Methodist appointment system, overcoming the threat of transfer for a full decade. At Charge Conference the spokesperson for the congregation stood up and addressed the district superintendent:

> Now, not that we would give you a hard time, but we just sort of dare you to move him.

1b. *Displacement.* A different sort of death modified the character of Corinth Baptist. It removed "the Godfather," Tom Layce, from the control of the church. "Mr. Layce and persons subservient to him held everything together—and down." He was so powerful and wealthy that projects were never finished by congregational effort. "We'd always look to him, and he would say, 'Well, I'll do the rest of it.'" Sitting in his properties office down the street from his bank, the "Godfather" reminisced:

> I was chairman of the board of deacons for twenty-five years, at first the youngest one of them, and now I'm a lifelong deacon. Was chairman of the finance committee, too. . . . I built one Sunday school plant—frame—just built that one myself. Built another Sunday school plant in 1947 but got some help on this one. The church used to stand on a hill on the other side of town. My father moved it to where it now is. I started out ringing the bell and putting wood in its stove.

But the recent newcomers to Corinth Baptist pay their own way, and, unlike the oldtimers, they had accumulated neither a moral nor a monetary debt to Layce. They allied themselves with Robert Foote, the new Baptist pastor. Said Layce:

> The newcomers are all on Robert's side; they all came in under him. And, if the old and the new disagree, we old ones would be outvoted. You can just see that and feel it.

In an epic scene that reminded observers of King John signing the Magna Carta, Robert and the newcomers wrested the power from Layce. For a century and a half the church had operated without a constitution and with no way to rotate deacons off the board. That was changed in conflict culminating in a confrontation between Layce's group and the newcomers in a private dining room of the local restaurant. Layce backed down. Robert, the pastor, remembers:

My first major hurdle was that we began to develop a constitution and bylaws. Heretofore we had always operated on oral tradition, and there was real opposition to changing this at first. "What do we need this for?" they would say, and they got real suspicious. . . . Throughout the fuss I never got the feeling my job was in jeopardy, but I was sure uncomfortable. One of the things about youth is that you think you were invulnerable.

Robert recites the benefits of displacing the "Godfather":

The first benefit was that we got new men, new ideas, new experiences. We then worked on education, the children's church. . . . Then we began to work up Wednesday Fellowship suppers and mission groups. We put all choirs under one roof. Our fiscal policies began to change; we began to get more money appropriated for missions, going for both home and foreign missions. The church is a lot warmer, even though larger, nowadays.

Edmund Leach explains the central motif of the Oedipal myth:

Roughly what it amounts to is simple enough: if society is to go on, daughters must be disloyal to their parents and sons must destroy (replace) their fathers. Here is the unreasonable, unwelcome contradiction, the necessary fact that we hide from consciousness because its implications run counter to the fundamentals of human morality. There are no heroes in these stories; they are simply epics of unavoidable disaster.[9]

The story of Oedipus shows repeatedly the murder and banishment required for the survival of the city of Thebes. First the dragon, then the Spartoi, then Oedipus' father, the Sphinx, and finally Polyneices are killed. Three banishments occur: Oedipus exiles himself from Corinth, and then is banished from Thebes; later his son Polyneices is also banished.

At First Baptist the idea of banishing Robert is mooted among some of the senior members in veiled language. "We want to turn Robert loose; he really needs time to study, meditate." "Our church is trying to relieve the pastor of duties so that he can devote full time to ministry." Tom Layce is more blunt:

I love Robert to death. But preachers after they've been around five to seven years become old preachers. They repeat the same sermons. The Methodist way of a preacher staying two or three years is much better than ours. But I'm not going to make any noise about this.

1c. *Death by rescue.* Bigelow Methodist killed the pastor who tried to rescue the church, stopping him before he really got started. The Briar Rose myth is the Sleeping Beauty tale in which the thick briar hedge imprisons the castle, protecting its sleeping occupants during their hundred-year slumber. The news of a sleeping princess spreads, and various kings' sons attempt to penetrate the briars to reach her, only to be impaled and killed by the thorns.

They were premature. Julius Heuscher writes of the adolescent: "His ideas though noble, delicate or princely, are still immature and brittle and cannot yet become a fully effective part of the adolescent's real life. They perish at the contact with the rude aspects of reality, just like the young princes who came too early to Briar Rose's castle."[10]

The king's son who came to Bigelow was told by his district superintendent (who himself had founded Bigelow nineteen years earlier) to shake them up: "Your vigorous approach to ministry is just what Bigelow needs now, and they will respond to it." Bringing a reputation as a successful pastor in a smaller and somewhat more naive congregation, Bill Prince unfortunately let it be known that he considered himself a missionary going to sluggish Bigelow. Before Bill's time the title of the church newsletter was first "The Briar Patch" and later "The Grapevine." When he came, he changed its name to "The Visitor." But, as Bill said a year later, "A master who wakens the dog stands the chance of being bitten." He was indeed bitten, and six months after that he was removed from the charge.

The congregation was not prepared for Bill. His predecessor was a much-loved "lazy good ole boy" who at the end of his Bigelow pastorate let the church lapse into lethargy. Given an opportunity to move to a better appointment in midyear, the predecessor left abruptly and did nothing to dispel the impression that the conference had forced that decision upon him. The bereft congregation impaled Bill with their anger. Bill had an aggressive style of ministry and a decidedly more canonic world view than did the Bigelow congregation:

> I have some definite ideas about what it takes to develop a dynamic, successful, good, local church. I am structurally oriented to the Methodist Church and I know how it is to be organized. Bigelow didn't have the right committees: no work areas, only chairmen. . . . Basically my sermons are all calls for commitment to the institutional church, the Church of the Living Christ. I expect a sermon to be a discipling process. Of course there are levels of commitment among people, but I try to conclude each sermon with a challenge that calls for a decision.

As one church official put it, "He came in like dropping *Mein Kampf* on my desk." Bill announced that the church would not have a "retreat" that year; its sessions would be called an "advance." He seldom took time off. He was tireless in the pursuit of what he considered a "positive, enthusiastic approach [that] was the type of ministry this church wanted."

"Bill," sighed one of the members, "has no capacity to be seductive."

Bigelow resisted Bill from the day of his arrival. They presented him with what he felt was a messy parsonage. He was not invited to intimate occasions of parish grief and celebration. Bill summed up the relationship a year later:

> I literally feel like I am preaching to a wall. They sit there with their arms crossed, saying, "O.K., let's get it over with and get home." There has been real,

gross rejection of my leadership. I am amenable to leaving because of the hell I've been through in the last twelve months and the hell yet to come.

Bill was glad to leave eighteen months after his arrival, and few members of the congregation regretted his leaving. Not being a watcher of *Saturday Night Live*, he missed the irony of Bigelow's youth referring to him as "Mr. Bill," the unseen television figure that macerated a doughboy every week.

2. THE THEME OF
PROFICIENCY

As characteristic as its response to crisis is each church's talent for trustworthy accomplishment. Each uses a predictable set of sharpened skills to achieve the group's immediate goals. The skills and their results form the dominant style of parish life, its dependable behavior.

2a. *Proof.* "Work" is the key word used by the Corinth Methodists to describe their proficiency. "Things just work like clockwork" at the church, "and the workings of the church are being worked by laypeople." Since the baby died, there developed a remarkable effort by members to ensure that attempted programs or projects were in fact successful. Sunday services were said by their participants to work. The sermon that Sam preached after his son's death was entitled "The Gospel of Jesus Christ: Thank God, It Works." Proficient work at Corinth Methodist was proof that the gospel message is true and church activity valid.

The power of the human Orpheus to coerce nature and the gods of the underworld was an extraordinary message in traditional Greek religion.[11] This image of human triumph helped make Orpheus founder and hero of the Orphic mysteries, a cultic practice noted for personal asceticism and accomplishment,[12] that demonstrated the immortality of the human soul. Followers of Orpheus expressed their accomplishment in rites, obscure to us, called *teletai* which, in Ivan Linforth's estimation, "acted like a sacrament to bring purification and release from the consciousness of wrongdoing, to renew the sense of vigor and vitality, and to give assurance of happiness after death."[13] Whatever the specific nature of these rites, they provided for initiates the proof that their souls would indeed cross in triumph the threshold of death, and that thereby they were not merely the mortal playthings of gods nor the hapless objects of fate.

Proofs of accomplishment abounded at Corinth Methodist. "They needed proof that they could keep a pastor for four years," Sam Singer said, and together they kept Sam for over a decade, not only by raising his salary each year beyond what he would make in another assignment but also by giving him a bonus each year from the surplus of an oversubscribed church budget. Earlier the congregation had complained that it had no purpose. A work group therefore sat down with Sam and wrote a Purpose Statement, an unexceptional compound sentence that thereafter appeared in each bulletin:

> In response to the call of Christ, the Corinth Methodist Church seeks to be a redemptive fellowship serving God and community effectively by: (a) enabling each person to achieve God's will through individual fulfillment; (b) providing religious training for all; (c) ministering to the community through service and witness.

This seemed to solve the issue. The church has proved it had a purpose. Church membership doubled.

But the rite of accomplishment most often employed was church work. When programs worked, it was a proof of the larger triumph of human transcendence. Members made sure things got done, and done abundantly, with everyone having something to work on. The church work groups doubled in size. "Sam is a conniver. He sees to it that every member is involved. Makes you feel like somebody." The church had to develop a three-year roster to accommodate volunteers for leadership positions.

The concept of hypocrisy took different forms in the two churches in Corinth. Among Baptists, for reasons that will later be evident, it meant taking both sides in an argument; among the Methodists it meant not living up to one's promise to work.

2b. *Adventure*. Corinth Methodist's proficiency was to prove its promises; Corinth Baptist's was to venture beyond the ordinary. The Baptists would oscillate between seasons of local frustration and global quest, contending in one moment among themselves and then setting out to the ends of the world. The half dozen airline pilots who attended church typified its prowess, but the "Godfather" was the prototype. In the 1920s Layce brought to railroadless Corinth its first automobile dealership and thereby loosed the town from its domestic tether. During the depression he loaded a bunch of Corinth men in the back of his truck and drove them all the way to Chicago to see the 1933 World's Fair.

Layce now fueled the frustration. Both churches in town needed larger buildings to accommodate their larger numbers, and the Methodists characteristically executed their funds campaign with aplomb, and with some smugness because the corresponding efforts of their Baptist neighbors were "down in the doldrums . . . God just doesn't seem to want us to build right now." Nor did Tom Layce. Layce made a $5,000 contribution for the Methodist building but said he was only going to put an organ in the new Baptist structure. Layce was said to be "holding his foot." The campaign, headed by one of the pilots, did not get off the ground until a rival bank in town gave the church a large loan. But until that occurred, they were "in a rut. . . . We need to push forward or drop backwards."

At the same time they quested to the ends of the earth. The teenagers were preparing for a revival in Kansas City; one of the pilots helped run a jungle aviation service for missionaries; another's daughter was a missionary in

Paraguay. A former pastor of the church was serving in Israel. An Australian evangelist campaigned at the church that summer. Methodists interpreted their mission largely as making Corinth a more effective community; the Baptists pressed their mission *only* beyond the gates of the town.

Constraint and journey mark the full life of Oedipus. As a babe he was pinned to the mountain, his feet pierced with a nail, and Claude Lévi-Strauss emphasizes the lameness implied in his name and that of his forebears.[14] Oedipus was then blocked at the crossroads by Laius, and later stopped by the Sphinx. But these events only temporarily check the larger unfolding of his life that carried him first to Corinth, then in flight to Thebes, and from there into exile, wandering for the rest of his life to Colonus, where he vanished, journeying into what Sophocles called "mysteries not to be explained."

An inner adventure at Corinth Baptist accompanied the outer quest, one that took the quester into scriptural territory. The Methodist members did not use Bibles, but many Baptists carried theirs to church, often had them in their briefcases and would spend some time each day reading them. "God's word is the road map," the pastor would tell them. A Baptist wife talked about her husband:

> I was amazed what was happening in Ron's life. He reads a lot, but he never was able to read the Bible. It "just doesn't say anything to me," he would say. But after all my illness happened, he picked up a Living Bible and he couldn't put it down. He kept getting so full of what it meant. . . . We then got into a neighborhood Bible study group and this really got us into the Bible. We've met every week for two years.

As one pilot put it, "We read God's instruction manual." Blocked at home, the Baptists searched the extrinsic worlds of earth and Scripture.

2c. *Curse.* Members of Bigelow Church exercised a different sort of proficiency, one directed perversely against opportunities for parish accomplishment. To typify their independent spirit they called themselves a "maverick" church, an unbranded beast who resists identification with any herd. The church skillfully resisted Bill Prince's canonic attempts to identify its household. A substantial number of participants asked that, even though they would remain members, their names be removed from the church's mailing list.

The pattern of putting down the church began before Bill came. Several leaders started in Bigelow's fourteenth year to say aloud that the church was "a waste of my time." At midpoint, in its fifteenth year, the church began its drastic decline in worship attendance, even though total membership continued to increase.[15] The church abused itself in other ways: it eliminated the posts of associate pastor and youth minister; it sold off its adjacent property. It in effect turned over the youth of the community to the Presbyterians when it closed its own kindergarten and day care programs. Presbyterian programs thereafter prospered, while Bigelow's dwindled. About the only program for which Bigelow received persistent community recognition was its service to retarded children.

The curse that impeded Briar Rose occurred in her fifteenth year, when, as predicted, she was pricked by a spindle and fell asleep for a hundred years. Before then her life abounded in all the blessings of the other dozen wise women, but, in spite of efforts of her father, the curse of the unrecognized thirteenth brought her down. Querulousness characterizes the story of both Briar Rose and Bigelow Methodist. Commenting upon Briar Rose, a Jungian analyst remarked: "In the anima also there is a certain nastiness, for the anima is primitive woman. Women, and man's entire anima, have a way of reacting to disagreeable situations by being downright nasty."[16]

Although other churches in the neighborhood continued to show promise, Bigelow did not. "We are in a declining situation," its leaders would tell each other, and they refined the knack of deflating ideas and enthusiasms that would suggest otherwise. Chief among the pessimists was Stan, who had arrested his own promising career in a big company to keep his family in the neighborhood. Once a district lay leader, Stan had mastered dour behavior. "He was everything I feared he would be," the 'good ole boy' pastor said about his meeting Stan. "He gave me nothing but problems the whole time I was there, not liking what was happening, either in weekly programs or on Sunday morning." Stan had a teenaged daughter who had been born with Down's syndrome, and it was Bigelow's program for retarded children that brought Stan's family to its somber fellowship.

3. THE THEME OF
PERVASIVE MOOD

A distinctive temperament also characterizes each of the congregations. Mood is more disposition than accomplishment. It displays the recurrent attitudes that affect how parish members measure and otherwise evaluate their situations.

3a. *Innocence.* At Corinth Methodist the mood is one of tranquillity and harmony. Unlike most gods and heroes, gentle Orpheus is neither pugnacious nor trapped in strife. Instead, his extraordinary musical talent resolves the contention of life, and he soothes both beasts and his aggressive companions. He lulls to sleep the dragon who guards the golden fleece, and later he so calms the tormentors of hell that they allow his entry and escape. Orphics distinguished themselves from the "unwashed" by a cleansed life (*Katharos Bios*) of controlled harmony, producing, according to J. R. Watmough, a "tranquility [that] is, above all, restrained and sober. It is a state of peace which flows naturally from the life of self-discipline and communion with the source of infinite *Eros*."[17]

I was struck by the innocence of worship in Corinth Methodist. Its sanctuary was unusually attractive, offering white walls and woodwork, with a fresh rosebud placed in each clear window at service time. Choir robes were pastel shades, and although the choir sat behind Sam Singer, facing the congregation, it did not counter his dominance. All attention was directed toward Sam. The congregation remained alert, passive, good-natured, with chins up to watch him. Sam only momentarily shunted that attention to the children, whom once in each service he called to the front of the church, re-presenting the innocence.

The symbols of First Methodist provided tireless encouragement for commitment. Dilemmas about the persistence of sin and the incongruity of life were not addressed; the service included neither a regular confession of sin nor an acknowledgment of ethical contention. Instead, Singer's message was deft but unequivocal, light but persuasive. "I preach for commitment," he repeatedly said. "I don't want people to *feel* good, as they do over in the Baptist Church, but to *be* good."

> Total commitment is what we need. "You must love me totally," God said, and not just have a batting average.

Like gentle Orpheus, Sam wooed people to innocence. His voice was so musical, in fact, that he would regularly sing religious songs as his sermon for the day. Sam traveled around the state as song leader for revivals and, while pastor at Corinth Methodist, made two recordings of gospel songs.

Members of the church frequently attested to its mood of harmony, comparing it with the conflict that seemed to mar the Baptist Church and the Methodists' own past. "Before Sam came, the church was divided; lots of dissension. Every time a new member came, he was not accepted. But dissension is now all gone; now you just don't have any."

3b. *Ambiguity.* "Baptists fuss and build" was the way that those in First Church Corinth described their contentious mood. Unless the sun shone brightly, their sanctuary tended toward gloom, its windows clouded by dark stained glass, its walls beige and furnishings a rich brown. Here the choir robes were gold and dark green, and their wearers sometimes noisily entered their seats after Robert Foote had begun the worship service. Robert shared both program and platform with the deacon of the week and the music director, between whom and Foote there was open competition. While the congregation respected and enjoyed Robert, their gaze also drifted to their Bibles and their neighbors. Announcements, prayer requests, and testimonies arose from the congregation at various points in the service. Children were not presented at the front of the church. Instead, what was called "the gall bladder report" was posted on a tripod there. The report listed the conditions of sick members and the needs of those requesting prayer.

The myth of Oedipus portrays life's ambiguity. "The killer you are seeking is yourself," Teiresias the prophet tells a righteous Oedipus who seeks the

murderer of his father. Earlier, Oedipus flees to avoid the possibility of parri-
cide and thereby kills his father. By ridding Thebes of the Sphinx, its menace, he brings the greater menace of plague to the city. "Show me," cries
Sophocles' chorus, "the man whose happiness was anything more than illusion followed by disillusion." In ultimate ambiguity Oedipus enters in love
the woman from whom he was born.

Harmony characterized neither the worship nor the politics of Corinth
Baptist. "Christ came to make us clean," Robert preached, "but, as Martin
Luther says, we have been liberated from prison but the stench and disease of
prison still lingers in our lives." "We think we are the masters of our fate," he
tells the congregation, "but the more I live the more I feel that events over
which I have no control shape my destiny. I am almost a pawn on a chess-
board."

Confession inaugurated the Baptist worship service, and the last congregational action at worship was to come forward to the altar to acknowledge
faults and shortcomings. Having had training in clinical pastoral education
(which Sam Singer had not), Robert more than most ministers found it easy
to disclose publicly his shortcomings. "How easily I run out of steam," he
confessed one Sunday. On another, he echoed the plight of Oedipus: "All of
us are blind. Not literally so, but handicapped in some way or another."

In addition to the political tension surrounding the "Godfather," First
Baptist expected trouble from its new members. "We need two churches.
This one is too big. We could separate the church we joined from the church
that joined us." Charismatics in the church generated another conflict that
aligned them opposite "seventy-five percent of the people who just sit there
and are scared to death of us." Sophocles' tragedies, Thomas M. Woodard
reports, "like the Greek world of the 5th century, presuppose inescapable,
unrelenting power struggles."[18] The paradoxical Oedipus, righteous and
guilty, fugitive and aggressor, figures the ambiguous mood of Corinth Baptist.

3c. *The big sleep.* "Bill," said one Bigelow parishioner, "do you think that we
are complacent?" "Would you believe docile?" Bill rejoined. "And I believe
that means dead." Many members joined Bill in considering Bigelow's life to
be dormant; a "sleeping giant," some said. "The fire has gone out." In its fifteenth year Bigelow's newsletter carried the motto "Where Dreams Become
Reality."

The fire went out when Briar Rose fell asleep, and everything else in the
castle slumbered. Bruno Bettleheim asserts:

> Whether it is Snow White in her glass coffin or Sleeping Beauty on her bed, the
> adolescent dream of everlasting youth and perfection is just that: a dream.
> The alteration of the original curse, which threatened death, to one of pro-
> found sleep suggests that the two are not all that different. If we do not want to
> change and develop, then we might as well remain in a deathlike sleep. During

their sleep the heroines' beauty is a frigid one; theirs is the isolation of narcissism. In such self-involvement which excludes the rest of the world there is no suffering, but also no knowledge to be gained, no feelings to be expressed.[19]

Bigelow's deep repose began after its decision not to build the large sanctuary projected in its original plans. In a meeting later hailed as "probably the most healthy conversation that ever occurred in the church," the congregation overwhelmingly voted not to take on the large debt of new construction but rather to remodel what they already had: a long, low fellowship hall. In consequence, pews were installed in the hall, carpet was laid, its windows outfitted with rich stained glass, and its ceilings deadened with thick acoustic tile. The resulting worship space looked and felt like a casket. "Everything seems to suck up the sound," complained a former associate pastor, who found the place too dark and soporific. "Things are so nice and cozy and soft in here!" exclaimed a visitor. Standing in a chancel sunk below the floor level because of the low ceiling, the altar is invisible to most of the congregation. When the pastor rises to preach, the lights further dim.

Throughout its life and worship Bigelow slumbered. "The church really doesn't want that much going on," said one untroubled member content with its inactive nature. Others were more concerned that Bigelow had "no central rallying point" and "no goals or objectives." Groups in the church virtually ran themselves; communication systems in the church fell into disuse; for a while the bulletin ceased publication altogether. "The church," said Bill, "is not yet a mature adult."

4. THE THEME OF
HOPE

Each of the churches also follows a quest that takes it well beyond its present accomplishment: it seeks a *telos*, a goal or outcome, promised but not provided in parish story. The proficiencies and moods of parish character are given further value in the deep faith a congregation places in its future.

4a. *Initiation*. Members of a church may identify the focus of their common hope with the phenomenon of warmth[20] and point to specific occurrences of warmth in places or phases of congregational life.[21] Members of Corinth Methodist experienced warmth at various physical and temporal thresholds that bound its life to its larger neighborhood. At these boundaries they encountered the outgoing love and concern that members considered the congregation's most valuable characteristic.

The immediate feeling of warmth. You just cannot come in here without someone speaking to you.

The warmth. I just feel a glow, an acceptance of people. They accept people for what they are and don't expect them to conform. We're constantly having one program after another to draw people in.

Such a threshold welcome

> reflects Sam Singer's personality. He's a very friendly, outgoing, easy type of person, and the visitor sees this. His personality has not taken hold until recently. Before that the church was dominated by an older and colder membership.

Sam's wife spoke of being strangely warmed at the death of her son, and members recalled their "characteristic afterglow" when they responded to a family that had experienced death.

People joined First Methodist without fulfilling prior requirements. Instead, the church met them where they were and beckoned them to cross the threshold. To serve children at their entry into education the church ran the best kindergarten program in town. "It's got to be the greatest—probably the turning point for our getting members, what with the young adults it reaches out to." Sam Singer himself marked this threshold:

> Sam has always been an integral part of the kindergarten. In other churches the minister is not seen at all by the kids, but here he comes by every day and speaks to them, and they love him, and they and their parents learn that the church loves them.

First Methodist produced an outstanding daily kindergarten program. The rest of the Methodist education program, not associated with threshold entry, was ill-resourced and ineffective. "We have just stopped teaching young people."

At Sunday school time Sam Singer was on another threshold. He went to a nearby lake to preach to crowds of one to two hundred unchurched people who stopped at an outdoor chapel before getting into their boats. Unlike his Baptist counterpart, Singer did not teach a Sunday school class. More important for him was to reach out to lonely, uncommitted people, to love them and invite them across the threshold. "The kids will not remember any of the Bible verses after twelve months," he would insist, "but they will remember the love you gave them. This is what the church is. We nurture, but for the implementation of love, and not for the acquisition of knowledge."

Plato complained that the Orphics

> persuade not only individuals but also whole communities that, both for the living and the dead, remission and absolution of sins may be had by sacrifices and childish performances that they are pleased to call initiations and which they allege deliver us from all ills in the next world, where terrible things await the uninitiated.[22]

The focus was the threshold, for, once initiated, the member was assured of perpetual, divine happiness. Orpheus was a liminal symbol because he was able to lead through hell's gate the dead to life. Orphism and Corinth Methodist hoped for a similar transcendence in their own initiations.

4b. *Growth.* Warmth was not generally described as a threshold characteristic at First Baptist. Rather, warmth was said to increase as initiates matured in membership, as they moved toward the center of the church and developed there toward God. "Warmth is in process," explained Robert Foote. During worship it did not occur for him in preliminary welcomes but in the "gall bladder times," when reports of troubles and requests for prayers "can be very warm and even get out of hand." A senior Eastern Airlines pilot talked about the fervor generated in his Sunday school class:

> We get so involved in Bible study that we go on and on, and that gives you a warm feeling, and the men are so anxious to get so involved in God's Word that they don't want to leave class to go to the worship service.

Growth rather than initiation was the prevalent aspiration of Corinth Baptist. While Robert Foote was as personable and outgoing as his Methodist counterpart, and his attractiveness brought new members into the church, the characteristic comment about Robert concerned his and the congregation's growth. "Robert's grown a lot since he has been here, and the church has grown also." "Robert has matured, and it is spreading to us."

So important was maturation to First Baptist that it introduced a Watch Care program for persons who wished to join the fellowship. The program was intended even for those joining from other Baptist churches. Contrary both to widespread Baptist custom and to the practice of Corinth Methodist, Robert did not extend the right hand of fellowship to persons desiring to enter the church. The candidates first had to undergo a four-week period of training. "People need to be born again," argued Robert, "but not again and again and again. After birth they need to grow."

Growth, no liminal events, draws the Oedipal myth to its *telos*. Oedipus' discovery that "the child grows into an adult, who grows into an old man" releases Thebes from bondage to the Sphinx. The motif recurs in the story of Oedipus himself: a babe abandoned, a young man at the crossroads, a mature ruler at Thebes, and an old man at Colonus.

> Despite all the instances one can find in the play to show that Oedipus turns away from knowledge of himself, he is more heroic than most men in his struggle to attain it. In his search for self-knowledge, Oedipus discovers resources of which he was previously unaware: a capacity for intellectual honesty that overcomes the pride that prohibits it, and a power of endurance that exalts him and those who, as chorus or audience, are involved in his destiny.[23]

"After one accepts Christ, what next? The command is to grow, to move on from milk to meat." Systems at First Baptist were therefore tiered to provide that growth. There were the adult choir, the young adult choir, the junior choir, the primary choir, and the beginning choir—"just like a feeder system," grinned the music director. Three handbell groups served different ages; four age groupings staged the Women's Missionary Union; and the Sunday school provided five levels for preschool groups, classes for every year until high school, two grades for high schoolers and four levels for adults. "Warm things started to happen when we started participating," said another member. "The church provided spiritual strength that we desperately needed at the time. It is a growth process. You don't take it in all at one time; you take it in little doses."

4c. *Awakening.* Members in sleeping Bigelow did not sense much warmth anywhere. "Just not an overly friendly church in my opinion," said a long-time participant. Their expectation was, rather, that if they really tried, they could bring about an awakening that would once again bring ardor to Bigelow's work. "The world," says Bettleheim, "becomes alive only to the person who herself awakens to it. Only relating positively to the other 'awakens' us from the danger of sleeping away our life. The kiss of the prince breaks the spell of narcissism and awakens a womanhood which up to then had remained undeveloped. Only if the maiden grows into woman can life go on."[24]

While new undertakings were belittled by some of Bigelow's powerful members, the projects were also invested with fervent hopes that they could wake the church up. Considerable anticipation accompanied the arrival of Bill Prince's replacement, but since he was close to his retirement, he did not ignite warmth and the congregation continued to languish. Some of the more charismatic members prayed for revival but then left the church. The expectation of many more people centered on a New Life Mission to be led by a distinguished Methodist official. Its meetings were well attended, and throughout its preparation and several days' execution there was "a spirit of expectancy . . . a hope not found here before." Participants signed cards on which they volunteered their efforts in new ways, but the cards were mislaid after the mission. Nevertheless, as one member put it, "You can see Spring coming." The congregation still awaits the new life promised first by the frog, then by the twelfth wise woman.

NOTES

1. Except for the titles "First," "Baptist," and "Methodist," all names of persons, organizations, and places are fictitious.
2. *New Larousse Encyclopedia of Mythology*, 192–93.
3. Edith Hamilton, *Mythology*, 103–5.
4. Francis P. Magoun and Alexander H. Knappe, trans., *The Grimms' German Folk Tales*, 182–85. Called *Dornroschen* in the German text, Briar Rose is also known as Heather Blossom and Rose Bud. Magoun and Knappe use Heather Blossom, but I have substituted the more familiar Briar Rose.
5. René Girard, *Violence and the Sacred* (Baltimore: Johns Hopkins Univ. Press, 1972), 31. Girard demonstrates the presence of violence throughout mythology, ritual, and cultural activity dependent upon ritual. The unifying rationale is the necessity of killing a sacrificial victim to protect human beings against their own inevitable escalation of retributive violence. "There is a unity that underlies not only all mythologies and rituals but the whole of human culture, and this unity of unities depends

upon a single mechanism, continually functioning because perpetually misunderstood—the mechanism that assures the community's spontaneous and unanimous outburst of opposition to the surrogate victim" (pp. 299–300).

6. "The mysterious union of the most evil and most beneficial forces is of vital concern to the community, and can neither be challenged nor ignored. Nevertheless, it is a paradox that totally escapes human comprehension, and religion humbly acknowledges its importance" (ibid., 86).

7. Samuel C. Heilman (*Synagogue Life*, 9–12) finds parallels between the two initial expulsions of authoritative members and the reports of Philip Slater about rejection of the leader in therapy groups. Through such violence, groups gain their solidarity.

8. W. K. C. Guthrie, *The Greeks and Their Gods* (London: Methuen & Co., 1950), 317; Martin P. Nilsson, *A History of Greek Religion* (New York: W. W. Norton & Co., 1964), 221.

9. Edmund Leach, *Claude Lévi-Strauss* (Harmondsworth: Penguin Books, 1970), 88. Cf. René Girard's treatment of the "violent unanimity" with which the scapegoat, primarily Oedipus himself, is destroyed by the society that benefits from his departure (Girard, *Violence*, 68–88).

10. Julius E. Heuscher, *A Psychiatric Study of Myths and Fairy Tales: Their Origin, Meaning and Usefulness* (Springfield, Ill.: Charles C Thomas, 1974), 164. Cf. Bruno Bettleheim, *The Uses of Enchantment: The Meaning and Importance of Fairy Tales* (New York: Random House, 1977), 233.

11. Guthrie, *Greeks and Their Gods*, 180.

12. J. R. Watmough, *Orphism* (Cambridge: Cambridge Univ. Press, 1934), 68–71.

13. Ivan M. Linforth, *The Arts of Orpheus* (Berkeley: Univ. of California Press, 1941), 166.

14. Claude Lévi-Strauss, *Structural Anthropology*, trans. Claire Jacobson and Brooke Grundfest Schoepf (New York: Basic Books, 1963), 274.

15. Average Sunday attendance at Bigelow:

12th year	326
13	360
14	416
15	428
16	403
17	378
18	365
19(Bill Prince's arrival)	315
20	284

16. Marie-Louise von Franz, *Problems of the Feminine in Fairy Tales* (Zurich: Spring Publications, 1972), 34.

17. Watmough, *Orphism*, 80.

18. *Encyclopaedia Britannica*, 15th ed., s.v. "Sophocles."

19. Bettleheim, *Uses of Enchantment*, 234.

20. Mircea Eliade, *Myths, Dreams and Mysteries* (London: Fontana Library, 1968), 146.

21. Gerardus van der Leeuw, *Religion in Essence and Manifestation* (London: George Allen & Unwin, 1936), 455.

22. Plato, *The Republic*, trans. H. D. P. Lee (London and Tonbridge: Whitefriars Press, 1955), 96.

23. *Encyclopaedia Britannica*, 15th ed., s.v. "Sophocles."

24. Bettleheim, *Uses of Enchantment*, 234

9

STORYTELLING

The purpose of telling a congregation's story with conscious reference to its mythic framework is to provide a fresh way to characterize its corporate life. The object is not simply to play a matching game that links a certain myth with the attitudes and actions of a certain local church. Although there is pleasure in the discovery of a myth that illuminates nuances in the events of a parish, the greater benefit of the exercise is its public expression. The considerable effort required to fit a myth to the cultural data of a congregation is best undertaken for the good of the church itself, not for one's private entertainment or academic purposes. A congregational story told with its mythic counterpoint helps church members to grasp how much their corporate life contains and means. It also prompts them to ask at the story's ending, "And then?"

Many churches fail to tell their story. They are paralyzed in prosaic self-description that follows depressingly predictable lines. They evaluate themselves by counting money, membership, and programs. Denying or ignoring the complexity of relationships in the congregation, they consistently proclaim their cohesion as a family. They tabulate the age, sex, race, and social class of their members. And they even equate themselves with the property they occupy. Such a pattern of self-reference reflects the aspects of household outlined much earlier: a mechanist side that focuses on numbers and tasks, an organicist side that portrays familial traits, a contextual side that stresses demography, and a symbolic side that may make property the household image.

In one sense the designations form a four-sided shell that defines the congregational household, representing the outer limit of creative self-portrayal in a community's life. But may it not also function as a protective device by which a parish conceals its essential life and shields itself from more telling and exciting self-knowledge? To concentrate upon numbers, programs, and family feelings may represent a flight from the ambiguous, demanding story of the group. Consider Daedalus and Briar Rose churches. Their intriguing dramas can be easily obscured by conventional self-description. Parish portrayal that ignores story is certainly simpler, and it undergirds piety as a private concern uninvolved with any vital household life.

A congregation can learn to tell its stories. It can search for their relationship to large epics and myths. It can argue about which is most apposite and can seek a variety of interpretations. In what might be a radical departure from its normal practice of self-description, the congregation can talk about the particularity and worth of its own character. Rather than reduce its self-image to that of a machine or an organism, the congregation might begin to give account of itself as the full, storied household the Bible promises it can be.

WHO EXPLORES CHARACTER?

The characterization of the church should be a collaborative undertaking. Although an examination of the setting—the world view—of a congregation might well be the work of a single individual, the development of an effective interpretation of the congregation's ethos requires a collective effort. This is true for several reasons. The first is the magnitude of the task. Not only does characterization involve a great deal of interview and observation, it also concludes with a number of attempts at narrative interpretation. To have several collaborators both divides the task and provides partners in the attempt to tell powerful stories.

Because myths are often troubling, even unflattering portrayals of character, the involvement of several people in their discovery has another advantage: it increases the likelihood that a congregation may be able to hear and ultimately to accept its own meaning. One church developed a helpful twofold grouping of people to explore the mythic dimension of its character. Doing the original search were a small group of lay investigators and the pastor. They reported to a larger group of members, who tried on the observations, stories, and myths that the smaller group proposed as important. Having refined the characterization in this way and made it the property of diverse representatives of the parish, the larger group then was able to portray and dramatize the story to the congregation as a whole.

A group of members whose talents are normally underused in a congregation may become leaders in the exercise of characterization. Social workers, psychologists, English teachers, raconteurs, and lovers of drama and literature bring special talents to the process. They already have an appreciation of culture in its broad sense and of the narrative link to social observation. Their collective memory of myths and tales also supplements the usually limited knowledge of a single investigator.

A final advantage of collective storytelling is that it tempers the fancies of any single interpreter. It is very easy in the late stages of developing a mythic framework to bend or break off the observations of parish ethos that contradict the myth. An individual examiner especially confronts this temptation.

Colleagues in the search for story can check this tendency in each other and together set a higher standard of accountability to the evidence.

The ministry of characterization does not begin with the presentation of the final story to the full parish. It begins in the conversations among collaborators who are forced to move beyond the standard ways of considering their parish. In their interviews and conversations with other members they then become engaged in what is essentially moral discourse, the determination of what constitutes the ethical stance of themselves and their group. In gathering and interpreting their collective ethos, they further participate as Christians in a prophetic ministry that sets forth the story of group in the light of God's covenantal history with all God's people.

METHODS OF INQUIRY

A team that seeks to characterize a congregation by narrative begins with methods of observation and interview. The general nature of this ethnographic approach is described in chapter 6. In the present section, several more specific ways are presented by which the effort to uncover the ethos of a congregation is pressed: (a) listening for narrative elements, (b) participant observation, (c) guided interviews for value patterns, and (d) corporate moral inquiry.

a. *Listening for narrative elements.* Short and longer stories constitute the bulk of everyday parish discourse. Thus some of the most valuable narrative sources are readily accessible, requiring the study team only to give a special kind of attention to the narratives they hear in the ordinary course of congregational life. Some of the tales are informal accounts shared among people gathered quite casually, perhaps after worship or between meetings. Other stories are recounted during programs and business sessions, and still others emerge in pastoral conversations.

The inquirers listen to, and possibly tape-record, the discourse. The stories it contains are later analyzed to detect at least the following elements:
  1. The points of stress or *crisis* that the narrative seeks to describe and resolve, and the nature of the resolution.
  2. Stereotypic characters and scenes portrayed in the stories and their proficient or otherwise typical *manner.*
  3. The atmosphere or prevailing *mood* depicted in the stories.
  4. Forms of *hope* or wish fulfillment projected in the discourse.[1]

These elements served to organize the stories told in the last chapter. They are the ones a congregational study team will use in discerning the structure of the congregational story and its mythic parallels.

b. *Participant observation.* The study team that seeks to identify a congregation by its character must, like the researcher looking for setting or world view, assume the role of observing participant, a posture that takes nothing for granted. The methods of participant observation are the same as those set forth in chapter 6, but the object of the inquiry is somewhat different. Inquiry about setting focuses on what the congregation assumes, presupposes, and believes. Research into ethos is oriented to capacities, behavior, and values. Thus the team must note the characteristic behavior of nuclear members and principal leaders, comparing it with the attributes and activities of marginal members. Actions must be recorded, especially those taken in instances of crisis and stress, because there values are patently at stake. Observers must pay special attention to the congregation's "street wisdom" about how things really get done; to evidence about what the congregation seeks to avoid; and to expressions of wishes, desires, and instances of their fulfillment. Etiquette, style, and stereotypic behavior are important. Clues about mood and values may be found in the way a congregation uses and decorates its physical space. Publications and bulletin boards may convey proficiency, style, and mood. Throughout the study the team keeps in mind the underlying question: What do members demonstrate is the preferable and reliable practice of their household?

c. *Guided interviews for value patterns.* Open-ended interviews that pose a predesigned series of questions permit members themselves to ponder their behavior and to develop their own ideas about what congregational actions intend. Some interviews should engage marginal members, who often bring a more critical interpretation to church behavior. Others are conducted among active participants. All informants are asked the same type of questions:

—What's the news around the church now?
—Tell me about your own association with this church.
—What changes have you noticed since you became a member?
—How is this church most likely to fall apart?
—What would you say were the most valuable characteristics of this church?
—What sort of talk dampens the spirit of this church?
—What distinguishes this church from [a nearby competitor]?
—What sort of church program or project is frustrating and unproductive?
—Think of a respected member. Without naming the person, describe the person's characteristics.
—Think of an embarrassing member. Without naming the person, describe the person's characteristics.
—At what points in church life do you feel closest to God?
—At what points in church life do you feel this congregation is in danger of losing touch with God?

Many of the guidelines laid down for world view interviews apply here as well, though again with a different object. It is important that interviewers concentrate upon the responses of their partners and not use the occasion to argue with them, to present an affirmative or alternative view, or to analyze what might be the motivation behind the respondent's answer. A "flat approach" from the interviewer is required. Such an approach tries to understand the interpretation of the informant and does not fall back into rejoinders of the interviewer or forward into psychoanalytic or sociological explanation. The object of inquiry is neither a negotiation between two opinions nor a second level explication of the informant's ideas. It is, rather, to understand as clearly as possible the interpretations of incident and value that informants themselves present.

d. *Corporate moral inquiry.* James Gustafson has proposed that local churches and other Christian groups become "communities of moral discourse."[2] What he has in mind is not the ongoing and largely unconscious operation of the inherent ethos of a congregation but its conscious attention to moral issues raised for the purpose of making a Christian decision about them. "By a community of moral discourse," Gustafson writes, "I mean a gathering of people with the explicit intention to survey and critically assess their personal and social responsibilities in the light of moral convictions about which there is some consensus and to which there is some loyalty."[3] He distinguishes such explicit gatherings from other occasions such as church business meetings and Bible studies where the consideration of ethical responsibility is an occasional and secondary occurrence.

Gustafson's basic idea is acknowledged in the following exercise, but greater emphasis is placed upon its descriptive dimensions than upon its prescriptive aspects. The transformative conclusion of the project is not, however, forgotten. A Christian community is, as Gustafson points out, bound to be concerned not only with its inherent system of values but also with their transformation in the light of Christian ethics. This exercise, therefore, is intended to assist the congregation in seeing both its inherent moral posture and its attempt to reach new decisions that reflect a more explicitly Christian character.

The exercise presented here differs from Gustafson's model in the attention it gives to exploring the existing value patterns in a congregation. It can easily miss the point, therefore, if its sessions are convened to develop a specific "right" response to a particular moral question, as discussions about moral issues usually are. Seminars in local churches that aim at moral discourse today frequently begin with a challenge to find the right answer. Such a process is implied in programs entitled "What is the Christian answer to . . . ?" Discourse conducted in response to such an introduction has several ethnographic handicaps, including the implication that some people present, notably the pastor, probably know the answer and that those who do not know it are there to be taught. That implication is likely to impede any corporate search for the actual attitudes of all participants.

A more exploratory discussion might begin from a different premise: "We all have deep opinions about this issue, and we want to see how they differ from and relate to each other." Less attention is placed on the conclusion, more on exploring the resources of the group. Several simple methods undergird the emphasis upon finding the given attitudes of people. People's understandings of their own viewpoints are recorded on newsprint. The ideas they offer are set down as statements, not, in the first instance, as arguments. Discussion is directed toward clarification and implication rather than persuasion. A moderator makes sure that all persons have an opportunity to express their positions. The formation of a consensus is considerably less important for this exercise than the development of an understanding of the range of values held by members of the same congregational household.

Beyond these perhaps obvious procedures to encourage participation and fair treatment of each member's contribution, an attempt can be made to claim the resources that narrative holds for elucidating character. A skillful leader might ask an individual venturing an opinion how that person came to hold it. The response will probably be a story of some significance that knits together both the given dimensions of a person's character (natural gifts and capacities, or those nurtured over a lifetime) and critical moments in which character has been formed by deliberate choice. Once the range of opinions (and stories) has been displayed, the leader might pose a question to the whole group: "Have we ever in this congregation faced an issue like this? What was it? When? How did we as a congregation respond?" Such questions will very likely provoke stories that portray the congregation's characteristic behavior and values. If the issue is a particularly difficult or controversial one, either for individual members or their congregation as a whole, it may be wise to *begin* the conversation in a narrative frame, using a carefully prepared case that poses the issue in a specific instance. A case lends some distance. Participants in the discussion may be readier to respond to a hypothetical example than to declare as their own an abstract moral position that brings them into direct conflict with others present.

These uses of narrative in moral discourse are more than clever devices. They are ways to introduce the possibility that the seeds of moral fortitude are already germinating in the rich history of the congregation's character. Sometimes the bringing to light of such history will provide precedents for moral courage ("If the last generation could take such bold measures, why can't we?"). In other instances, the account of characteristic decisions of the past may display traits or patterns that the congregation now sees it must modify or reject. But in either case the telling of stories grounds the possibilities for future decision and action in the particularities of character. Such a grounding casts in new perspective issues that may at first have seemed

unwelcome impositions from outside the characteristic life of the congregation and its members.

Like other methods, the practice of corporate moral discourse requires
careful recording and a later search for dominant themes. The team of parish
investigators meets together to compare observations and to develop descriptions of congregational character it observes in members, situations, and conversations.

THE SEARCH FOR MYTH

As the themes of congregational ethos become clear to the team, it begins
the search for representative myths. There are countless myths in the world.
An early collection, *The Mythology of All Races*, completed in 1932, runs to
twelve volumes plus an index and represents only a small number of myths
now known to exist in literate and nonliterate societies.[4] Especially at a time
in which relatively few people have learned even the so-called classic myths of
Greece and Rome, there naturally arises a question about how to locate a suitable tale within the plethora of myths.

What might seem at first glance to be a great aid in the search may not, in
fact, prove to be much help. Shortly after the anthology cited above was completed, Stith Thompson began to publish his six-volume *Motif-Index of Folk-
Literature.*[5] Motifs for Thompson were the significant details that compose
full-fledged narratives. He classified the motifs of all the stories found in *The
Mythology of All Races* and in four hundred other collections and studies of
the folk tales that appear in ballads, fables, and other forms of traditional expression. One can dig into this feast of themes in two ways. The first way is to
follow Thompson's elaborate but sensible classification scheme that divides
the motifs into major subjects (category B, for example, refers to animals, D
to magic, T to sex). Within each subject, he factors out a clear but complex
subdivision of parts (in section B: mythical animals, magic animals, animals
with human traits, friendly animals—and each of these types is then further
subdivided). A second way into the collection is through the final volume's
fascinating alphabetical index (e.g.: "Abbot caught in sin permits monks to
sin," or "Lost object found by throwing spade at ghost"). A standard reference item in university and many municipal libraries, Thompson's *Index*
is worth a search through its intricate system for references to themes that
emerge in the exploration of a congregation's ethos. The motifs may prove to
be too specific, however, for sensing the gestalt of the folk tale, and the
reader may tire of following false leads before finding something that parallels the value pattern of the congregation. But other investigators may have
better fortune, or learn to work Thompson's system better, than I.

I follow the more pedestrian and time-consuming practice of reading and
rereading a relatively few anthologies of myths and tales best known in the
West. My primary sources are Edith Hamilton's collection of Greek, Roman,
and Norse myths,[6] plus one of the translations of Grimms's fairy tales,[7] and

the Larousse encyclopedia of myths throughout the world.[8] Once I find several likely candidates among the tales, I try to read everything written about them available in a library with large holdings in the humanities. When the short list includes a Greek myth, as it usually does, I go first to its extensive and analytical treatment in Robert Graves's anthology.[9] The collaboration of several teammates, especially if they are students of literature, is an invaluable help to such a search.

I have been pressed to elaborate a procedure for deciding which specific myth to employ. That is difficult to do. Like many other activities of ministry—rendering a theological judgment, structuring a sermon, being present to persons in acute crisis, discerning the plan of action and strategy to which a congregation is called at a particular moment in its life—choosing a myth requires the complex interworking of rational judgment, adequate information, emotional openness and self-awareness, intuition, sensitivity, prayerful reflection, and more. It helps if one begins the search already steeped in mythic materials. The choice is usually easier if, as earlier urged, it can be made by a group of inquirers. But finally, as for other acts of ministry, there is no technique whose workability is guaranteed in every case.

There are, however, some tests of appropriateness once a choice is tentatively made, though these lend only a general sort of ratification to the choice, not empirical certainty of its rightness. An appropriate myth is, for instance, one that is recognizable or learnable, not so obscure that its elements compound a church's uncertainty about the unusual topic of their character. Moreover, the myth should illuminate the four basic elements of congregational character that have been mentioned before and utilized in each of the stories of churches presented in these latter chapters. In other words, the description of parish ethos and its mythic "genius" should be analogous at the following points: (a) the characteristic response to the crisis; (b) the style of behavior characteristically deemed most effective; (c) the pervasive mood; and (d) the characteristic expection and hope. Finally, a myth should encapsule the major features of a congregation's ethos. In a recent book I described the character of a New England congregation according to the myth of Zeus and his Olympian abode.[10] More than just elements of the myth and the church's ethos were in consonance: the parish had about it the jovial, Olympian atmosphere that characterized both myth and social situation as a whole.

WHEN AND HOW ARE
STORIES TOLD?

A congregation possesses both a story and stories. When I speak of the singular story of a parish, I mean to represent the dramatic coherence of the group's experience through time and circumstance. I would speak in a similar manner about the story of America or the story of a social movement or family. But I also recognize the changing, multiformed nature of any story that portrays a living community. No single, specifically worded story fully identifies the life of that group. Its plot continues to unfold and thicken and twist, its character slowly to develop, its setting perhaps to adjust or shift. Because the community has subsidiary stories and related plots, no specific story can be final or definitive. As it accounts for the ongoing nature of the parish, narrative is modified and requires retelling.

This pliant narrative process suggests a type of storytelling that occurs in a variety of modes and occasions. There can be no single event, no opening night, that presents a conclusive version of the story to its congregation. The story should instead reform itself and recur throughout parish life, the better to illuminate the ongoing activities of the household.

A congregation concerned about the prosaic quality of its self-understanding might therefore begin to tell its story in circumstances that before had encouraged the other types of self-description: mechanist accounts of numbers and program, organicist projections of family, contextualist categorizations of age, class, and the like, and formist symbolizations of property or other important totem. Possibly, out of such storytelling would emerge a new sense of parish identity, appreciative of the congregation's corporate nature, accepting yet critical of its collective character. Consider four scenes ripe for storytelling.

Scene One: An annual parish meeting given to long program reports, statistics, and financial statements. The recitation of such reports might be halved in length to make time for a group to dramatize the previous year, not in terms of congregational accomplishments but in terms of its crises, typical actions and moods, and specific hopes.

Scene Two: A sermon that usually refers to the familial qualities of the congregation. Instead, the preacher might concentrate upon a mythic aspect of the congregational life in the previous month—the spirit, hero, or creature that seems to have been inhabiting the place—and wrestle with the way the gospel both emerges in that aspect and transforms it.

Scene Three: A parish planning session that, contending with the realities of a transitional neighborhood, desperately seeks strategies for the congregation's survival in the midst of discouraging demographic information. Rather than concentrate upon the factors that describe the alienation of the church from a context with difficult social characteristics, the session might tell itself the story of why its present members do in fact participate in the church and how their own story approximates the social hopes of those now inhabiting the neighborhood.

Scene Four: An altar guild gathering usually devoted to cleaning and embellishing the church's chancel. Putting aside, for the moment, its polishing and sewing, the guild might instead consider the people who sit in the pews, where they sit, what they think, how they participate not only in the liturgical drama but also the larger drama of the church's life.

The scenes are only illustrative. They show some uses for parish story where now there tend to be none, as ways to give fresh sight and hope to members caught in the flat routine of standard parish self-understanding.

Telling the story develops the identity and mission of a congregation in at least three ways. By establishing the setting of the story of a local church, its picture of the world, narrative proclaims corporate nature. The congregation in story is not permitted to reduce itself to numbers of individual contributors of money, names added to the church rolls, or ticket holders at congregational programs. Story instead weaves a living fabric of common episode. Church members become actors integral to an encompassing drama. Narrative also provides, as this chapter argues, a ministry of *characterization* that particularizes the congregation by displaying in mood and incident the unique ethos of the individual parish. Through characterization, story reflects the specific configuration of moral choice and historical circumstance that identifies each local church. In the next section I turn to the action of story, its plot, that conveys both collective memory and corporate hope, past and future, in the present bodied moment. Narrative thus acknowledges what we have been and done, but in the presence of the world story, the gospel, that gives the *telos* to even the small stories of local parishes.

NOTES

1. See a somewhat similar list for the analysis of group myth in Dexter C. Dunphy, *The Primary Group: A Handbook for Analysis and Field Research* (New York: Appleton-Century-Crofts, 1972), 281.

2. James M. Gustafson, *The Church as Moral Decision-Maker* (Philadelphia: Pilgrim Press, 1970), 83–95.

3. Ibid., 84.

4. Louis Herbert Gray, ed., *The Mythology of All Races: In Thirteen Volumes* (Boston: Marshall Jones Co., 1916–1932).

5. Stith Thompson, *Motif-Index of Folk-Literature: A Classification of Narrative Elements in Folk-Tales, Ballads, Myths, Fables, Mediaeval Romances, Exempla, Fabliaux, Jest-Books, and Local Legends*, 6 vols. (Bloomington: Indiana Univ. Studies, 1932–1936).

6. Edith Hamilton, *Mythology*.

7. Francis P. Magoun and Alexander H. Knappe, trans., *The Grimms' German Folk Tales*.

8. *New Larousse Encyclopedia of Mythology*.

9. Robert Graves, *The Greek Myths* (Harmondsworth: Penguin Books, 1955).

10. James F. Hopewell, "The Jovial Church: Narrative in Local Church Life," in Carl S. Dudley, ed., *Building Effective Ministry*, 68–83.

PART FOUR

THE PLOT OF PARISH STORY

10

THE ACTIONS OF PLOT

This chapter's revision coincides with my second hospitalization for cancer. Again my friends join me in my room. Our struggle for stories to encompass this new reality differ from those told earlier when my disease was first discovered. Our new accounts are more intricate; now they recount our common history lived in the light of my illness, a three-year collaboration that, among other intentions, battles my death.

What thickens our present tales is their richer plots. Neither the settings nor the characterizations we employ in our storytelling have changed notably. But plot has gathered our meantime actions, choosing and weaving them into now more eventful narratives.

This section of the book explores the nature of plot in the congregation. The major aspects of parish story already examined, setting and characterization, depict features of congregational life that—though by no means immutable—usually remain the same over long periods of time. Respectively, they represent a church's persistent views and its values. Plot, by contrast, traces the occurrence and consequence of changing events. Plot relates the unfolding activity of a group, its unsettled venture through time and circumstance. Plot tells what happens.

Studying the diachronic, or ongoing, nature of plot requires an exploratory device different from those used to investigate the synchronic, or simultaneous, aspects of setting and character. Remember the typology of literary genres used to distinguish the variety of congregational world views, and the corpus of world myths employed to interpret congregational ethos. Although both literary genres and myths themselves contain evolving stories, their usefulness in examining setting and character rests primarily upon their capacity to preserve abiding patterns of views and values. Because plot conveys change and chance in a story, it requires other tools for its examination.

One such tool can be fashioned from terms commonly used to describe what plot accomplishes. Plots are customarily said to link, unfold, thicken, and twist. The terms depict important distinctions among the actions of plot:

a. Plots *link*. They collect and concatenate past events, giving order to action and an identity to the actors. (In my hospital room we recall various
   happenings in the last three years that typify our common experience
   and present feelings.)
b. Plots also *unfold*. They show cause for story's development or dissolution, thus giving reasons for the present situation and evidence of the
   likely future. (Our hospital tales seek by sequencing certain events to
   understand our current predicament and to anticipate what might happen next.)
c. Plots *thicken*. They acknowledge happenings that counter the independent unfolding of action, thus depicting the tension and *agōn*, or struggle, of life. (Our narratives must address problems in our own fellowship, and our involvement in other predicaments.)
d. Plots *twist*. They discover an unexpected indeterminate action that
   transforms for good or ill the character of the actors. (We also witness
   among us the rare graceful event that redeems our plight.)

One evening a group of pastors and church consultants related a pungent
array of stories that depicted the congregation that each served. I shall use
their anecdotes to probe at greater depth the various actions of plot.

Plots link

One of the actions of plot is linkage, the drawing of a story line from
among the entanglement of various happenings. A myriad of events occur in
any day of parish life. If W. H. Auden is correct in his assertion that the day's
events in the life of an average person could fill a novel, an account of the activity of a congregation in the same period might occupy several shelves.
That huge account would be called a chronicle. Containing every detail of the
congregation's activity, from the singing of a syllable to the turning of a door-
knob, the chronicle would have no plot. In fact, reflecting the raw cascade of
time itself, the account would have no beginning, development, or end. It
would record an unremitting flow of happenings.

An important function of plot is to make human sense of this formless rush
of incidents. Plot links by recalling only a few events from among everything
that has happened, thus changing chronicle into history. By recollection—
what Plato called anamnesis—a community reduces its association with the
chaotic immensity of its past. And plot's linkage of remembered events helps
create its subject's present identity.

Here is a story whose plot links a few incidents to represent the identity of
a congregation in a culture disposed to deny it.

Adhering to its own denominational heritage rather than to local religious custom, a small congregation of Brethren in rural Texas developed an unfortunate
reputation among its neighbors for not being a "Gospel Church." To mend its
image the congregation decided to host one of the Gospel Sings for which the

region was well known. Groups from other churches arrived with all their per-cussive enthusiasm and performed with such vigor that the plant on the piano danced to the floor. Finally the terrified quartet of the Brethren Church offered up their own calm hymn, and no one clapped or stomped. The pastor felt that all was lost, but the noise of the other numbers was sufficient exorcism, for there-after neighbors told him, "You really got a Gospel Church."

In the long history of the relationship between the congregation and its neighbors, many other events occurred, most of them ambiguous or opaque in their significance. Plot reaches into that jumble to give sequence and co-herence to a story that comes to stand for the complex life of this congrega-tion.[1]

The power of plot to give coherence is often acknowledged in the charge that the stories of congregations about themselves are frequently self-con-gratulatory or constructed to justify the miserable moments of parish life. But plot can also reveal matters that congregations would rather hide than ex-plain, such as the pulpit one Episcopal congregation must keep in its boiler room:

> Defying both the rector and the vestry of a young Episcopal congregation, a pow-erful member and his cronies wrestled a huge pulpit of his own acquisition into the nave of the new church building. Rather than counter the challenge of this heavyweight, the rector preached from the pulpit the following Sunday. But members had to retreat to the rear of the church in order to see him. The pulpit remained in the sanctuary for several months while the rector refused to use it and the donor refused to remove it. Finally it was inched to a neutral corner in the boiler room.

Note how bland and inaccurate the portrayal of these last two churches would be were a report of the music program to replace the tale of the Gospel Sing or an account of the order of worship to obscure the story of the boiler room pulpit. A congregation's identity depends upon the unique link that plot forges with certain events in its past.

Plots unfold

Plots do more than recollect the past, however; they also disclose the un-folding of the present. "In a closely contrived plot," René Wellek and Austin Warren state, "something has happened in time: the situation at the end is very different from that at the opening. To tell a story, one has to be con-cerned about the happening, not merely the outcome."[2] A good plot ripens former events to reveal the present, and from the present seeds a likely fu-ture. Parish plot is a scenario that demonstrates a causal sequence in congre-gational life.

Unless incidents unfold, their succession loses meaning. Persons in de-spair, for example, find little plot in their experience. They see their lives in-stead as just one damn thing after another.[3] Communities as much as indi-viduals require the unfolding action of plot, the recognizable development of life toward fulfillment. Note how plot unfolds a situation that, without its narrative expectation, might prove intolerable to its participants.

> Although frequently given to public acts of social and religious consequence, a pastor especially shook his flock when he helped by extralegal means to bring Hispanic refugees into the United States. The church board, listening to the murmurs of city fathers and picturing the flight of funds and members to more placid parishes, decided to fire the pastor. But his adventurous nature had also attracted many supporters who disputed the board's claim that the majority of members wanted the pastor discharged. A specialist in conflict management was appointed to break the impasse, and a final vote revealed that most members wanted to keep their minister. The minority opposition felt not only repudiated but also vindictive. They left the church, knowing their departure destroyed the congregation's financial base. Today, a pensive remnant lives on with its pastor in increasingly shabby surroundings.

Were the church not sustained by a plot that shows cause for present conditions, the congregation would probably disintegrate. "Plots," says Wesley Kort, "are images of recognizable processes, particularly of growth or dissolution."[4] They respond to the question "How come?" disclosing in this instance why a recently respectable and secure congregation now finds itself in dignified desperation.

Although both explicate the course of human action, plots are substantially different from theories. A social scientist might distill from the refugee incident the hypothesis that there are certain predictable community responses when attempts are made to help people marginal to its corporate life. Social science would test this hypothesis by careful comparison of parallel situations. If confirmed, the hypothesis would contribute to theories that could be used in making more or less accurate predictions of the outcomes of similar situations. The theory would contain causal conclusions that, as Northrop Frye points out, confer the right of science to say "hence." The future orientation of plot, however, conveys the more concrete but uncertain prospect which is implied, as Frye says, in story's conjunction, "and then."

Both scientific theory and story address the future of a local church. Theory provides a relatively few abstract principles of which a particular parish might in time become an illustration. With a different sort of anticipation, plot projects the future. We are not sure of the outcome, but we are certain that it is the complex images of the storied present that are cast forward into the future. Neither theory nor story in fact reveals what is to come, but narrative brings to the future the stuff that will give it particularity. Theories predict, while plots unfold.[5]

Plots thicken

Plots also complicate their story line by recognizing elements in life that counter its simple unfolding. When we say that a plot thickens we mean that it has incorporated contradictory evidence that gives the story a strained intricacy. Thickening is inevitable. "All plots," say Robert Scholes and Robert

Kellogg, "depend upon tension and resolution,"[6] and Kenneth Burke demonstrates the inescapable dialectic found in both fictional and historical dramatizations.[7] Although we are socialized to think that tension marks an embarrassing and probably unnecessary failure in ministry (one recent book for pastors asserts that "conflict was not God's plan for humanity"), the *agōn* of individual and corporate life is inextricable from a congregation's plot.

Parishes in the thick of things do not escape tension:

> To dramatize their commitment to the destitute of a troubled Northeastern city, an action group of a blue-collar United Church of Christ congregation arranged a march from their church building to an ecumenically supported food center. Carrying banners and sacks of food, and following a bagpipe player, the group set out under the eyes of other, disapproving, church members. The trip went smoothly enough, except that an alcoholic male parishioner who loved to touch women draped himself over the female pastor throughout the parade.

Many local church histories are written without reference to the elements that produce tensions and strains, in this case the neighborhood poor, doubting church colleagues, an incongruous parade, and an amorous drunk. Histories concentrate instead on dates and accomplishments; they avoid the tension that accompanies the complicated struggle to maintain and enliven any community. Most local church histories are therefore boring. It is not just prurience that makes us itch to learn the real story behind the usual church account of names and projects. It is much more a spiritual longing to participate in the tensed complexities and contradictions that roil our actual lives.

The conflicting intentions of several groups thicken the following plot:

> The only black Episcopal congregation in its diocese, in distinction from other diocesan mission churches, founded itself without headquarters support and proudly maintained itself without diocesan aid throughout its history. It accepted, however, a diocesan proposal that it organize a conference to discuss how it could obtain better clergy leadership from its own ranks. The diocese sent in various experts and observers, including a white person, frustrated elsewhere in her desire to gain ordination. When the congregation faltered in its own conclusions, she announced, "I will be your priest." The participants received this unanticipated development with apparently great joy and immediately accepted her offer. But during the next week the congregation dismissed its wardens and vestry and never communicated further with the candidate who had volunteered her services.

We listen to these stories with their strange tensions, preferring them to thin, placid success stories because they recognize in their plots not insignificant or random events but the world's own thickening. The recent spate of books about church fights and leader burnout[8] examines aspects of the church's thickening plot. Acute moments in parish conflict now attract increasing numbers of specialist consultants. The analyses used by most students and referees of distress do not, however, go far enough. Constrained by a market that demands immediate results, consultants concentrate upon features of agony that are isolable and responsive to treatment and tend to ignore the deeper and abiding dialectic of congregational life that stirs up the fights. Several of the books on church conflict begin with learned quotes that suggest that anything worthwhile begins in conflict but ends in reconciliation. That understanding is less than half the story. Things also fall apart, and much at stake in the household life of the congregation never approaches resolution. To advise churches that all their distresses have solutions palliates pain at the expense of allowing the church to experience its thick connection with the suffering of the wider world.

Plots twist

Plots also represent an action more irregular than the linkage, unfolding, and thickening described already. In so doing, they acknowledge the possibility of transformation. Like other groups, a local church is not bound to the images of its recollection, or the inevitability of sequential development, or the persistence of tension. Occasionally there occurs in corporate life an unanticipated and apparently deviant twist that transmutes the course and character of the group. Twists are better recognized when they occur in concrete situations than when they are defined or described in generalized theories about change, because, by their nature, twists contort the accepted definitions of things. Here are two accounts, one of a twist initiated by a pastor, the other the result of congregational action.

Sometimes the plot of the church is twisted by deliberate action of leaders who realize that an important element of congregational life is wrong and who therefore force its change. In the following story, leadership is provided by a pastor who institutes a costly modification in the way the parish views its relationship with God:

> Were members of a United Methodist church to have described the holiest moment of the year for their congregation, they would uniformly have cited the warm, candlelit hours of Christmas Eve when families would arrive whenever it was most convenient for them for a private Communion at the altar. Each group would wait discreetly outside if another family were already present. Once alone, the family would silently move forward to the pastor, who would first hug and greet them and then provide Christ's body and blood for the kneeling kin. Tears would fall. Families felt a strange closeness.
>
> In the view of the new pastor, however, the Christmas message was getting lost in this moist intimacy. Christ was born, he preached, to a world as disparate as shepherds and kings, not merely to nuclear families, and the way the church witnessed God's new embrace at Christmas should be by congregation-wide Communion, not private huddles at the altar. He announced that future Christmas Eve services were to be held at a set time for the whole congregation.
>
> The church's millionaire member withdrew his pledge. Many members felt that their Christmases had been spoiled. The first year only the pastor's family showed up at the service. A year later, some other members joined them.

Sometimes the twist occurs in spite of well-intentioned leadership:

> At diocesan urging, a Roman Catholic congregation sought to start a parish council that would institute the principles of local lay leadership advocated in the

documents of Vatican II. The organizational efforts of the pastor and his rural church members, however, went nowhere. The priest made speeches about democracy; the flock listened quietly but passively. Finally a woman in her sixties stood up. "Monsignor," she said, "let me say something. I have been sitting here listening to all these words and thinking that I am just a farmer. Have run my own farm for thirty-eight years. Then the more I listen the more I realize: *You couldn't run a farm.* Now let's get this council working."

That cracked the mold: heavenly patriarchy collapsed into matriarchal farmland earth. The bravery of an older layperson twisted millennia-old patterns of parish authority.

But twists are not necessarily acts of heroism, and they do not always bring benefits. Some are accidents, like the change initiated by the death of the pastor's son in Corinth Methodist Church. Some are catastrophes, killing the church. Nor is their occurrence the prerogative or even the consequence of newly installed pastors who feel compelled to turn around their new congregations. Especially in the case of churches that suffer the entry of different, eager pastors every few years and that become indifferent to their prodding, new leaders are advised to appreciate the church's existing story before attempting to twist it. They should first learn the other actions of a congregation's plot: the years of local linkage, the unfolding and thickening which have happened only partially through the ministrations of a pastor. All actions of plot need attending. The twists of a congregation's plot are infrequent and uncertain, and they are not the ultimate measure of ministry. It may be considerably more significant for a congregation to face its thickening circumstances than for it to try to twist its nature.

THE FUNCTIONS OF PLOT

Notice how stories differ from program description, the almost automatic form for summarizing parish life. Reports about a local church usually fix upon such regularities as worship services and committee meetings, not upon the plot that unfolds and twists. But formal, regular activities are relatively infrequent occurrences in the total activity of a congregation. Program description fails to account for most of the collective behavior that moves the church from one moment to the next. In spite of what most annual reports of congregations seem to attest, program descriptions do not sum up what happens in church or in society. Plots do. Analyzing parish narratives through the actions of their plots throws light on the nature of the congregation in several significant ways.

First, it demonstrates that congregations are capacious. They collect occurrences that otherwise might be dismissed as eccentric or irrelevant. The fact that such irregular events as aid to Hispanic refugees can be typified as actions of plot gives evidence that congregational life possesses a larger coherence than its sequence of liturgies and standard programs by themselves suggest. The ongoing corporate life of the local church is not a muddle of atomic incidents connected merely by the regularities of church worship and organization. Rather, a larger, hermeneutically richer story knits together the manifold existence of the parish household.

Plot analysis also displays the ubiquity of issues of power in congregational
life. The very terms of analysis—link, unfold, thicken, and twist—suggest
the work of power throughout local church events. All the anecdotes told that
evening by the pastors and consultants deal more or less openly with political
power: its absence, acquisition, contention, transfer, or consequence. The
changes in location of the big pulpit are accomplished by contending forces.
The food parade is a symbol of power's absence. In facing the pastor, the
farmer represents the transfer of power. To acknowledge the plot of the congregation is to recognize the political nature of God's household.[9]

Third, analysis of parish plot demonstrates the historical nature of the
congregation. The local church is more than a narrative setting, an assembly
of ideas about the world that floats among those who hold them. Nor is the
parish merely a narrative characterization, an ethos held in common by otherwise dissociated people. Despite our aspirations, congregations are not
timeless havens of congenial views or values. By congregating, human beings
are implicated in plot, in a corporate historicity that links us to a specific
past, that thickens and unfolds a particular present, and that holds out a future open to transformation. Congregational story is a household confession
that recognizes the continuing participation of the church in the passage of
events. This theme regulates the final chapters of this book. First, in the remainder of the present chapter, I examine how the actions of congregational
plot parallel the struggles for survival of people everywhere, but especially
the poor and oppressed. In the next, I explore the complex relationship between the common human undertaking of a congregation and the Christian
story. Then ways of interpreting Christ's plot in and with the world are proposed in story form in chapter 12. Finally, all three major elements of narrative are reexamined for their meaning for the congregation's wider ministry
and mission.

Last and most significant, congregational plot—capacious, political, and
historical—testifies to the symbolic relationship that exists between the rich
drama of church life and the struggle of the world's peoples. Christianity did
not, of course, create narratives and their attendant plots. Story is found in
all societies, as essential to their own life and meaning as it is to the survival
and identity of the Christian congregation. To explore the narrative structure
of the local church by examining its elements and their representation is to
participate, perhaps unknowingly, in a much larger adventure into how human societies everywhere struggle to communicate and maintain themselves.
Understanding the local church story is subversive: this act of apparent self-
reference brings to consciousness the symbolic forms and processes that bind
together all humanity. The narrative structure that holds together the congregation binds it as well as to the world's communities.

THE IMPLICATIONS OF PLOT

Factors in the struggle of a people to exist as a corporate body are set forth in the four-function paradigm of Talcott Parsons.[10] Although the adequacy of his analysis is challenged by other theories, especially those focused upon social change,[11] Parsons's model provides a useful delineation of the actions implicated in a group's toil to perpetuate itself. According to his theory, an organization must fulfill four functional imperatives if it is to survive. First, to sustain its identity an organization must preserve its values, history, and meanings. Parsons calls that action *pattern maintenance*. Second, the group must provide norms and means that give its members a coherent unity: the imperative of *integration*. Third, the organization by *adaptation* must develop the resources and skills to modify itself. And, fourth, members must function within a system of governance that enables them to accomplish *goal attainment*. Together the four functions encompass the activities that give a social structure both its equilibrium and its capacity to evolve through time.

Among suffering people, however, Parsons's functions are more often represented by their contradiction than their accomplishment. Thus pattern maintenance is less characteristic of their life than the obliteration of cultural pattern, and integration less a present reality than its opposite, alienation. In like manner, poverty overtakes the resources and skills required for the function of adaptation, while oppression prevents the possibility of goal attainment. For the marginal societies of the world, therefore, the four functions of Parsons are much less achievements than the distant intentions of a grinding struggle to ameliorate cultural amnesia, alienation, poverty, and oppression.

The fourfold fight waged by the world's poor is also expressed by the actions of plot in the local church. What is experienced in its own historical, political plot are movements that are pale but authentic forms of the life-and-death struggle waged by oppressed peoples. Can the congregation grasp

— that plot's *linkage*, in the stories of both congregations and poor societies, marks the struggle for recollection of the past so that cultural identity, the pattern, is maintained in the face of cultural obliteration? The fight of a Brethren church to protect its identity in an overwhelmingly different religious ethos is structurally identified with the toil of sub-Saharan people to maintain their negritude in spite of massive Western influence.

— that plot's *unfolding*, in the stories of both congregations and poor societies, characterizes the attempt to attain group goals in the face of oppression and other obstructing factors? A story like that of the pastor who sponsored refugees unfolds as pastor and congregation hold firmly to their principles in the face of bitter opposition. By similar action, peoples throughout the world struggle to attain their goals in societies dominated by oppressive political and economic systems.

— that plot's *thickening*, in stories of both congregations and poor societies, describes a society's labor to acknowledge alienated elements or members, whose activity now repudiates any orderly incorporation? Proud of its identity and independence, the black Episcopal church entered a divisive time when outside interventions thickened its plot. The quest for integration, an internal social health and wholeness, is a thickening that also occupies countries torn by civil war and peoples segregated into colors and classes.

—that plot's *twist*, in stories of both congregations and poor societies, seeks the potential of a group to adapt its nature to meet new circumstances and reflects a struggle to lay hold of the skills and resources that enable transformation? Although threatened by the withdrawal of resources, the Methodist church offering Christmas Eve Communion was able to transform itself because of the skill and fortitude of its prophetic pastor. The energetic strivings of poor and oppressed societies against considerable odds presuppose the possible twists of plot.

The congregation by its household narrative can mediate the entry of the individual into the fullness of the world, making manifest how the biography of a member is woven into the story of all human society. This mediatorial ministry of the local church can be probed, as suggested earlier and proposed at greater length in what follows, by exploring the setting, character, and plot of the congregation. In a church's narrative setting, its world view, though idiomatic, is nonetheless oriented within the genres of all Western literature. The world's mythology portrays the genius of a congregation's character within a global labor of mythopoesis. And the plot of the local church, as just argued, is pitched within the struggle of humankind for significance and survival. Involvement in the local church can be itself a twist: a parochial venture that turns out to be a worldly risk.

NOTES

1. "Ordering the world at a spontaneous level of story telling implies that the search for coherence in the universe is not futile; it testifies to a primal conviction that reality lays itself open to being ordered in a comprehensible way" (John Navone, *Towards a Theology of Story* [Slough, England: St. Paul Publications, 1977], 39).

2. René Wellek and Austin Warren, *Theory of Literature* (New York: Harcourt, Brace & Co., 1942), 222–23.

3. "When someone complains—as do some of those who attempt or commit suicide—that his or her life is meaningless, he or she is often and perhaps characteristically complaining that the narrative of their life has become unintelligible to them, that it lacks any point, any movement towards a climax, or a *telos*" (Alasdair MacIntyre, *After Virtue*, 202).

4. Wesley A. Kort, *Narrative Elements and Religious Meanings* (Philadelphia: Fortress Press, 1975), 62.

5. "Unpredictability and teleology therefore coexist as part of our lives; like characters in a fictional narrative we do not know what will happen next, but nonetheless

our lives have a certain form which projects itself towards our future" (MacIntyre, *After Virtue*, 201).

6. Robert Scholes and Robert Kellogg, *The Nature of Narrative* (New York: Oxford Univ. Press, 1966), 212.

7. Kenneth Burke, *A Grammar of Motives* (New York: Prentice-Hall, 1945).

8. John C. Harris, *Stress, Power and Ministry* (Washington, D.C.: Alban Institute, 1977); Speed Leas and Paul Kittlaus, *Church Fights*; Douglass Lewis, *Resolving Church Conflicts: A Case Study Approach for Local Congregations* (San Francisco: Harper & Row, 1981); Larry L. McSwain and William C. Treadwell, Jr., *Conflict Ministry in the Church* (Nashville: Broadman Press, 1981); John M. Miller, *The Contentious Community: Constructive Conflict in the Church* (Philadelphia: Westminster Press, 1978); Charles L. Rassieur, *Stress Management for Ministers: Practical Help for Clergy Who Deny Themselves the Care They Give Others* (Philadelphia: Westminster Press, 1982).

9. Cf. Johann Baptist Metz's use of narrative and memory in his political theology in *Faith in History and Society*. Although Metz views the categories of narrative and memory as essential for Christian solidarity with the world, his categories refer primarily to the collective experience of the church universal expressed in theological terms (memory of the dead, apocalyptic hope, etc.).

10. Talcott Parsons, *The System of Modern Societies* (Englewood Cliffs, N.J.: Prentice-Hall, 1971), 4–28; With Edward Shils, Kaspar Naegle, and Jesse Pitts, eds., *Theories of Society: Foundations of Modern Sociological Theory* (New York: Free Press, 1961), 36–41; *Social Systems and the Evolution of Action Theory* (New York: Free Press, 1977), 43–53, 111–16.

11. For a comparison of Parsonian and Marxist analyses, see Marie Augusta Neal, "The Comparative Implications of Functional and Conflict Theory as Theoretical Frameworks for Religious Research and Religious Decision Making," *Review of Religious Research* 22 (Fall 1979): 24–50.

11

CHRIST AND EROS

Membership in a local church implies both identification with the plot of its corporate activity and also an attraction, through that history, to the Other whom the congregation proclaims its Lord. Accepting the sticky consequences of a particular social commitment and covenant, a church member participates also in narrative reflection and storied praxis. Through their members, congregations consider their own story. At certain moments, most often in their worship and acts of mission, congregations intensify their own search for the meaning of their corporate lives. It is in these events, which often seem to be parenthetical moments in church life, that the local church represents its participation not only in its own story but also in that of God.

Recently a pastor invited members to develop a "time line," in order to deepen the congregation's consciousness of its plot. Assembled one evening in the church basement after eating, the members adjusted their chairs toward a wall on which was tacked a long strip of butcher paper with a horizontal line drawn a third of the way down from the top. The years through which the church had lived were marked on the line, earlier years ticked closer together than those more proximate to the present. The pastor encouraged members to talk about what had happened in each year, and, as they talked, a scribe noted key phrases in the stories at the appropriate place on the paper: "great music festival," "administrative mess," "Mrs. Chairperson dies," "young people ask for a different type of worship," "new kitchen." Over the line were written events important to the larger community and world: "recession," "Vietnam," "new highway." As the evening passed, the pace of storytelling quickened, and more difficult and embarrassing tales began to emerge. At the end, people signed the chart at the point they themselves had entered the church's life.

Throughout the following week, members kept adding other events important to the story. By the following Sunday the record had so enlarged in significance that it was moved from the basement to the rear wall of the sanctuary, where it still hangs. Occasionally someone adds further elaboration or comment.

Thus members of one church posed graphically the fundamental issue of their worship. The story of the congregation, they demonstrated, is not an activity separate from and subordinate to the story of God; the stories of congregation and God belong in the same room, united though in tension, the first reflecting human history, the latter the definition, acceptance, and evaluation of that history by the Being within, yet beyond, history's comprehension. The stories are blended in worship. The congregation's members, as God's household, stand between the symbols of the two stories, one figured on the rear wall, the other sounded and signed from the chancel. In the crossfire of symbols, the members represent Christ's body, the manifestation of God within signs of their flesh and culture.

To speak of this conjoining I shall first tell about Christ, the incarnation of God, and then Eros, the personification of culture, as they embody the life of the parish.

THE CHARACTER OF CHRIST

It is now much more difficult for the local church to give an account of Christ than in former centuries. As I conducted world view interviews I was surprised how infrequently, in even conservative Protestant congregations, the name of Christ was mentioned in response to questions about crises such as death, family instability, or world catastrophes. Although the name of Christ is regularly used by church members in the intensive, self-identifying acts of worship and evangelism, it seems now to be infrequently employed to fathom situations that challenge personal or corporate identity. The formidable pedagogy developed by the church to inculcate the person of Christ into the total world view and ethos of Christian life has today largely failed, the house of authority, to use Edward Farley's image, having collapsed.[1]

Structures within which the congregational household has for millennia made its home have lost an earlier power both to explain the world in Christian terms and to form behavior by norms readily acknowledged as those of Christ. The authority of Scripture, dogma, organization, and theological reasoning that once constituted the church, the *ekklēsia*, has waned to the point of inconsequentiality for most Christians trying to make sense of their existence.

Can *paroikia* with its thick culture built from direct human interaction survive the cave-in of its surrounding *ekklēsia*? If the congregation is nothing more than a division of the larger church, the local unit of a national and international apparatus, then its future is grim indeed. Little in the activity of the overarching organizations of the church today provides compelling reasons for belonging to a congregation. If the foundering of denominational and ecumenical offices and the quandaries of theological faculties are current indications of a loss of coherence that will in time debilitate all congregations, then church membership is hardly worth the effort.

But consider the tenacity of the local church. Congregational structures appeared before the time of Jesus but became the primary social expression of his presence. The congregation then abided the growth of ecclesial apparatus and the establishment of canon and dogma; it endured councils and conventicles; it persisted through reform, counterreform, and enlightenment. As Christianity spread throughout the world, the local church has taken root in cultures more readily disposed to other social forms—kinship, for instance, or civil association. The congregation continues today in the face of criticism and announcements of its recent or impending death. But conventionally shaped congregations, a third of a million of them in the United States, still serve Christians as the principal forum for their faith. Even redundant congregations of the elderly may (to the puzzlement of church executives) defy extinction, because such churches often assimilate still other aged persons who replace the members who die.

Ernst Troeltsch proposed reasons for the persistence of the local church. Troeltsch sought to accept the critical methods of modern thought and to acknowledge their devastating consequences for the structures of *ekklēsia* but also "to preserve Christianity as redemption through faith's constantly renewed personal knowledge of God."[2] Seeking the essence of Christianity, Troeltsch threaded his way between arguments for the knowledge of God by linguistic formulation and other arguments that discovered the path in mystical encounter.[3] He located the bond between humanity and God in the cultic life of the community. He did not specifically cite the congregation as the locus of the worshiping Christian community, nor was he sanguine about the long continuation of any institutional form of the church, but his acuity in aligning the essential faith of Christianity with its cultic expression in specific communities provides an explanation for the present strength of the local church. Christ, he proposed, is the "support, center and symbol" of the worshiping Christian community:[4]

> For as long as the peculiarly Christian-prophetic religion bearing within itself the Stoa, Platonism and various other elements continues, all possibilities of a community and cult, and so all real power and extension of belief, will be tied to the central position of Christ for faith.[5]

The Christ made manifest by the worshiping community is not, in Troeltsch's argument, primarily a principle or a contemplative symbol but the historical personality who actually began the church and focused its intersubjectivity:

> It was the requirement of community and cult which gave to the personality of Christ its central position. They continue to give it this central position. Where community is dissolved into free and isolated religious convictions of individuals and the cult is transformed into mood and reflexion, there too the link with Jesus

is less prominent. Even where it is apparently preserved intact, we have instead of Jesus the inner Christ or the free mystical presence of God in the soul. Where on the other hand this weakness and dispersion is abandoned in favour of a return to community and cult, this brings with it a renewed emphasis upon the significance of Jesus' historical personality.[6]

The person of Jesus drawn from New Testament accounts is the Christ represented in worshiping communities. The biography of the founder thus in a peculiar way nourishes the plot of the congregation. The historical fact of Jesus, who lived, taught, died, and triumphed not only stands at the remote beginning of any congregation but also concretizes the hope that the congregation finds in its present existence.

Although Christ is central to the congregation, his effective presence in its corporate life is elusive. Today the grace of Christ is guaranteed neither by the traditional certainties of the church nor by the contemporary designations of social sciences. There are at best tentative intimations of Christ in the life of the congregation, and his presence is hardly captured by what current observers wrongly label a congregation's sacred time and sacred space. A congregation given to the cultivation of sacred "hot spots" in its life, whether liturgical or emotional in form, may amplify the linking action of congregational plot—the association of events for the purpose of identity—but the vivid occurrences do not in themselves qualify as sacred moments. The nuance of Christ is more likely to appear when expressions of congregational culture are summarized. As the Other, Christ is there defined by the whole but not derived from it. The Christ of faith nuances the extensive whole of corporate experience rather than any one intensive congregational event.

The Eucharist, far from representing the sacred isolation of Christ from the fullness of plot, is the sign of their association. Nowhere else is the relationship of Christ and a local church's total culture more succinctly presented, displaying the variety of plot actions and evoking the presence of Christ. "The absolute invariable nucleus of every eucharistic rite known to us," according to Dom Gregory Dix, is its fourfold action:

(1) The offertory; bread and wine are "taken" and placed on the table together.
(2) The prayer; the president gives thanks to God over bread and wine together.
(3) The fraction; the bread is broken. (4) The communion; the bread and wine are distributed together.[7]

In Holy Communion the fact of Christ is proclaimed in conjunction with the elements of cultured grain and grape, in conjunction with humanly formed words, vessels, and gestures. As (1) an offering worthy of God and God's people, the goods of Eros are *linked* to Christ. By their presence over which (2) prayer is uttered they are *unfolded* in their divine significance. In (3) fraction their meaning is *thickened* to show their brokenness. And through (4) Communion their intention is *twisted*, transformed into the eternal banquet for all peoples. Essential in itself to the worshiping congregation, the Eucharist also symbolizes a larger liturgy played throughout the whole life of the local church. The Eucharist is the underlying paradigm for recognizing the actions of Christ and Eros throughout the life of the parish. To understand their mutual working, the nature of Eros must first be defined.

THE CHARACTER OF EROS

The myth of Eros attributed a human urgency to the cosmos, an interpersonal passion to seize form and meaning, thousands of years before our current understanding of the social construction of reality. Eros is popularly characterized today as little cupid, who instigates love affairs among gods and mortals. Behind the mischief, however, lives an earlier and considerably more formidable deity whose nature incites both ancient philosophers and contemporary theologians to recognize humanity's creative force.

On the whole, theologians are more likely than philosophers to be suspicious of Eros. In *Agape and Eros*, Anders Nygren sharply distinguishes Christian faith from Eros piety, which he considers the early church's "most dangerous rival"[8] and today the seducer of the human soul toward impossible attainment. Eros represents the striving of people for an ideal world, an acquisitive love of the beautiful and the good. Eros promises a salvation gained by human initiative. Erotic desire signifies the possibility of a self-generated fulfillment that satisfies personal need and rewards worldly accomplishment.[9] Against this urge of the world Nygren pits the agape of Christ through whom God by divine initiative offers the free gift of salvation. Eros builds from the ground up, seeking to realize for himself the beautiful and the good;[10] Christ by contrast reaches down, sacrificing himself, redeeming by uncalculating love the undeserving world.

Dietrich Bonhoeffer has a similar estimation of Eros. In *Life Together*, his stirring essay on Christian fellowship, he just as sharply differentiates the society of Eros from the community of Jesus Christ.[11] Although human reality, the realm of Eros, generates notable creativity, aspires to "the highest and the best," and lovingly seeks "human ties, suggestions, and bonds," such erotic practice for Bonhoeffer is self-serving and basically untruthful about life. Christian society lives instead according to a spiritual reality that discloses the truth of God and the occasion of agape, "the bright love of brotherly service."

In distinction from Nygren and Bonhoeffer, Troeltsch's interpreter H. Richard Niebuhr defines the relationship between Christ and Eros as more subtly interwoven. Christ for Niebuhr actually focuses and mediates both the agapaic movement of God toward the world and the erotic press of the world toward God.[12] Niebuhr's analysis seems to me to explain what actually happens in a congregation's plot. The toil of Eros is essential to congregational story because, as Niebuhr perceived, Eros signifies far more than the contradiction of agape love: Eros is an image of culture itself, the expressive stuff

without which the proclamation or incarnation of the Christian story is incon-
ceivable.

So basic is Eros to the composition of the universe that Hesiod names him
third in the order of creation:

> First of all, chaos came into being, next broad-bosomed Earth, the solid and eter-
> nal home of all, and Eros, the most beautiful of the immortal gods, who in every
> man and every god softens the sinews and overpowers the prudent purpose of the
> mind.[13]

Primordial Eros couples the cosmos, creating its forms, firing its process,
constituting its harmony. Eros is the overpowering, softening, possessive energy that gives things their shape and linked significance.

In today's view, culture gives the cosmos its shape and linked significance.[14] We no longer believe that our perceptions stem from something innate. Left to themselves, our sight and senses would be like those of newborn
children not yet taught the figure and meaning of things. It is only through
our initiation into the web of culture, into the intricacy of our language, that
chaos becomes the images, sequences, and ideas that compose the world we
know. Culture gives the world its understood nature. Culture is not just the
human representation and manipulation of nature; it is, for its human fabri-
cators, the underlying order of the cosmos itself.

Eros is thus a narrative symbol of our creative, grasping culture. His story
posits the settings, characterizations, and plots by which all people find their
way in a world that without story would recede into the formlessness of
chaos.[15] Eros is our narrative struggle to signify the value and consequence
of our existence.

In the *Symposium*, Plato recalls another tradition, one that identified Poverty and Plenty as the parents of Eros, thus emphasizing the daimon's double
nature that, on the one hand, is "always in distress," yet, on the other, is
"bold, enterprising and strong." This apposite joining of necessity and resource, of want and power, generates for Plato the erotic transaction.[16] A
similar union characterizes our present understanding of the creation of culture.

Culture, on the one hand, is the child of Poverty. Culture is the scenario,
Ernest Becker writes, that humans construct in the face of death to counter
the final deprivation that causes their obliteration.[17] Whether the ultimate
deficiency of death threatens my own life, or the integrity of a political system, or the future of people born and living in hopelessness and squalor, the
collective response of death's subjects demands their constant weaving and
repair of webs of significance that constitute a shared culture and common
story. I noted how the plot of common story deals with the threats of cultural
amnesia, oppression, alienation, and death. Similarly, story's setting fights
against the menace of absurdity, which is the denial of ordered scene. And

the character of a group's story represents a reaction to anomie, social decay that evokes both the Latin sense of "no name" and its Greek cognate of "no norm." Thus the terror of want spawns Eros. An ultimate poverty compounded of absurdity, amnesia, and the rest provokes an erotic quest for intimate community, the thirst for goodness and beauty, and the desire for meaning.

Nygren and Bonhoeffer nevertheless mistrusted this acquisitive grasp of Eros, and even Plato found him "terrible as an enchanter." Should we shy away from Eros? If we do, we avoid certain dangers. But unless we also engage him in a certain way, acknowledging the struggle that society consistently wages against chaos, we are left with a lonely need to address the absurdity in private. Without the passion of society for meaning, the search for significance becomes a desperate private quest. As long as one disregards the culture's own imperative to remember, to give things their shape, to assign their purpose and importance, one labors for these ends in terrifying isolation. I wrote these words shortly after my first operation for cancer:

> I learned last week how I will probably die—with a bit of luck, some time from now, but now a particular tiger in a pack has been pointed out to me as the one that will run me down. What has been most helpful in my distress has not been, as I would have expected, the counsel and concern of those friends who dared approach me person-to-person, providing talking therapy ("How do you feel about it?") or sure gospel formula. What has proved most comforting has been my sense, conveyed also by friends, of being part of a body—my seminary, my church, my family—that itself seeks meaning in distress. Anxiety recedes.

Eros offers the good news that none of us strives alone for meaning. My individual distress is also the distress out of which culture emerges. My own distress is not resolved, but it enlists the relentless struggle of the whole community.

But Eros is also parented by Plenty. His engendering also depends upon a resourceful counterpart: the rich human imagination that creates the forms and links and sequences by which we recognize the universe. Out of the fertile plenitude of Eros comes the opulent language of word, mark, and gesture. The narrative nature of erotic culture, moreover, is displayed in myths so compelling that they shape society's sense of itself. It is the symbolic capacity of culture that creates works of literary expression, drama, music, dance, and the fine arts. By Eros are made the world's tools and artifacts, the disciplines of inquiry, the events of human development and association. In its imaginative action, culture gives some attributes even to our understanding of God, because the concepts of creation, redemption, sanctification, Lord, grace, and salvation reflect society's metaphorical labor. Whatever objective reality our various views profess by such terms, that reality is signified by images compounded in culture. Eros expresses in part the nature and being of God.

THE CONGREGATIONAL
SETTING

Congregations are the church's erotically capacious households. Other organizations are specialized for particular ends. Seldom do other social organizations include both children and the aged; seldom do they rely upon members with diverse careers and educational preparations. Once joined, the noncongregational bodies of the church often gently pressure members into uniform patterns of behavior or attitudes. Among the structures of the church, only the congregation persistently addresses the diverse personal goals of its members.

Two stories, one of Eros and one of Christ, occur in the local church. This book has examined primarily the narrative that the congregation historically enacts through its day-to-day behavior and by its particular views and values. Comparable attention has not been given to the Christian story upon which the local church by its local story stakes its ultimate identity. Several recent books provide an opposite imbalance, emphasizing the congregation's normative relationship to Christian narrative.[18] "The social-ethical task of the church," says one, ". . . is to be the kind of community that tells and tells rightly the story of Jesus."[19] It is the contention of this book, however, that persistently and seriously as a congregation may present as its own the Christian story, it nevertheless enacts a cultural narrative identified by myths quite distinct from the story of Jesus.

No local church escapes Eros and, therefore, a narrative structure that draws upon the world's stories. It is no more reasonable to expect a Christian community to lose its peculiar erotic nature than it is to anticipate that Christian individuals will discard their own unique identities in following Christ. But the good news of Christ does not require that one's culture be obliterated in redemption. H. Richard Niebuhr exposed the inadequacy of attempts to free Christianity from culture:

> Christ claims no man purely as a natural being, but always as one who has become human in a culture; who is not only in culture, but into whom culture has penetrated. Man not only speaks but thinks with the aid of the language of culture. Not only has the objective world about him been modified by human achievement; but the forms and attitudes of his mind which allow him to make sense of the objective world have been given him by culture.[20]

In his typology of approaches to the Christ and culture problem, Niebuhr repudiates the contention of groups identified by his "Christ against culture" category who feel they can withdraw from their secular environment:

> When they meet Christ they do so as heirs of a culture which they cannot reject because it is part of them. They can withdraw from its more obvious institutions and expressions; but for the most part they can only select—and modify under

Christ's authority—something they have received through the mediation of society.[21]

The plot that tracks the connection between Christ and Eros in congregational story will be one that reflects not Niebuhr's "Christ against culture" category but his four other types of interaction between the two powers in human life. Rejecting the possibility of isolating Christian experience from a cultural matrix, Niebuhr cites four different motifs by which the relation between Christ and culture has been perceived:

   a. The *"Christ of Culture"* approach sees no essential conflict between Christ and Eros. Christ is the comprehensive fulfillment of culture, and culture the given expression of Christ. Culture is accepted as the present representation of God's grace and kingdom.

   b. *"Christ Above Culture"* recognizes present culture as a stage in the development toward divine perfection of a world that is now both holy and sinful. Eros is acknowledged as the necessary synthesis of divine and human activity that leads, by both revelation and human reason, to a full future salvation.

   c. *"Christ and Culture in Paradox"* proposes an inevitable dialectic between the sinfulness of culture and the graceful action of God within the world. Eros is tolerated as the inescapable, evil stuff of human life through which divine wrath and mercy must nevertheless occur.

   d. *"Christ the Transformer of Culture"* expresses the hope that even fallen culture can by the power of God be redirected to regain the kingdom that the Fall contradicts. Eros in all his activities is interpreted as the object of conversion that by radical transfiguration fulfills the intention of God for the world.

Niebuhr treats these contradictory understandings of Christ's association with culture as motifs advanced by different theologians and schools of thought through Christian history. Although he recognizes strands of the other approaches present in each theological position, he argues that a particular interpretation emerges in most situations as the most prominent,[22] and he enjoins Christians to reach their own "final" choice.[23] The study of the struggle of congregations to grasp the relationship of Christ to their own culture suggests, however, that all four motifs are constantly in play: it is difficult to find one theme dominating the others. Niebuhr's several motifs of Christ and culture are also the several actions of a Christian congregation's plot and, like those actions, are required for a coherent story. In the plot of the local church the story of Christ weaves itself throughout the erotic narrative, sometimes accepting and affirming the church's story as it stands (thus *linking* Christ and Eros), sometimes teasing (or *unfolding*) the congregational narrative toward the promise of the kingdom, sometimes prophetically contradicting the erotic story by disputing (thus *thickening*) its development, and sometimes actually transforming congregational culture by *twisting* its plot.

THE PLOT

Consider the relationship of Christ and Eros in the plot of young Smithtown Church.

Urgent Eros, striving for shape and meaning, stirred the minds of those who first thought about creating Smithtown Church. The early phone calls among potential members and the initial conversations in the shopping malls and around dinner tables conjured up a variety of churchly images. The planners worked from models in their heads that erotically joined images of fellowship, piety, work, and various loyalties to form a congregation they felt would be worthy of God. Although some disputes developed and a few initial planners fell away, ideas and images meshed sufficiently for the founders to begin, a half year later, their first services and other activities. They gained approval from their denomination, gave themselves a name, and announced to the community that they constituted a church. Eros linked them, unfolded their practice, thickened their collective life with frustration and challenge, and twisted a loose aggregate of individuals into a local church.

Eros *linked* them. So far in this book I have concentrated upon the temporal and ideational aspects of this linkage. Let me here focus upon its spatial and operational dimensions, the manner in which the people of the congregation took space and energy and, by the imaginative working of Eros, forged the links that helped to compose their household.

From the very first, participants grouped their borrowed chairs in a Sunday arrangement that suggested their intention of becoming a church, and they stood, bowed, and mingled in spatial relation to one another. Much of their attention centered upon their first building. Despite the fact that they did not have much money, their intended church structure had to be distinctive from other dwellings, proclaiming both to themselves and to their community that they were a Christian congregation. They and their architect accomplished the distinction by special roof lines, windows, and doors. A cross and a large sign further announced their purpose. Their mutual bond to faith became even more obvious in the new sanctuary. There another cross was placed in a central position, along with a pulpit and altar furniture. An open Bible, candles, stained glass, and tracts in the rear further surrounded them with an identity as people of God.

So did certain modal members of the young congregation. Carl Dudley speaks of the "saints" of a congregation, a few members whom the rest of the household may not emulate but nevertheless appreciate for the authentic way they exemplify the common faith. The saints helped to undergird Smithtown Church's new identity. A distinguished gentleman, prominent in the denomination, sat up front and typified the influence of the larger communion on this congregation. The ordained minister of the congregation, Sarah Peters, also filled linkage roles, especially priestly functions that presented and explained the symbols of the faith.

When they gathered each Sunday, the members performed further operations fashioned from the craft of Eros. They sang music, they assumed pious and attentive attitudes, they listened with appreciation to the complex exposition of Scripture, they responded with signs of warmth to moving parts of the service. Their common identity was further reinforced by church school classes held before the service, in which both children and some adults were knit together as much by their personal interaction as by the lesson material they studied.

Eros not only links the behavior of Smithtown Church to its identity, Eros also *unfolds* its action in relation to its goals. Once again Eros uses space, roles, and repetitive processes to further the plot. Smithtown sanctuary's primary erotic function was linkage; other areas of the building contributed more directly to the congregation's unfolding. Its office, corridors, and administrative rooms existed to promote the goals of the church, because it was within them rather than in the sanctuary that decisions about the future of the parish were made and directives enacted. Artifacts greatly different from those in the sanctuary developed the unfolding: telephones, office equipment, a plethora of paper products, bulletin boards, and other signs, including those that say "directory" and "exit."

Modal persons were again instrumental for Smithtown's unfolding. Most typical was the benefactor, whose support was required for any major physical or programmatic development in the congregation. Dudley identifies in this vein a group of members who are as important to the church's unfolding as his "saints" are to its linkage: the "organizers," people whose participation promotes the accomplishment of goals. Various processes of the church likewise enabled the unfolding of its plot: campaigns, committee meetings, elections, as well as the less conscious political and socializing actions of the parish. Pastor Peters functioned more as ruler than as priest in the unfolding process, the resourcer and executor of many of the church's programs.

Further, Eros *thickened* the plot of Smithtown Church, introducing both the complications that prevent its smooth unfolding and the means for integrating these differences within the church's story. Though they jointly resolved to begin a church, Smithtown's first members were a heterogeneous group, diverse in age, background, and status, and at variance with one another about the nature of the church they all were committed to develop. The resulting conflicts thickened Smithtown's plot. No rational administrative unfolding resolved fundamental disparities; nor did linking the plot to God in prayer bring solutions. Eros thus provided another set of cultural actions designated by the term of thickening.

Space, roles, and repetitive processes played a role in the thickening. Kitchen, fellowship hall, and group and counseling rooms served the purpose of integrating Smithtown's diverse members, bringing them from their sometimes dissonant private lives to a sense of shared community. The erotic artifacts in these areas were again distinctive. Food assumed a central place.

So did furniture more comfortable than the pews that link and the straight chairs that seat the unfolding of administration. Lighting softened; how things feel and touch became a paramount concern.

Certain types of people and processes served the thickening. One modal person was the cook, a member seldom seen outside the kitchen, present for every gathering, welcoming all sorts and conditions of hungry parishioners without regard to their beliefs or their capacity to contribute to the accomplishment of the church's program. Dudley's third group of distinctive church members are the "socializers," the people who come to life in organizing the games, dinners, and other gatherings that enable heterogeneous people to unite in common fellowship.

Thickening involves cultural processes that attend both the tension within the church and the tension between the church and its environment. Within the church were not only social gatherings but also the various sorts of care groups and age-defined fellowships that collected persons otherwise alienated from the ongoing functions of the congregation. But in its thickening, the church also addressed the dissonant world beyond the congregation: there it undertook a variety of mission and evangelistic programs and continued as well its sometimes discordant relationship to its denomination. In the thickening aspect of Smithtown's plot, Ms. Peters fulfilled a pastoral office, gathering and healing the flock while also urging that the church direct itself to the healing of the world.

THE TWIST

Is the planting and nurturing of a church such as Smithtown a fundamentally Christian activity? Every act and image mentioned has its counterparts in other religions. The graceful and loving presence of Christ may well be active within the kinds of events just reported, but both faith in Christ and appreciation of the abundant fertility of Eros resist the facile equation of specific parish events with the activity of Christ. A reluctance to identify, say, Smithtown's campaign for building funds or its development of a church school as peculiarly Christian work springs from convictions about the elusive otherness of even an incarnate savior. To lock Christ into particular actions of the congregation runs the risk of idolatry and just plain folly. This tentativeness springs not from an absence of faith but from faith's opposition to the guarantee of God in any concrete human construction, even those widely identified as most sacred.

Christ may not be presumed within each of the actions of plot, but Christ may, indeed must, be sought there. How Christ is present in and to the erotic culture of Smithtown Church must be the overriding ethical concern of its ministry. Sermons are suspect that do not wrestle with the topic of Christ's presentation within the specific plot of the listening congregation. Administrative and counseling sessions that do not labor to understand the association of their action to Christ are likewise misguided. But to cultivate Christ as a numinous moment in the outworking of church activities would miss the point. The purpose of discerning Christ in relation to Eros is the ethical one made by H. Richard Niebuhr. Christian ministry must constantly and publicly ask of its congregation's plot:

— Does this parish activity reflect a linkage that permits the recognition of the "Christ of Culture," in which the person of Christ is reflected in and through what occurs?

— Or is this a congregational activity that must unfold toward the goal perceived in the designation "Christ Above Culture," the understanding that the action's present nature, while acceptable, nevertheless requires development toward a more adequate realization of the kingdom?

— Or is this church activity deep in the thickening that represents "Christ and Culture in Paradox," dangerously but inextricably caught in evil and endured because even in its situation Christ is witnessed?

— Or does this parish activity require twisting, in obedience to "Christ the Transformer of Culture," radically converting its nature to conform to the person of Christ?

The last question is the most difficult. The most important twist in congregational life is its mission. Mission for a congregation means the crossing over of the boundaries of its cultural matrix into a world where the congregation's household webs of significance no longer obtain and the household is threatened by different discourses, stories, and social forces. In mission, the congregation meets its own erotic death, but the crucified Christ, outside the wall that encloses the familiar, also awaits the encounter:

> So Jesus also suffered outside the gate in order to sanctify the people through his own blood. Therefore let us go forth to him outside the camp, bearing abuse for him. For here we have no lasting city, but we seek the city which is to come.
> (Heb. 13:12–14, RSV)

With mortal consequences for its own erotic structure, the congregation in mission seeks the Christ who on his cross marks the *oikoumenē* beyond the parochial boundary. The congregation does not in mission propel outward the Christ it already knows from its internal history. Rather in hope, seeking the city which is to come, the congregation exits from its own structures and safeties to find the Christ who appears in societies whose histories repudiate the local church's unfolding plot.[24] How a congregation that currently avoids the quest might twist itself outward to Christ is the topic of the next chapter.

NOTES

1. Edward Farley, *Ecclesial Reflection: An Anatomy of Theological Method* (Philadelphia: Fortress Press, 1982), 3–168.

2. Ernst Troeltsch, *Die Bedeutung der Geschichtlichkeit Jesu für den Glauben* (Tübingen: J. C. B. Mohr (Paul Siebeck), 1911), translated by Robert Morgan and Michael

Pye, *Ernst Troeltsch: Writings on Theology and Religion* (Atlanta: John Knox Press, 1977), 191.

3. George Rupp, *Culture Protestantism: German Liberal Theology at the Turn of the Twentieth Century* (Missoula, Mont.: Scholars Press, 1977), 30.

4. Morgan and Pye, *Ernst Troeltsch*, 202.

5. Ibid., 205.

6. Ibid., 203.

7. Dom Gregory Dix, *The Shape of the Liturgy* (London: Dacre Press, 1945), 48.

8. Anders Nygren, *Agape and Eros*, trans. Philip S. Watson (Philadelphia: Westminster Press, 1957), 162.

9. Ibid., 170.

10. Ibid., 175.

11. Dietrich Bonhoeffer, *Life Together* (San Francisco: Harper & Row, 1954), 31–39.

12. H. Richard Niebuhr, *Christ and Culture* (New York: Harper & Brothers, 1951), 27–29.

13. Hesiod, *Theogony*, 56.

14. Peter L. Berger and Thomas Luckmann, *The Social Construction of Reality: A Treatise in the Sociology of Knowledge* (Garden City, N.Y.: Doubleday & Co., 1966). "The basic form of social objectivation is language. Language analyzes, recombines and 'fixes' biologically based subjective consciousness and forms it into intersubjective, typical and communicable experiences. The metaphorical and analogical potential of language facilitates the crystallization of social values and norms by which experience is interpreted. It is this edifice of semantic fields, categories and norms which structures the subjective perceptions of reality into a meaningful, cohesive and 'objective' universe. This universe, 'reality as seen' in a culture, is taken for granted in any particular society or collectivity. For the members of a society or collectivity it constitutes the 'natural' way of interpreting, remembering, and communicating individual experience. In this sense it is internal to the individual, as his way of experiencing the world. At the same time it is external to him as that universe in which he *and* his fellow-men exist and act" ("Sociology of Religion and Sociology of Knowledge," *Sociology and Social Research* 47 [1963]: 421).

15. "Not to have a story to live out is to experience nothingness: the primal formlessness of human life below the threshold of narrative structuring" (Michael Novak, *Ascent of the Mountain, Flight of the Dove: An Introduction to Religious Studies* [San Francisco: Harper & Row, 1971], 52).

16. *The Dialogues of Plato*, trans. Benjamin Jowett (New York: Liveright Publishing Corp., 1927), 223.

17. Ernest Becker, *The Denial of Death* (New York: Free Press, 1973).

18. Stanley Hauerwas, *A Community of Character*, 1–52. George W. Stroup, *The Promise of Narrative Theology: Recovering the Gospel in the Church* (Atlanta: John Knox Press, 1981), 132–69.

19. Hauerwas, *Community of Character*, 52.

20. Niebuhr, *Christ and Culture*, 69.

21. Ibid., 70.

22. Ibid., 44.

23. Ibid., 253.

24. Jürgen Moltmann, *Theology of Hope: On the Ground and Implications of a Christian Eschatology* (London: SCM Press, 1967), 304–38.

12

WILTSHIRE'S
WORLD STORY

The most analyzed congregation in America today is a church in New England that agreed in 1981 to submit itself to the scrutiny of a score of investigators who sought to understand how their different methods might work together when trained on the same object. Ethnographers, sociologists, psychologists, theologians, case study writers, and organization and management consultants observed the congregation and searched through church documents and transcripts of member interviews. The analysts later compared their findings in several conferences and finally recorded them in a book.[1] Because a consciously multidisciplinary approach to comprehending the life of a congregation had never before been attempted, the book, *Building Effective Ministry*, represented an important advance in the study of the local church. The difficult project was more successful, however, in analyzing the problems of Wiltshire Church than in suggesting how the church might address them. Chief among the findings was the consuming degree to which Wiltshire Church cultivated its private life and the self-centered values of its affluent neighborhood. But neither the social analysts nor the organization and management consultants provided much help to Wiltshire's leaders or to similar churches that want to change such a situation.

Whatever external investigators and consultants may accomplish in a congregation, its specific future still depends overwhelmingly upon its reaction to the information it gains about itself. Finally, it matters more what a congregation tells itself than what it is told. Deft analysis or intervention can, at best, resource the attempt of the local church to understand or change itself. Transformation requires a different order of knowing than that which outsiders provide.

The self-knowledge a congregation requires to study and alter itself is predominantly narrative in its form. Stories ranging from gossip to gospel compose the substance of what members say to each other about their household identity and task. Interpersonal communication occurs by symbol and is conveyed largely in story. Though preachers, analysts, and consultants may sometimes wish it otherwise, there is no connective tissue among members that directly transmits meaning except the symbolic interaction of the members themselves. Members can individually hear the words of a sermon or analytical presentation, but their corporate response depends upon the signals they subsequently trade with each other.

Taking up where the book on Wiltshire Church left off, this chapter suggests ways by which the congregation itself might, comprehending its own story, better understand its nature, circumstances, and mission. We shall start with a synopsis of the story Wiltshire Church tells itself and then show how an awareness of the narrative might help the church achieve deeper reflective and performative significance.

This account assumes the accuracy of the case study that begins the book about Wiltshire.[2] After a fictive introduction, the case study divides the plot into eight periods. The same form is employed in the synopsis that follows, and each period is identified by the title given to it in the case study.

1. Company town—company church

Members of the Adams family, who owned the major industry in the town of Wiltshire, had built without assistance from the townspeople both the first and the present church building, the latter a replica of a beautiful Anglican church in England but made from the same sandstone used to construct the Adams factory. The family had continued to control and maintain the church in a manner resembling the factory's oversight of the community. The patriarch would annually cover any deficit in operating the church. For decades the church had languished, a congregation of elderly people served by pastors who were themselves "tired old men, ready for retirement." In 1970 the last Adams patriarch, who had long been the church board chairman, and three other trustees died, causing great consternation among parishioners.

2. Sid Carlson appointed to Wiltshire

The Methodist bishop thereafter negotiated with Sid Carlson, a pastor known for his unusual managerial and preaching effectiveness, about the Wiltshire appointment. Before accepting the post, Sid, disguised as a corporate representative seeking a new business site, "checked out" Wiltshire. Officials welcomed Sid in disguise. He closely examined both the civic and religious institutions in town. In accepting the appointment, Sid entered a listless church that was losing members, while its surrounding community was rapidly growing. To consolidate the congregation he quickly: (a) collapsed the two ill-attended Sunday worship services into one, (b) removed 221 inactive persons from the church rolls, and (c) reduced the administrative board from 55 to 15 members. Because he found them incompetent, Sid fired both the veteran church secretary and the choir director. An angry choir met to consider petitioning the bishop to remove Sid, but Sid, uninvited, attended their meeting and challenged their authority. The choir backed down, as did the 55-member administrative board, which voted itself out of existence. Sid used executive force, not standard Methodist procedures, to make these changes. With moral indignation he disclosed that members contributed an average of only 25 cents each to the church each week and that they sent their children to church school in a building that violated seventeen fire code regulations. To address both failings Sid led the congregation into major debt that simultaneously required a more substantial contribution to retire it and permitted the renovation of the church school building and parsonage.

3. Growth in Wiltshire Church

The tactics worked. Over a hundred new members, drawn from the community's transient, upwardly mobile, middle-class executives, joined the church each year. Sid deliberately adapted the activities of the church to meet the conscious needs of a congregation composed of relatively young parents attracted to Wiltshire by its seclusion and good schools. "They really buy a school, not a home." Church school and youth work therefore became strong program features. Sid developed an uplifting worship service that included excellent music, and he used the pulpit to address the personal and family problems that accompany executive life: skepticism about the Christian faith and disenchantment with the American Dream, broken homes, tensions at work, appliances that malfunction, traveling spouses, children who drink and use drugs. To befriend such wary, wistful people Sid rejected the ministerial stereotype. He dressed, cursed, behaved, and managed his work like a dynamic corporate executive. No longer impotent, the church under Sid's leadership became an attractive and popular institution. "If you can't join the country club, join Wiltshire Church," the saying went. Wiltshire Church developed the reputation of being "the best show in town."

4. Recent changes

In the latter part of the 1970s, however, the combination of a compliant congregation and a forceful leader began to unravel. A similar shift occurred in the town itself. Wiltshire residents who commuted in order to work for other businesses had recently wrested control of the town from citizens loyal to the old Adams Company. They blocked, for the first time, a plan of the Adams Company to expand its business. Similar challenges confronted Sid Carlson. Members once eager to follow his leadership lost their zest, and Sid, turning fifty, lost some of his as well. Anxious about the future he: (1) entered a D. Min. program, the exams for which he failed, (2) pressed for better retirement provisions, (3) considered quitting the ministry, and (4) went to see a psychiatrist. Members increasingly criticized three aspects of what seemed to them arrogant behavior of pastor and church: neither Sid nor the congregation adequately participated in Methodist conference functions;

they gave scant evidence of traditional Christian piety; they did not, except in some personal ways, concern themselves with the poor.

5. Administrative board retreat

At a recent retreat the administrative board of Wiltshire Church spent its first hour exploring the identity of the church: its character, goals, and image. The lay leader drew up a summary, deprecatory statement: "I hear us saying we are a community of individuals who profess a belief in Christ, who have a limited or nominal belief in his teachings and the extension of his work, and who pose very limited responsibilities on becoming part of our group." Sid sat at the edge of the group and did not enter into its discussion.

Then the tenor of the meeting changed. Breaking his silence, Sid turned the discussion to a consideration of staffing needs, and the group spent the rest of the morning examining issues raised by the departures of the Sunday school superintendent, the minister of visitation, the assistant pastor, and the youth leader. After lunch, attention shifted to needs for extra Sunday school space and the inadequate insulation of the present education wing. Because there were not enough funds in the current budget to finance a new church school building, a vote on the construction advocated by Sid was postponed.

6. Pastoral housing proposal

During the last three years of the decade members had debated whether they should erect a new church school building, but another, more covert, building venture brought the church to open conflict. In early 1979, Sid had revealed that he was considering job offers elsewhere, and, to keep him at Wiltshire, several close friends in the congregation developed a plan to help Sid buy his own house. They contrived the proposal without the knowledge of the administrative board chairman, without approval of the bishop, and in opposition to conference regulations. The supporters viewed a private house as a way not only of retaining Sid but also of releasing him and his family from the constant attention of parishioners that the present parsonage adjoining the church encouraged. Sid liked the idea.

When presented to the administrative board in the fall of 1979, however, the proposal met a variety of objections. Some board members objected to the hidden negotiations, which were technically "out of order." Others doubted that the church members would submit to simultaneous campaigns for a church school building and for Sid's house. Some were concerned that the plan tied the church to Sid indefinitely, others that Sid already made more money than any other minister in the district. Worry about the bishop's reaction and uncertainty about precedents for relationships with future pastors further darkened the issue. The board tabled the proposal for further study. Sid became angry. "They don't give a goddamn about me," he said, feeling unsupported by those whom he had served for ten years. In a later

public meeting he vilified one of the objectors. Further conflict and complaints led the administrative board chairman to cancel all further official discussion of the housing proposal and to call a special meeting of the board, ex-
cluding Sid, to discuss objections to several aspects of Sid's behavior.

7. Tensions increase

Feeling its own authority usurped, the Pastor-Parish Relations Committee
objected to the meeting called by the administrative board chairman to
discuss complaints against Sid. The meeting ended without decision, and
shortly thereafter the church member abused by Sid resigned from the administrative board. Other members expressed their concerns about Sid's be-
littling those who did not agree with him and his breaking of confidences. Sid
began to raise questions about the church's renowned music program. It was
rumored that the organist and choir director would resign, thereby deepening
the alienation of the choir from Sid.

8. Building proposal

It was widely recognized that the church school building was small and
poorly constructed. Classes spilled over into Sid's study and also across a
busy street into rented quarters. The building itself could not be heated adequately and was ill-equipped for emergencies and handicapped people. Yet
the members of the church were uncertain about their capacity to raise sufficient funds to build a new building. The present levels of attendance and giving seemed dependent upon the continuing presence of Sid Carlson, but the
increasing discomfort with Sid and his own dissatisfaction with his lot suggested that he might leave. The administrative board continued to postpone a
decision about construction, and, tired of the mounting difficulties of Wiltshire Church, the chairman of the board resigned his post.

THE SETTING OF AN
ISOLATED CHURCH

Because it follows a case study format, the Wiltshire story ends with the
chairman's resignation and the important issues of the story unresolved. But
enough of the story has by then been told to sketch the church's plot and to
pose the major question the plot raises for Christian ministry: How might
Wiltshire Church address its alienation from the life of the world that surrounds and sustains it? How might it—entangled as it is in problems of self-
preservation—participate instead in the larger quest of humanity for redemptive community?

Others might identify another problem as the central one: ineffectiveness
of leadership and administrative arrangements, for instance. If this were the
key problem, the solution might be the removal of Sid Carlson. From another perspective, the problem might be identified as one of damaged relationships among members, the repair of which might be found in building up

a fellowship that encourages greater love and less animosity. Such managerial and therapeutic approaches in Wiltshire's case seem to me, however, to miss the depth of its trauma. The church was autistic. Probably to a greater degree than most other churches, Wiltshire conducted its affairs and generated its problems without reference to any larger church, society, or deity. It suffered, to be sure, from symptoms of ill will and maladministration, but these difficulties only exacerbated the more basic problem of Wiltshire's blindness to the rest of the world.

Note the evidence of its isolation. Church members were residents of a community dedicated to separating itself from the business life of its inhabitants in the nearby city. Wiltshire was dubbed a "Shangri-La" and was characterized in a news article as having a "drawbridge mentality." Upwardly mobile executives retreated to Wiltshire each evening. The attraction of the town, said its mayor, was "the ability to live in a suburban community and yet have . . . your own island. You can not only get in between the ridges every night, you then go and get in between the birches and elms. You can really isolate yourself."

Although the executives, restored by their overnight respite in Wiltshire, would return each morning to the realities of the workday world, they left their church behind, among the trees. Wiltshire Church was part of the retreat, like the town's country club. The church's recent success in recruiting members was due in good measure to the pastor's attention to private needs of those members. To further secure its seclusion, the congregation avoided links with either its denomination or its larger society. Sid Carlson provided the primary example. He was said to be "really turned off by Methodism," attending his annual conference only on its opening day and finding all Methodist structures burdensome. Nor did he cultivate the social dimension of his ministry. He said he had "minimal interest in impacting major social and economic problems in the community." Wiltshire Church sanctioned the independence of its pastor. It placed none of its members on denominational committees; it spent less than 4 percent of its budget on social outreach.

A similar isolation marked the beliefs of the congregation. At its retreat, the administrative board characterized the faith of Wiltshire Church by its distinction from the board's understanding of Christian orthodoxy: "We are a community of individuals who profess a belief in Christ, who have a limited or nominal belief in his teachings and the extension of his work." Other references are made to the church's agnosticism. When members of Wiltshire Church took the world view test described in chapter 6, the congregation made the highest empiric and lowest charismatic scores of any church yet tested. There was near the town of Wiltshire an eminently successful charismatic church that drew its members from roughly the same population as the United Methodist Church, suggesting that it would have been possible for Wiltshire Church itself to take a different spiritual tack, but instead the congregation, in its sermons and education programs as well as its informal conversations, emphasized its distrust of both standard orthodox and adventurous charismatic forms of Christian belief.

Ministry in a church as alienated as Wiltshire usually takes one or another form of scolding. The scolding asserts standards of benevolence, piety, and denominational conformity, and then demonstrates how far short of the mark a church like Wiltshire falls. Sermons and other pronouncements take on the prophetic task of criticizing a negative performance. Since the accomplishment of Wiltshire in its congregating fails to measure up to ethical expectations, its culture is treated as an inferior undertaking to be nagged toward improvement.

Prophetic critique conducted through the medium of scolding has several drawbacks. Because its manner is antagonistic, there is the temptation not even to attempt such an approach to a group as politically and economically powerful as Wiltshire Church. Persons or groups with strong commitments to social action or evangelical faith often shun direct engagement with Wiltshire-like churches, dismissing them as lost to the cause, and instead issue more general pronouncements that avoid the nastiness of encounter with specific congregations whose values oppose their own. Words that chastise, moreover, have difficulty making their way into the idiom of the congregation under censure. Criticisms in such a setting are usually deflected or rationalized. Although straightforward, specific talk about the shortcomings of a congregation has its place, its power to transform a church in contemporary times is not very much in evidence. Wiltshire Church patently serves a class of capitalist society that reinforces the individualistic posture and management style of the church. The congregation is further captive to the privatistic values of the American suburb. Its sophisticated membership and financial independence still further diminish the chances that it will be willing to listen to scolding. Wiltshire therefore seems a poor prospect for any usual type of prophetic critique. Might prophecy take another form?

The argument of this book is that the culture of even a church as isolated as Wiltshire contains its own prophecy. Instead of judging Wiltshire's story by external standards of merit, I would rather labor within the story to find its own dimensions of human value and transformation, its own linkages and twists. Like any other society, Wiltshire Church congregates itself by languages of association. Within those languages are the structure and images of all human imagination and their potential for both social cleavage and coherence. Rather than berate Wiltshire, I would seek to show how the story itself implicates Wiltshire Church in the life of the wider world.

One such implication resides in the church's world view. Members of the congregation consider their own beliefs, if not nonexistent, at most pale versions of Christian orthodoxy. Their empiric outlook, however, is integral to the circle of world view interpretations laid out earlier in this book. Human groups do not withdraw from the business of determining the setting of their own story. Wiltshire's faith is not, as it suspects, an infidelity to a Christian canon not its own, but a participation at a different point in a full round of interpretation. Each point in the compass of world view options involves, as earlier observed, its own oppositions and ancillary alliances. Far from being a withdrawal from faith, the highly empiric position of Wiltshire Church in fact represents a familiar way by which human society everywhere has attempted to wrest meaning from the chaos of life.

Were I a leader of Wiltshire Church, I would try to plumb the richness of what the church now interprets as rejection of Christian belief. I would point out that Wiltshire is dependent upon a worldwide imaginative struggle to gain an ironic distance upon traditional assertions about life and cosmos. I would attempt to show that what members identify as their doubt about Christian claims can also be viewed as reliance upon a genre of interpretation that has a reciprocal relationship with other, quite different genres of Christian belief. Wiltshire agnostics do not in fact remove themselves from the business of believing. In their reflection of certain interpretations they engage in a practiced and patterned negotiation familiar in the settings of many other human narratives.

The opportunites for taking Wiltshire's world view seriously might arise in sermons, classes, or informal conversations. Whatever the occasion, the common intention would be to show that the congregation's lack of orthodoxy is itself an arc of rich human interpretation that, rounded into a circle, enfolds all expressions of belief. If members were to begin to see in their own constructions the working of an entire world, what would be gained would be a sense of participation in a common human struggle for meaning.

THE CHARACTER OF THE
ISOLATED MEMBER

"I look upon myself on Sunday mornings as addressing a congregation of wistful hearts," Sid Carlson reported. "I am basically addressing a secular, agnostic congregation of people who are drawn to the church because they find themselves with children and suddenly begin to sense that they want to give the kids some kind of background." What sort of background is unclear. Although most church families at Wiltshire had successfully climbed up the corporate structure of business, the view from the top hardly supplied an integrating vision. Sid spoke of members' disillusion "with the American dream of the two-car garage and the house in the country—divorce—kids drinking and using pot—job conflicts—the plumbing leaking and your husband in San Francisco—the family needs [are] monumental." Not only was the church isolated from any larger imaginative working of humanity, individual members and families likewise saw themselves as separated from any larger social struggle to gain shalom for the world.

Wiltshire Church aligned itself to provide solutions that would fit the bureaucratic individualism of its members. It altered its program to supply the managerial and therapeutic ethos that, Robert Bellah argues, pervades a culture that has lost its communal values.[3] In Bellah's view, American culture is dangerously individualistic. It informs persons that their worth depends upon what they as independent agents make of life. To function in a society so atomized requires that each person become an efficient party to contractual arrangements that constitute the fabric of any collectivity, from large corporations to nuclear families. Effective management is required to fulfill the utilitarian goals of the social unit: each member has private goods that are parlayed to greatest advantage by efficient administration. But witness the disillusionment of Wiltshire's members. The free-standing individual also has needs that efficient management cannot fulfill. Thus an individualistic society requires a concomitant: a service intended to heal the emotional and physical suffering wrought in the individual's private lot in competitive society. Bellah identifies the managerial and the therapeutic as the twin hallmarks of the ethos—bureaucratic individualism—that now affects American life.

Hence in responding to the personal needs of its members, Wiltshire Church concentrated upon providing efficient administration and elaborate therapy. Sid Carlson cleared out the awkward elements, such as the oversized administrative board, that impeded effective congregational operation. He reduced the church rolls to active members; he streamlined committees and bypassed reactionary participants. Most important of all, he took personal control of the operation. Sid was a person "who knew how to take charge of a situation in the best corporate sense," and he ran Wiltshire as a chief executive officer might be expected to do. At least during the earlier years, programs under Sid's management met with surprising success. Sunday services, church school, youth fellowship, social occasions, and meetings functioned with businesslike efficiency. There were few complaints about Carlson's autocratic style, because he organized the church to work like a finely tuned engine.

Nor did Wiltshire Church neglect the therapeutic needs of its members. The church was called the "sanctuary" for parishioners in pain. "It is the place that provides nurture and caring for those who must go out of the sanctuary and do battle in a fundamentally exciting and positive world." The pastor himself was gifted in helping people in personal crises, and the God that he preached was a deity tuned to help people: a loving Father, a compassionate Son, and an available and forgiving Holy Spirit. People experiencing loneliness, anxiety, and failure found in Wiltshire Church a haven in which they could be healed.

By its efficient operation and attentive care of its members, the congregation reinforced the surrounding privatized culture. Members could treat such a well-managed church as a sort of corporation in which they bore limited personal liability. Further, the well-run church augmented their sense of singular worth, because each person had contracted to support "the best show in town" much as—with little else in common—fans support a winning sports team. Even those disappointed about their own accomplishments had confidential recourse to the church, where the pastor was poised to help them cope.

In learning to hear its own story, a congregation beckons its members to share a corporate life that challenges their excessively private identities. Stories knit people into large wholes. Stories give people a collective character that repudiates individualism. The narrative of Wiltshire Church may recount, in the main, managerially and therapeutically tinged events, but their being bound into the form of a story witnesses a continuing communal drama that cannot be reduced to the atomized experiences of isolated members.

Wiltshire's story therefore requires strong characterization to pit it against its members' tendency to disintegrate corporate history into their private dramas. Unless vivid tropes and a memorable script present Wiltshire's story, it cannot become good news to members now secluded in their separate egos. A myth must be found that illuminates Wiltshire's story. The myth of Zeus on Olympus serves that purpose.[4]

Edith Hamilton summarizes the myth:

> The Titans, often called the Elder Gods, were for untold ages supreme in the universe. They were of enormous size and of incredible strength. . . . The most important was Chronus, in Latin Saturn. He ruled over the other Titans until his son Zeus dethroned him and seized the power for himself. . . .
> The twelve great Olympians were supreme among the gods who succeeded to the Titans. . . . The entrance to [Mount Olympus] was a great gate of clouds kept by the Seasons. Within were the gods' dwellings where they lived and slept and feasted on ambrosia and nectar and listened to Apollo's lyre. It was an abode of perfect blessedness. . . .
> Zeus became the supreme ruler. He was Lord of the Sky, the Rain-god and the Cloud-gatherer, who wielded the awful thunderbolt. His power was greater than that of all the divinities together. . . . Nevertheless he was not omnipotent or omniscient, either. He could be opposed and deceived.[5]

There are significant correlations between the narrative of Wiltshire Church and the Zeus myth. I sort some out according to the analytical categories advanced in chapter 7.

Crisis and resolution

Life at Wiltshire Church under the Adams family and within the Adams Company was chronic and saturnine, captive and dull. Chronus kept all his offspring, save Zeus, in his belly. But Zeus by deception escaped the imprisonment and forced old father Chronus to vomit up his children. The overthrow of the Titans ensued. Four trustees died in 1970. Zeus threw out the old leadership and established himself as supreme ruler. So did Sid Carlson.

Manner

Zeus was an arbitrary and dictatorial ruler, using thunderbolts to punish those who dared oppose him. But not only did he punish the wrongdoer, he also advised the suppliant, giving counsel to seekers who came to his shrine. Carlson was a "one man show" at Wiltshire, a person of exceptional management gifts who ran the church and who got his way not only because of the acquiescence of corporation-minded members but also because he had a habit of "getting people," ridiculing them with his thunderbolts. But Carlson was also the pastor who provided therapy for souls who found their way to his shrine.

Mood

The mood, by Jove, was jovial. Remote Olympus was the land of the blessed. The gods lived in marvelous houses and enjoyed the best food and entertainment. Wiltshire, equally remote from the cares of mortals, provided comparable residences and entertained its members in "the best show in town." Members gained jovial solace: they were loved and accepted in the Olympian sanctuary.

Expectation

The Olympian gods were ultimate but not spiritual powers. Spirituality is marked by aspiration to or inspiration by a power beyond oneself. But the Olympian gods, though immortal, partook of no such transcendence. They themselves were beyond control, beholden to none. Likewise, the members of Wiltshire were beautiful, successful people in whose veins seemed to run the ichor that would make them immortal. They were oriented not to the Other but toward personal ultimacy, either for themselves or their children. They expressed, through Sid, their disdain for anything larger than themselves—social issues, church, or deity—that would command their obedience and deny their private sense of immortality.

To characterize Wiltshire as Olympus is to resist the prevailing ethos of bureaucratic individualism that denies binding myth, indeed *any* binding force other than utilitarian contracts. The Zeus myth is not a pretty story, but its very aptness and ugliness might awaken its actors both to their plight and to their Christian promise: that Zeus, like Eros, intertwines with Christ who redeems the storied body.

THE PLOT OF AN
ISOLATED GOD

The individualism of Wiltshire churchgoers and the isolation of their church from the larger society were not unrelated to the way they demarcated the presence of God in distinct events within the total life of the congregation. Two sorts of occurrences at Wiltshire seemed to its members to manifest the Holy: the sermon and the music program. Both transpired within what many observers would call "the sacred space" of Wiltshire Church's sanctuary, and both represented instances in what the same observers might call "the sacred time" of Wiltshire's ongoing history. But isolating God in

these events diminishes both the nature of God and the significance of the total life of the corporate household. It suggests that God inhabits only packaged moments in history and that the bulk of life lived outside those moments is profane. I contend that the exclusive concentration of Wiltshire and
many other churches upon sermon and sacrament and beauty to reveal the
presence of God defeats their attempt to embody the fullness of Christ's plot
for the congregation.

There is no special area in a church building that can be justified as sacred
space any more than there is authenticated sacred time within particular parish history. Wiltshire undertakes powerful ritual actions in its sermons and
music that may seem unusually holy. But the perusal of the total plot does
not support a distinction between sacred and profane events. The characteristics of so-called sacred time—symbolic intensity, deep emotion, repetitive
corporate behavior—do not cluster only in special moments and places. All
household life is caught up in the creation of the cosmos. No act escapes the
tremendum of death. The entire story is sacred. Particular ritual behaviors distinguish the Sunday morning service from the rest of Wiltshire Church's
plot, but their performance marks more a mode of story's unfolding, not the
congregation's only appointment for entry into God's real presence.

The limitation of God's presence to isolable sacred times in Wiltshire
Church also restricts an understanding of what constitutes moral behavior. If
God is linked only to its worship, a consequence is that a congregation's other
struggles to survive and find meaning are stripped of religious meaning. The
obvious structural connection between its total life and the life of other human societies is then obscured because that connection does not merit divine
designation.

Wiltshire could be challenged to face its isolation from the world by proclaiming all its space and time as in some sense holy. To discover that the entirety of the physical space and historical time it shares is of God might check
its relentless habit of restricting meaning to hot spots in its worship and to
crises in the lives of its individual members. Finding in its plot the negotiation of Christ and Eros in spaces heretofore considered inert and at times of
its common life regarded as incidental or profane, Wiltshire Church could
begin to appreciate its implication within the working of all social space and
time. For Wiltshire is a participant, whether it acknowledges it or not, in a
long and broad history that bears a similar erotic patterning to Wiltshire's
own. It is not merely the congregation's Eucharist that follows the fourfold
action of plot, in which elements are taken or unfolded, then blessed or
linked, then broken in the act of thickening, and finally distributed in a twist
that foretells the kingdom banquet. The entirety of Wiltshire's story performs a larger liturgy equally disposed to divine presence.

Were the congregation of Wiltshire to discover this intertwined work of
Christ and Eros throughout its corporate history, it might better comprehend
its participation in the full pattern of human striving for worth and meaning.

If the church could see within the peak moments of its worship not the point but the paradigm of its total life, and understand that its sermons, prayers, and music do not only meet personal needs but, more important, also symbolize the whole struggle of an embodied people, then the congregation might better grasp its solidarity with peoples throughout the world who labor to voice their own significance. It would be easy to demonstrate how Wiltshire, like Smithtown Church in the last chapter, used space and modal persons to enact its plot. But even the gritty recent political history of Wiltshire Church can be shown to participate in universal forms of symbolic behavior. In each of the eight periods demarcated by the case study, a single action of plot characterizes the period and another action is there repressed. The account of Wiltshire's corporate life weaves its way through a texture of linkages, unfoldings, thickenings, and twists that constitute a way of identifying far-reaching strands of social behavior. To understand their mesh within one community provides coordinates by which to place the community within the world.

Plot actions within Wiltshire's story of conflict and self-interest play out the following pattern:

1. *Company town—company church:* The era of subordination to the Adams family was remembered primarily by its attention to *linkages*: the physical and economic associations of the church with the Adams Company, the replication in Wiltshire of a historic Anglican church structure, the adherence of the church to the lives and fortunes of the Adams lineage. Notably absent from the plot was any *thickening*, complicating reference to conditions and events that contradicted the bond of the church to power and prestige.

2. *Sid Carlson appointed to Wiltshire:* Here is a *twist*. Some old leaders died, others were turned out of office by the new pastor in an administrative transformation that paralleled simultaneous changes in program, worship, and pastoral style. *Linkage* to older patterns and persons suffered.

3. *Growth in Wiltshire Church:* An *unfolding* of Wiltshire's plot followed Sid's alterations. The congregation steadily grew. Its church school developed. The church became attractive to new executive families moving into Wiltshire, but service to their private needs further diminished the *linkage* of Wiltshire to Methodism, orthodox beliefs, and wider community concerns.

4. *Recent changes:* The plot *thickened* in the frustrations of the later 1970s: Sid, turning fifty, worried about his career and retirement; members became increasingly restless under his autocratic leadership. An earlier zest for church development disappeared. The possibility of *twist* resourced by decisive leadership and member enthusiasm diminished.

5. *Administrative board retreat:* The attempt of the board to *link* itself by exploring its identity was defeated by Sid's refusal to participate and his shift of attention to matters of *unfolding:* appointments to staff vacancies and the modification of the education wing.

6. *Pastoral housing proposal:* Each of the final three periods in the case study shows the further *thickening* of Wiltshire's story. The housing proposal surfaced the deepening tension between a group supporting Sid and those opposed to the scheme. The orderly *unfolding* of church process was repudiated in several ways: the group acted behind the backs of the administrative board and against Methodist conference regulations; and the group was aware that opposition to its scheme might well subvert the continuing leadership of Sid Carlson in guiding the church.

7. *Tensions increase:* The very title of this period suggests its *thickening.* Wiltshire's administrative board and Pastor-Parish Relations Committee were at odds; Sid and a board member got into a fight; animosity grew between Sid and the choir director. The potential for any *twist* disappeared in Wiltshire's administrative paralysis: a compromised pastor, an almost nonexistent staff, and church committees suspicious of each other.

8. *Building proposal:* In a final *thickening,* the proposal for a new education building was opposed because of doubts about the capacity of the church to finance the construction. And, in the final, tense action of the case study, the administrative board chairman resigned. Once again conflict-laden issues prevented the church's *unfolding.* Decisions were postponed; Wiltshire Church expressed uncertainty about its direction and its power to achieve its goals.

More is at stake in Wiltshire's recent history than an administrative crisis. The congregation might well diagnose the problems of these years in managerial terms, but in so doing, it would miss the opportunity to see in its thickenings and unfoldings the immediate narrative of Eros and Christ. The erotic labor of a body given Christ's name is the local instantiation of the world struggle, with all its frustrations and potential for disaster. For Wiltshire to seek its full story with that story's resonances throughout the forms of human suffering and human imagination would open the congregation to its redemptive promise.

Story is the larger liturgy of the congregation. Its local outworking reflects the structures of human societies that struggle to exist throughout the world. By gathering into its local telling the manifestations of setting, character, and plot, and by linking its structure to that of other people's stories, narrative overcomes the notion that we are atomic individuals justified by our private works. In faith we yield to a larger work that is God's economy for the world.

NOTES

1. Carl S. Dudley, ed., *Building Effective Ministry*.

2. Ibid., 3–20.

3. Robert N. Bellah, "Discerning Old and New Imperatives in Theological Education," *Theological Education* 19 (Autumn 1982): 7–29.

4. For a fuller exposition of the consonance between the Zeus myth and the Wiltshire story, see James F. Hopewell, "The Jovial Church: Narrative in Local Church Life," in Dudley, *Building Effective Ministry*, 68–83.

5. Edith Hamilton, *Mythology*, 24–27. Cf. Hesiod *Theogony*, VIII–XII.

13

EPILOGUE: THE MINISTRY AND MISSION OF CONGREGATIONAL STORY

Narrative can be a means by which the congregation apprehends its vocation. Though I have written this book in part to set forth what I think is a neglected perspective among scholars, researchers, and consultants who study congregations, at the end of the ministerial day it matters less whether private analysts understand the narrative features of the congregation than whether the congregation itself understands those features. If through greater sensitivity to its stories a local church better discerns its constitution and mission, the effort of narrative analysis will have a significant result.

That a congregation communicates by narrative is not merely a descriptive fact. It is also a normative intention of Christian ministry. A healthy congregation, like a healthy family, is one that understands and tells its stories. Neither families nor parishes can, in any event, escape some kind of narrative exchange, but their vigor in part depends upon the degree to which they know that they know these narratives. Parish self-understanding, like that of a family, depends upon its perception of itself in a particular time and form, with a memory of its past and the capacity for an open yet characteristic future. A vital congregation is one whose self-understanding is not reduced to data and programs but which instead is nurtured by its persistent attention to the stories by which it identifies itself. Thus a congregation that wants to deepen its perception of what it is and where it is going should consider what James Hillman called "restorying,"[1] the conscious employment of accounts by which its corporate life is structured and interpreted. To ignore story, or to treat it lightly, is to miss a major way by which a congregation may come to terms with its identity and calling.

The central argument of this book is that narratives, like sacraments, can be signs that do things. As J. B. Metz reports, a story can have a practical and performative aspect, not just a descriptive function.[2] Three potent actions of ministry are latent in the stories that a congregation tells about itself. They correspond to the major sections of the book. First is the ministry of *evocation* present in congregational storytelling: the development of an awareness "that we are." Second is the ministry of *characterization*: the deepening of the sense of "who we are." Finally there is the ministry of *confession*: the congregation's acknowledgment of "what we are."

a. *Evocation*. If uncorrected by story, the subtle message of a congregation portrayed primarily by its statistics and programs is that members are essentially private contributors to the church who volunteer their presence, time, funds, and energy to constitute its being. Much of the current understanding of Christian commitment begins with the individual, who, supposedly, from a personal stock of time and resources provides for the church. Storytelling represents a different way of considering commitment, one that depicts members as agents in a drama, not donors to a program. By its ministry of evocation, parish story incorporates participants in a common entity. Narrative establishes "that *we* are." It works against the notion that the congregation is a loose aggregate of miscellaneous souls whose relationship to each other is summed up in the private contribution that each makes to an unsubstantiated whole.

A major function of parish story, therefore, is the formulation of a larger setting for the self, one that situates the individual as part of a society and a world. In establishing a setting, narrative acknowledges that what "I" am only gains sense in the matrix that "we" are. "I" do not as donor create the corporate entity and the world that holds it; rather, "I" figure as actor in the larger narrative that group and world provide. Insofar as parish story is told with attention to its setting, then, we state that we are not adrift as atoms in a chaotic soup. By narrative we are comrades in common story, first with those who play out the story in our congregation, but ultimately with all people who in communal discourse inhabit the world. Jesus cleansed the temple of symbols that suggested that worshipers by their private donations of money and animals could constitute the temple's activity. The temple, his action suggested, did not require such gifts. It was the house of God: its corporate prayer constituted the worshipers and formulated their setting.

Any congregational setting or world view, particular and idiomatic as it may be, evokes the commonality even of those who do not adhere to it. For each particular view is formed in negotiation, sometimes in contention with its opposite, often in conspiracy with a different but partly allied view. Thus empiric Wiltshire links itself, in one way or the other, to a wide array of divergent views and those who hold them. Thus my hospital visitors and I, as different and even contradictory as were our various views of my plight, found that our telling of world stories evoked among us a corporate ministry.

b. *Characterization*. "A man's sense of his identity," Stephen Crites says, "seems largely determined by the kind of story which he understands himself to have been enacting through the events of his career, the story of his life."[3] The story told by Hero Trinity enabled the congregation to consider its peculiar identity. The second ministry of parish narrative is to articulate the character of the congregation, the persistent distinctiveness that individuates the church from its setting and from other bodies. Ministers, I noted much earlier, refer to the unique character of the church as its personality. But character is a more adequate term to describe the full ethos of the parish, its specific pattern of dispositions and values. It is in its distinctive experiences through time that these traits and norms are expressed, and story is the vehicle that accounts for them. Telling the story identifies the parish's moral particularity, the finite role and behavioral dimensions of the church's life.

The conscious use of myth in the ministry of characterization does more than merely sharpen the story. It also encourages a more authentic storytelling and thus a more faithful ministry. Wendy O'Flaherty explains. We can best understand our own myths, she says, "by translating them into other myths, by drawing them back into that internal hub where our own reality, our own nature, intersects with the myths preserved by tradition, by culture."[4] Finding the mythic resonance of congregational story is not an eccentric action, diverting the group from real self-knowledge. The correlate myth, rather, draws perception toward O'Flaherty's hub, the center of human characterization. "Properly understood," she continues, "myths provide a conceptual system through which one may understand and thereby *construct* a universal reality, a roundhouse where we can move from the back of one person's reality to another's, passing through the myth that expresses them all."[5]

There is always the danger of distortion in relating stories about one's church, accentuating the achievements and minimizing the failures. A greater danger of distortion occurs, of course, in the congregation that totally neglects its story, but even in the best of tellings there persists the temptation to flatter the teller or the audience. What O'Flaherty reports about myth, however, is that using it consciously provides a means of directing the narrative to ordinary social constructions of reality. Myth seldom flatters; it reminds us of our labor to interpret ourselves in an uncertain world and of our commonality with other societies in the labor. An entirely objective assessment of congregational character can never be gained by any means. But telling the congregational story in counterpoint with mythic parallels may give it greater chance of being a "true" story.

When the corporate story and myth are not used to characterize the tellers, the group finds other ways to account for its condition. When a parish lacks a narrative sense of its corporate identity, it will probably assume that its nature is the aggregate of personal stories of individuals prominent in its life. It therefore may glorify or, by scapegoating, condemn such persons out of all proportion to their actual consequence. Frequently these projections focus on the pastor, who, without the constraint of the larger parish story, is extravagantly praised or blamed for the condition of the congregation. Parish story tempers the tendency to create goats and heroes, providing in their stead a corporate identity by which to characterize the happenings of the church.

It is now several years since Bigelow Church first told its Briar Rose story, and it still wrestles with the implications. A new team of pastor and young assistant have been appointed to the church, and members voice the hope that "the suitor has now penetrated the thorns." "We were a teenaged church," says one member, "and now we are waking up." "The myth of Briar Rose was still active until the fall of 1981," says the assistant pastor, "but members have now got restless and have dug themselves out of the thistles." Bigelow members have focused on the problem of their frail identity. They feel that they have now consolidated their programs and financial prospects and that their sense of community has measurably increased under the care of their new pastor. Anger is still expressed about the manner in which earlier ministers did not "parent" them in a way that would have permitted their childhood "innocence, beauty, and wonder" to bloom a bit longer.

Has Bigelow escaped the Briar Rose myth? A number in the congregation believe that the tale no longer characterizes the church. Some have speculated, though based on little new research, that the church may now live in consonance with another fairy story: Cinderella. Bigelow is today known by passers-by as the Pumpkin Church because of the tons of pumpkins that its young people sell in its yard before Halloween. Prince Charming may have come to the church in the form of its new pastor, who is significantly more acceptable than his immediate predecessors. In the terms of this new myth, the church considers itself treated poorly by its former pastor-parents, who, it feels, abused, ignored, and abandoned it. "Sandwiched," as it says, "between two great churches," Bigelow persistently compares its poorer lot with two sister Methodist churches. Prince Charming, moreover, promises a castle, for he is leading a movement to build a new sanctuary to replace the present casket-like structure in which Bigelow worships. Bigelow feels, like Cinderella, the possibility of transformation.

What matters here is not which myth to employ. What is significant is that Bigelow has learned to wrestle with the nature of its character by the use of narrative. It is able by metaphor to talk publicly about its serious problems, more able than most churches I have encountered. It is also more clear and candid about its hopes. Without platitudes or promotional rhetoric it can express its dreams and talk about awakening and new life. It has, through narrative, come to terms with the particularity of its character.

c. *Confession*. Confession, like story, involves both an exercise of memory of what has occurred and the anticipation of what might happen next. In story, especially in a confessional form that stakes parish life within the gospel story, the congregational plot develops from a remembered past through a confessed present to a promised yet open future. Narratives relate the possibility of transformation, the unpredictable outcome of present congregational actions and decisions. To tell the congregational story, therefore, is an act of confession in which the parish acknowledges that while it is the principal author of its plot, and accepts the design of its past and the nature of its present, in the light of God's story for all humankind it also resolves to claim a transformed future.

Unless its corporate story is confessed, a congregation may drift in despair. Unless the plot is found that connects its actions and identifies their course, corporate life has no point, no conclusion. How does the recounting of the story to date set up the future? Charles Winquist likens it to homecoming, a return to dwelling:

> Storytelling can be allied to homecoming because homecoming is more than the collection of actuality. It is more than a bare statement of our facticity. Homecoming is a re-collection of experience. Our remembrance is an interpretation. We tell a story about the actuality of experience to lift it into a context of meaning that speaks out of the reality of possibility as well as actuality. The *prima materia* of meaning encompasses the possibilities from which the particularity of historical fact is made determinant. The re-collection of experience attends the fullness of the reality. As strange as it may seem, re-collection allows us to think ahead to the original ground of experience and become conscious of the finality of meaning that coincides with the origination of the actual.[6]

In telling the story of the congregation, we unravel its plot. Perhaps our version is less authentic than others yet to be told, but only in relating it does the congregation begin to come to terms with its symbolization of the way things have been for it. Then, as Winquist suggests, the group struggles by story to acknowledge the ground of its corporate existence and the possibility that projects it toward the end of all being.

Those proposing to undertake the recollective, confessional, and transforming ministry of plot must be warned, however, that this aspect of congregational story is, in J. B. Metz's word, "dangerous." "Memory and narrative," says Metz, "only have a practical character when they are considered together with solidarity and solidarity has no specifically cognitive status without memory and narrative."[7] A local church examining its own plot explores at the same time its inescapable identity with the actions of all groups: their linkages, unfoldings, thickenings, and twists. Thus a fortuitous irony awaits those congregations whose white, American, middle-class representatives are most likely to buy this book and employ some of its methods. If such relatively affluent communities do in fact attempt to move beyond their technically and psychologically sophisticated understandings of themselves to tell their household stories, they will encounter there the narrative of groups deprived of technical and academic sophistication who have little but story by which to understand and modify their corporate existence. Churches curious about their own story embark on a "dangerous" activity that might show their solidarity with the world's poor and oppressed peoples.

An example of the danger lies close at hand. In the previous chapter, I argued that plot indicates the participation of the congregation in history. Consider how a congregation's deepening awareness of its historicity parallels the struggle of oppressed people reported by Paulo Freire. Freire states that human groups gain consciousness of their selfhood only as they recognize themselves in the pregnant sequence of time. They "develop their power to perceive critically *the way they exist* in the world *with which* and *in which* they find themselves [when] they come to see the world not as a static reality, but as a reality in process, in transformation."[8] Liberation first requires that a people discover their own historicity:

> Strictly speaking, "here," "now," "there," "tomorrow," and "yesterday" do not exist for the animal, whose life, lacking self-consciousness, is totally determined. Animals cannot surmount the limits imposed by the "here," the "now," or the "there." . . . Through their continuing praxis, men simultaneously create history and become historical-social beings. Because—in contrast to animals—men can tri-dimensionalize time into the past, the present, and the future, their history, in function of their own creations, develops as a constant process of transformation.[9]

By understanding their presence in time and their creative participation in its unfolding, people overcome their sense of life's immutability and find courage for a transformed future.

Most popular notions of the future of the local church today are technical concepts that work by formula, not history. The notions build upon regularities that use numbers and statistical trends to predict the outcome of the congregation. Pictured in this mechanistic light, congregations suffer in a state resembling the dilemma of the unselfconscious, ahistorical peoples described by Freire: they do not know their plot. They do not understand the storied continuity that moves by the transfiguring power of links and twists. One of the tragedies of mainline churches that lost so many members in the 1970s was that their leadership was better equipped to offer them computer-produced documentation of their decline than to help find meaning in the changing story of each community. But the survival of the local, middle-class American church is less than half its story. In finding the forms of its own narrative, it meets also the labor of the human race in the larger struggle for meaning and freedom.

By its witting participation in its own stories the congregation becomes a mediating structure by which individuals ally themselves with the people of the world. Deepening its consciousness of the cultural forms and social processes that constitute its own household, the parish functions as a halfway house that initiates the once isolated member into the struggles of society at large. Local churches are seldom judged to have this capacity. More frequently, observers maintain that present-day congregations are unlikely to escape their captivity to local interests and private religiosity. But the congregation, by both tradition and demonstrable narrative composition, is more powerfully associated with the struggle of the whole church, the *oikoumenē*, than often recognized. Parish resources are, as argued before, capacious, sensitive to the issues of power, open to history. If a congregation persistently wrestles—in sermon, class, and conversation—with its own memory and narrative, it can profoundly deepen its sense of identity with the suffering of the world.

I am not minimizing the power of social and psychological forces that mold a congregation's conservative outlook and behavior. I am proposing, however, an alternative to the usual means employed to goad the local church to social responsibility: appeals based on shame, sympathy, and scriptural injunction. The approach through parish story is different, subversive, dangerous. Unlike the other methods, it instructs us first to watch ourselves: how we set and characterize our story, how our own plot moves through history. Shielded neither by statistical and programmatic facades of self-description nor by normative proclamations about what the church should be, we look at our finite, culture-bound symbolisms and find in them our idiomatic expression, but also structures wrought by the imaginative labor of all humanity.

THE CHURCH IN
THE WORLD

I want to end close to where I began, locating my argument among those of others who care about the local church. The fundamental differences among us, I believe, have to do with the various ways we envision the parish in mission within the larger world. Mission in its Christian sense means crossing the boundary between the domestic and what lies beyond the parish household. In an early chapter, I envisioned the congregation peering out of certain windows to interpret itself in the light of the part of the horizon it saw there. But congregations do more than orient themselves to one of a variety of world interpretations. They also live in engagement with the world that extends beyond, and through, their own identities.

Stephen Pepper, in his *World Hypotheses*, again assists me. Earlier I used, somewhat covertly, a version of Pepper's categories to distinguish the various approaches that analysts make to understand individual congregations.[10] Here I return to Pepper's original intention and consider the root metaphors by which various thinkers have understood the world. I then search these metaphors for the place of the church within them.

Pepper finds four distinct arguments for what constitutes the world and its operation. He terms these hypotheses the contextualist, mechanist, organicist, and formist positions, and he demonstrates how philosophers and scientists have based their theories on one of the four. If our interest is the mission of the Christian church and the gospel to which that mission witnesses, we must pay close attention to what composes the world that the church engages. Pepper provides four different images.[11]

In Pepper's *contextualist* category, the world is the exciting and disturbing texture of current events. Missional engagement in such a world means embracing the consequences of today's incidents, the events to be related in tomorrow's newspaper and other chronicles. It requires the parish to recognize its dependence upon the circumambient forms of its place and epoch and to accept as its own nature the world's problems and opportunities. A contextualist understanding of the world requires the passion of the church, the suffering of the world's issues. Most present characterizations of world events include oppression, injustice, and anxiety. For the church to undertake its mission in a contextually conceived world compels its presence in such distress and ambiguity.

Pepper's *mechanist* category portrays the world as a machine. By this metaphor the world is understood according to the regularities of its forces. Causal laws explain it. Scientific treatises rather than newspapers record its workings. Mission in such a world entails action rather than passion, impact instead of suffering. To be the church in a mechanistically conceived society is to be an initiating agent that changes the lives of those the church reaches out to touch. The congregation applies the laws of human and social behavior to the world to transform it.

Pepper's *organicist* hypothesis views the world as developing toward a final integrated reality which is unapparent in its present state. In an organic process the world unifies its disparate parts, overcomes obstructions, and grows toward wholeness. A congregation in an organicist world has a different sort of mission: it uses its corporate life as a prototype of the world process. Accepting the heterogeneity of its members, the congregation takes upon itself a synthesizing activity for the world at large and strives to develop a paradigmatic fellowship, a foretaste of the ultimate community of all humanity. Eschatological vision rather than scientific treatises reveals the organicist world. Both the world and the kingdom to come occur in microcosm in the local church. In an organicist hypothesis the part discloses the whole. The life of a single parish stands for the ultimate fellowship, the *koinōnia*, that all people will have among themselves and with their God.

There is a fourth world hypothesis that suggests still another way. The *formist* category of Pepper figures the world as a collectivity of structures. Different entities participate in this collectivity in different ways to derive their particular identities. Such a world rests upon the evidence of similarity, the correspondence of certain images and patterns with others, and the argument that such consonance implies a common form or structure in which similar objects participate. It is upon such a perception of the world that this book relies. To note, as I do, the correspondence between the exploits of Trinity Church and the journey of the Hero, or between sickbed tales and the genres of literature, is to propose a formist view.

This view also has as its base a missional purpose. I have been trying to convey a fourth and underused way in which the church exists in the world. Mission in my view involves a witting participation in the world's meanings, an appreciative acknowledgment of forms of signification by which societies from the first have labored to shape and point their communities. The world in this formist argument is witnessed not so much in newspapers, scientific works, and eschatological vision as in literature and other symbolic structures.

Many missiologies assume that there are essentially two forms of mission: evangelism and service, a vertical obligation that brings people to God and a horizontal duty that requires Christians to support other human beings. The mission of the congregation in the world is actually more complex. It includes the witness and participation in social action that mechanist and contextualist understandings of the world imply. It also involves the paradigmatic modeling that an organicist interpretation promises. And, fourth, it requires that the local body identify certain of the world's imaginative structures that give life its meaning. The gospel is conveyed through all four modes of mission. The gospel also represents the astonishing news that a local church can suffer in the world, change it, symbolize its outcome, and be subject to its interpretive structures.

Pepper's formist hypothesis permits me to picture the congregation as a dwelling within a larger house. That, in fact, is close to the manner in which early Christians figured their own distinctive nature.[12] They called themselves the *paroikia*, the "sojourning," that inhabited the *oikoumenē*, the "big house" or "world." In early Christianity, *paroikia* was the temporary frame of a Christian community that represented its corporate life in the big inhabited house, the *oikoumenē*. By emphasizing the temporality implied in the concept of *paroikia* the New Testament conveyed the alien nature of parish in its larger setting and the sojourning of Christian groups in the world.[13] By patristic times, however, the spatial aspect of *paroikia* also proved useful because it designated the prolonged physical existence of Christian community in the world. Often in distinction to *ekklēsia*, the whole catholic church, *paroikia* as parish came to signify the persistent dwelling of the individual congregation.[14]

Viewing the parish as house within the world house emphasizes its participation in the frame of all language. Human imagination as a whole provides the particular idiomatic and narrative construction of a congregation; its members communicate by a code derived from the totality of forms and stories by which societies cohere. In such a picture, local church culture is not reduced to a series of propositions that a credal checklist adequately probes. Rather, the congregation takes part in the nuance and narrative of full human discourse. It persists as a recognizable storied dwelling within the whole horizon of human interpretation.

NOTES

1. James Hillman, "Archetypal Theory," in *Loose Ends* (New York and Zurich: Spring Publications, 1975), 4.

2. Johann Baptist Metz, *Faith in History and Society*, 207.

3. Stephen Crites, "Myth, Story, History," in *Parable, Myth and Language*, ed. Tony Stoneburner (Cambridge: Church Society for College Work. 1968), 68.

4. Wendy Doniger O'Flaherty, "Inside and Outside the Mouth of God: The Boundary Between Myth and Reality," *Daedalus* 109 (Spring 1980): 120.

5. Ibid., 121.

6. Charles E. Winquist, *Homecoming: Interpretation, Transformation and Individuation*, American Academy of Religion Studies in Religion no. 18 (Missoula, Mont.: Scholars Press, 1978), 108.

7. Ibid., 183.

8. Paulo Freire, *Pedagogy of the Oppressed* (New York: Herder & Herder, 1968), 70–71.

9. Ibid., 88–89, 91.

10. See chap. 2, n. 5.

11. There exists an obvious relationship between the four categories of Pepper and the four genres of Northrop Frye. A contextualist understanding of events linked to the indeterminate world at large invites the romantic adventure; the mechanist hypothesis about the predictable regularity of action poses instead the ironic rejoinder; organicist images of an ultimate integration tend to the comic; and formist perceptions of adherence to structured pattern are more tragic in their orientation. Correlations of these and other fourfold typologies presented throughout this book are, however, at best imprecise and at worst diminish the richness of the varied interpretive options that constitute a congregation's web of meanings.

12. Gerhard Friedrich, ed., *Theological Dictionary of the New Testament* (Grand Rapids: Wm. B. Eerdmans Pub. Co., 1967), 5:851–53.

13. 1 Peter 1:17; 2:11, but note Eph. 2:19. Abraham is the prototypical sojourner in Acts 7:6; Heb. 11:9; Israel in Acts 13:17.

14. Adolf von Harnack, *The Mission and Expansion of Christianity in the First Three Centuries* (New York: G. P. Putnam's Sons, 1908), 1:408–14.

APPENDIX

WORLD VIEW TEST
(1982)

Listed on the following pages is a series of questions about God and human situations that different Christians answer in different ways. We want you to choose **one** answer from each item that would come closer to your own opinion than any other.

Example:

00. To me God's presence is:
    a ☐ knowing I am doing his will
    b ☐ my awareness of the beauty of creation
    c ☒ the power of the universe within me
    d ☐ his physical closeness

There are no right or wrong answers to these questions. There is only your answer. BE SURE TO CHECK ONLY ONE BOX IN EACH QUESTION!

1. At its best my faith is:
   a ☐ concerned for humanity's highest values
   b ☐ filled with the Holy Spirit
   c ☐ born again in Christ
   d ☐ aware of my own divinity

2. When I die:
   a ☐ God will continue to bless and keep me
   b ☐ I shall then be with Christ
   c ☐ I journey on toward greater oneness with God
   d ☐ what will be, will be

3. When I see a picture of a starving child, I think that:
   a ☐ if everyone did God's will, this would not happen
   b ☐ the child is nevertheless a spiritual being nourished in other ways
   c ☐ we live in an unfair society
   d ☐ God is with him and can ease his troubles

4. I feel that I mature as I:
   a ☐ seek and receive God's gifts
   b ☐ follow God's plan for me
   c ☐ learn to love
   d ☐ realize the divine potential within me

5. Jesus Christ provides:
   a ☐ salvation from my sins
   b ☐ miraculous power in my own life
   c ☐ an example of life in tune with the absolute
   d ☐ freedom and self-reliance

6. I get in touch with God primarily through:
   a ☐ deep study of the Bible
   b ☐ experiences of God's presence with me
   c ☐ close human relationships
   d ☐ shutting out the world and communing with my innermost self

7. Worship is most meaningful:
   a ☐ at times of mystery and silence
   b ☐ when the Word is faithfully heard
   c ☐ in the midst of a caring community
   d ☐ when God's Spirit is manifested

8. When a young mother has cancer:
   a ☐ I know she could find real peace in the Bible
   b ☐ I know that life often contains great suffering
   c ☐ I must realize that all things work together for highest good
   d ☐ I pray that God will heal her

9. Were a person close to me dying, I would:
   a ☐ find strength to persevere
   b ☐ expect comfort from God
   c ☐ recognize how divine life sheds the limits of this world
   d ☐ stress the importance of the state of that person's salvation

10. In the worst times of my life I find:
    a ☐ the divinity within me shows my troubles to be less crucial
    b ☐ comfort in verses from the Bible
    c ☐ patience until better times
    d ☐ God blessing me in new ways

11. Some non-Christian people claim the ability to predict the future. I think:
    a ☐ these predictions may reflect their contact with universal intelligence
    b ☐ they are empowered by the devil
    c ☐ they are probably mistaken
    d ☐ the only disclosure of the future is that written in Christian scripture

12. I would like the next pastor of my church to be gifted in:
    a ☐ presenting sound Christian doctrine
    b ☐ bringing in God's power
    c ☐ deepening our fellowship with each other
    d ☐ uncovering the untapped powers of the mind

13. In the future I want to:
    a ☐ ask God for all the blessings God has in store for me
    b ☐ cultivate deeper levels of consciousness
    c ☐ really get into the Bible
    d ☐ be honestly who I am

14. As I see it, the world:
    a ☐ contains a mixture of good and bad
    b ☐ is only the surface expression of divine reality
    c ☐ is the place where God is emerging victorious
    d ☐ would improve were we to fulfill the mission God has given us

15. When someone I knew died, I was basically:
    a ☐ consoled that death is an illusion of this world
    b ☐ thankful for (or concerned about) the person's relation with Christ
    c ☐ strengthened by God's closeness
    d ☐ troubled by the loss

16. God enters my life most decisively in:
    a ☐ my deep commitments
    b ☐ answers to prayers
    c ☐ the peace and harmony I discover
    d ☐ the rules by which to lead a good life

17. After I got acquainted with the new pastor in my church, I hope that
    we would:
    a ☐ see each other as ordinary friends
    b ☐ share testimony about our wonderful growth in Christ
    c ☐ explore the signs that reveal God's truth
    d ☐ learn together from God's scripture

18. As a citizen I follow the laws of my country because:
    a ☐ disobedience obscures the divine pattern
    b ☐ I agree with the laws
    c ☐ God blesses those who pray and obey
    d ☐ I am to obey the authorities

19. God speaks to me:
    a ☐ through the words of the Bible
    b ☐ through the power I share with all of life
    c ☐ through meaningful human relationships
    d ☐ sometimes directly

20. When someone I love is very ill, I pray that this person:
    a ☐ be miraculously healed
    b ☐ accept the will of God in this situation
    c ☐ gain awareness of healing participation in divine perfection
    d ☐ be skillfully cared for by doctors

21. Satan is:
    a ☐ an old way of talking about evil in the world
    b ☐ a name for the illusion that blocks full consciousness
    c ☐ the ruler of the damned
    d ☐ active in individuals today

22. Were my family to suffer deep financial loss, I would:
    a ☐ look for God to change the situation
    b ☐ nevertheless prosper according to principles of divine abundance
    c ☐ adjust and go on
    d ☐ obey God

23. Earlier this year a neighbor complained that a ghost was in her house. I think that:
    a ☐ it could be a demon and be driven away by the power of Christ
    b ☐ she should move beyond such negative forms of thought
    c ☐ such a strange occurrence should lead her to God
    d ☐ there is probably a scientific explanation for her experience

24. When someone grows senile, I think that this situation is:
    a ☐ part of God's will that someday we may understand
    b ☐ a temporary condition not truly showing his continuing progress toward God
    c ☐ still ripe for God's blessing that person
    d ☐ just an unfortunate fact of life

25. In the next decade our nation:
    a ☐ will be faced with critical decisions
    b ☐ could escape its present level of discord
    c ☐ will be punished if it fails to live up to its covenant with God
    d ☐ must claim the power and guidance of the Holy Spirit

26. To me a horoscope drawn up by an expert:
    a ☐ is dangerous because it brings ungodly powers into your life
    b ☐ is wrong because God, not the stars, determines my life
    c ☐ may be helpful
    d ☐ may be entertaining but is otherwise worthless

27. In listening to a sermon I feel dissatisfied unless the minister preaches:
    a ☐ about our unity with God
    b ☐ a spirit-filled message
    c ☐ a convicting message from the Bible
    d ☐ with reference to everyday situations

WORLD VIEW TEST
INSTRUMENT SCORE SHEET

Circle the letter of the answer that you gave to each of the questions. (If you left the question unanswered, mark an x in the space provided.)

At the bottom of each column write the number of responses that you circled in that column.

Copy the number of responses in each column into the grid on the next page. Your total number of responses should equal 27.

					Unanswered
1.	a	c	b	d	____
2.	d	b	a	c	____
3.	c	a	d	b	____
4.	c	b	a	d	____
5.	d	a	b	c	____
6.	c	a	b	d	____
7.	c	b	d	a	____
8.	b	a	d	c	____
9.	a	d	b	c	____
10.	c	b	d	a	____
11.	c	d	b	a	____
12.	c	a	b	d	____
13.	d	c	a	b	____
14.	a	d	c	b	____
15.	d	b	c	a	____
16.	a	d	b	c	____
17.	a	d	b	c	____
18.	b	d	c	a	____
19.	c	a	d	b	____
20.	d	b	a	c	____
21.	a	c	d	b	____
22.	c	d	a	b	____
23.	d	c	a	b	____
24.	d	a	c	b	____
25.	a	c	d	b	____
26.	d	b	a	c	____
27.	d	c	b	a	____
	(Em)	(Ca)	(Ch)	(Gn)	

WORLD VIEW TEST
INSTRUMENT SCORE SHEET
(continued)

CANONIC (tragic)	GNOSTIC (comic)	CHARIS-MATIC (romantic)	EMPIRIC (ironic)	UN-ANSWERED
Ca	Gn	Ch	Em	

To chart your score:

a. Determine the horizontal axis

If canonic score is larger than gnostic:

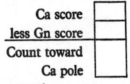

$$\begin{array}{r} \text{Ca score} \\ \underline{\text{less Gn score}} \\ \text{Count toward} \\ \text{Ca pole} \end{array}$$

If gnostic is larger than canonic:

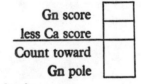

$$\begin{array}{r} \text{Gn score} \\ \underline{\text{less Ca score}} \\ \text{Count toward} \\ \text{Gn pole} \end{array}$$

b. Determine the vertical axis

If empiric is greater than charismatic:

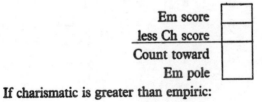

$$\begin{array}{r} \text{Em score} \\ \underline{\text{less Ch score}} \\ \text{Count toward} \\ \text{Em pole} \end{array}$$

If charismatic is greater than empiric:

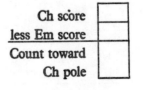

$$\begin{array}{r} \text{Ch score} \\ \underline{\text{less Em score}} \\ \text{Count toward} \\ \text{Ch pole} \end{array}$$

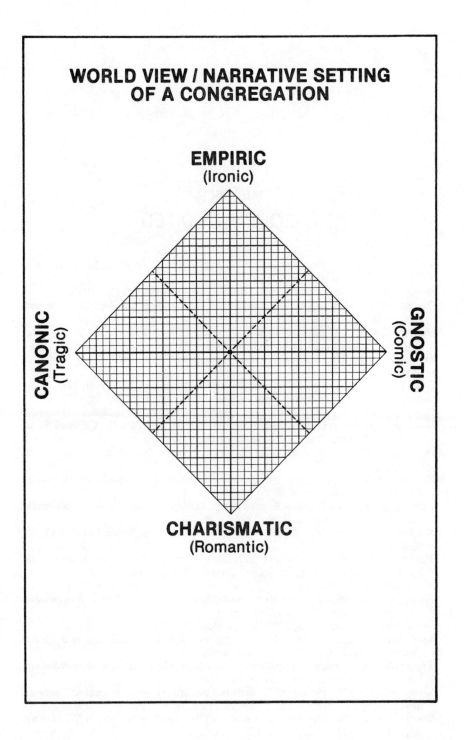

WORLD VIEW / NARRATIVE SETTING
OF A CONGREGATION

EMPIRIC
(Ironic)

CANONIC
(Tragic)

GNOSTIC
(Comic)

CHARISMATIC
(Romantic)

WORKS
FREQUENTLY CITED

Anderson, James D. *To Come Alive!: A New Proposal for Revitalizing the Local Church*. New York: Harper & Row, 1973.

Berger, Peter L. *The Sacred Canopy*. Garden City: Doubleday & Co., 1967.

Douglas, Mary. *Natural Symbols: Explorations in Cosmology*. London: Barrie & Jenkins, 1970.

Dudley, Carl S., ed. *Building Effective Ministry: Theory and Practice in the Local Church*. San Francisco: Harper & Row, 1983.

Freilich, Morris. *Marginal Natives: Anthropologists at Work*. New York: Harper & Row, 1970.

Frye, Northrop. *Anatomy of Criticism*. Princeton: Princeton Univ. Press, 1957.

Geertz, Clifford. *The Interpretation of Cultures*. New York: Basic Books, 1973.

Hamilton, Edith. *Mythology*. New York: New American Library, 1940.

Hauerwas, Stanley. *A Community of Character: Toward a Constructive Christian Social Ethic*. Notre Dame: Univ. of Notre Dame Press, 1981.

Heilman, Samuel C. *Synagogue Life: A Study in Symbolic Interaction*. Chicago: Univ. of Chicago Press, 1973.

Hesoid. *Theogony*. Translated by Norman O. Brown. Indianapolis: Bobbs-Merrill Educational Publishing Co., 1953.

Leas, Speed, and Paul Kittlaus. *Church Fights: Managing Conflict in the Local Church*. Philadelphia: Westminster Press, 1973.

MacIntyre, Alasdair. *After Virtue: A Study in Moral Theory*. Notre Dame: Univ. of Notre Dame Press, 1981.

Magoun, Francis P., and Alexander H. Knappe, trans. *The Grimms' German Folk Tales*. Carbondale: Southern Illinois University Press, 1960.

Mead, Loren. *New Hope for Congregations*. New York: Seabury Press, 1972.

Metz, Johann Baptist. *Faith in History and Society: Toward a Practical Fundamental Theology*. New York: Seabury Press, 1980.

New Larousse Encyclopedia of Mythology. London: Hamlyn, 1959.

Roof, Wade Clark. *Community and Commitment: Religious Plausibility in a Liberal Protestant Church*. New York: Elsevier, 1978.

Turner, Victor W. *Dramas, Fields and Metaphors: Symbolic Action in Human Society*. Ithaca, N.Y.: Cornell University Press, 1974.

Westerhoff, John H., and Gwen Kennedy Neville. *Generation to Generation: Conversations in Religious Education and Culture*. Philadelphia: Pilgrim Press, 1974.

Winter, Gibson. *The Suburban Captivity of the Churches*. Garden City, N.Y.: Doubleday & Co., 1961.

INDEX